Anonymous

A Leaf in the Storm a Dog of Flanders, and Other Stories

Anonymous

A Leaf in the Storm a Dog of Flanders, and Other Stories

ISBN/EAN: 9783337814977

Printed in Europe, USA, Canada, Australia, Japan

Cover: Foto ©ninafisch / pixelio.de

More available books at **www.hansebooks.com**

A LEAF IN THE STORM;
A DOG OF FLANDERS

AND OTHER STORIES.

BY

OUIDA,

AUTHOR OF "IDALIA," "TRICOTRIN," ETC.

COPYRIGHT EDITION.

WITH A PREFACE WRITTEN BY THE AUTHOR
FOR THIS EDITION.

LEIPZIG

BERNHARD TAUCHNITZ

1872.

PREFACE.

By desire of my esteemed friend and publisher, the Baron Tauchnitz, I beg to state that the present edition is the sole one authorised by me for Continental circulation. The edition issued by Messrs. Asher and Co. of Berlin was produced by them unknown to me. After its appearance that Firm addressed me offering payment and stating that they held piracy in abhorrence, and respected the rights of authors even where those rights were unsecured by legal exactitude. To obtain the belief of authors in the sincerity of these sentiments I would beg to suggest to the Messrs. Asher that it will be wiser in future to abstain from appropriating a literary work until they have secured the writer's permission to make profits from it. I take this opportunity to request all Continental residents and travellers who may purchase my books out of England to be so kind as to remember that all my works are assigned by me to Baron Tauchnitz, and to him alone, and that all other editions issued for Continental sale are an invasion of my rights and probably likewise an imperfect version of my writings.

OUIDA.

Florence, May 30.

CONTENTS.

	PAGE
A DOG OF FLANDERS.	9
A BRANCH OF LILAC	72
A PROVENCE ROSE	179
A LEAF IN THE STORM	245

A DOG OF FLANDERS.

I.

Nello and Patrasche were left all alone in the world.

They were friends in a friendship closer than brotherhood.

Nello was a little Ardennois—Patrasche was a big Fleming. They were both of the same age by length of years, yet one was still young, and the other was already old. They had dwelt together almost all their days: both were orphaned and destitute, and owed their lives to the same hand. It had been the beginning of the tie between them, their first bond of sympathy; and it had strengthened day by day, and had grown with their growth, firm and indissoluble, until they loved one another very greatly.

Their home was a little hut on the edge of a little village — a Flemish village a league from Antwerp, set amidst flat breadths of pasture and corn-lands, with long lines of poplars and of alders bending in the breeze on the edge of the great canal which ran through it.

It had about a score of houses and homesteads, with shutters of bright green or sky-blue, and roofs rose-red or black and white, and walls whitewashed until they shone in the sun like snow. In the centre of the village stood a windmill, placed on a little moss-grown slope: it was a landmark to all the level country round.

It had once been painted scarlet, sails and all, but that had been in its infancy, half a century or more earlier, when it had ground wheat for the soldiers of Napoleon; and it was now a ruddy brown, tanned by wind and weather. It went queerly by fits and starts, as though rheumatic and stiff in the joints from age, but it served the whole neighbourhood, which would have thought it almost as impious to carry grain elsewhere as to attend any other religious service than the mass that was performed at the altar of the little old gray church, with its conical steeple, which stood opposite to it, and whose single bell rang morning, noon and night with that strange, subdued, hollow sadness which every bell that hangs in the Low Countries seems to gain as an integral part of its melody.

Within sound of the little melancholy clock almost from their birth upward, they had dwelt together, Nello and Patrasche, in the little hut on the edge of the village, with the cathedral spire of Antwerp rising in the north-east, beyond the great green plain of seeding grass and spreading corn that stretched away from them like a tideless, changeless sea.

It was the hut of a very old man, of a very poor man—of old Jehan Daas, who in his time had been a soldier, and who remembered the wars that had trampled the country as oxen tread down the furrows, and who had brought from his service nothing except a wound, which had made him a cripple.

When old Jehan Daas had reached his full eighty, his daughter had died in the Ardennes, hard by Stavelot, and had left him in legacy her two-year old son. The old man could ill contrive to support himself, but he took up the additional burden uncomplainingly, and it soon became welcome and precious to him. Little Nello—which was but a pet diminutive for Nicolas—throve with him, and the old man and the little child lived in the poor little hut contentedly.

It was a very humble little mud-hut indeed, but it was clean and white as a sea-shell, and stood in a small plot of garden-ground that yielded beans and herbs and pumpkins.

They were very poor, terribly poor—many a day they had nothing at all to eat. They never by any chance had enough: to have had enough to eat would have been to have reached paradise at once. But the old man was very gentle and good to the boy, and the boy was a beautiful, innocent, truthful, tender-natured creature; and they were happy on a crust and a few leaves of cabbage, and asked no more of earth or heaven; save indeed that Patrasche should be always with them, since without Patrasche where would they have been?

For Patrasche was their alpha and omega; their treasury and granary; their store of gold and wand of wealth; their bread-winner and minister; their only friend and comforter. Patrasche dead or gone from them, they must have laid themselves down and died likewise. Patrasche was body, brains, hands, head and feet to both of them: Patrasche was their very life, their very soul.

For Jehan Daas was old and a cripple, and Nello was but a child; and Patrasche was their dog.

A dog of Flanders—yellow of hide, large of head and limb, with wolf-like ears that stood erect, and legs bowed and feet widened in the muscular development wrought in his breed by many generations of hard service. Patrasche came of a race which had toiled hard and cruelly from sire to son in Flanders many a century—slaves of slaves, dogs of the people, beasts of the shafts and the harness, creatures that lived straining their sinews in the gall of the cart, and died breaking their hearts on the flints of the streets.

Patrasche had been born of parents who had laboured hard all their days over the sharp-set stones of the various cities and the long, shadowless, weary roads of the two Flanders and of Brabant. He had been born to no other heritage than those of pain and of toil. He had been fed on curses and baptised with blows. Why not? It was a Christian country, and Patrasche was but a dog.

Before he was fully grown he had known the bitter gall of the cart and the collar. Before he had entered his thirteenth month he had become the property of a hardware-dealer, who was accustomed to wander over the land north and south, from the blue sea to the green mountains. They sold him for a small price, because he was so young.

This man was a drunkard and a brute. The life of Patrasche was a life of hell.

His purchaser was a sullen, ill-living, brutal Brabantois, who heaped his cart full with pots and pans and flagons and buckets, and other wares of crockery and brass and tin, and left Patrasche to draw the load as best he might, whilst he himself lounged idly by the side in fat and sluggish ease, smoking his black pipe and stopping at every wine-shop or café on the road.

Happily for Patrasche—or unhappily—he was very strong: he came of an iron race, long born and bred to such cruel travail; so that he did not die, but managed to drag on a wretched existence under the brutal burdens, the scarifying lashes, the hunger, the thirst, the blows, the curses and the exhaustion which are the only wages with which the Flemings repay the most patient and laborious of all their fourfooted victims.

One day, after two years of this long and deadly agony, Patrasche was going on as usual along one of the straight, dusty, unlovely roads that lead to the city of Rubens.

It was full midsummer, and very warm. His cart was very heavy, piled high with goods in metal and in earthenware. His owner sauntered on without noticing him otherwise than by the crack of the whip as it curled round his quivering loins.

The Brabantois had paused to drink beer himself at every wayside house, but he had forbidden Patrasche to stop a moment for a draught from the canal. Going along thus, in the full sun, on a scorching highway, having eaten nothing for twenty-four hours, and, which was far worse to him, not having tasted water for nearly twelve, being blind with dust, sore with blows and stupefied with the merciless weight which dragged upon his loins, Patrasche, for once, staggered and foamed a little at the mouth, and fell.

He fell in the middle of the white, dusty road, in the full glare of the sun: he was sick unto death, and motionless. His master gave him the only medicine in his pharmacy—kicks and oaths and blows with a cudgel of oak, which had been often the only food and drink, the only wage and reward, ever offered to him.

But Patrasche was beyond the reach of any torture or of any curses. Patrasche lay, dead to all appearances, down in the white powder of the summer dust.

After a while, finding it useless to assail his ribs with punishment and his ears with maledictions, the Brabantois—deeming life gone in him, or going so nearly that his carcass was for ever useless, unless indeed some one should strip it of the skin for gloves—cursed him fiercely in farewell, struck off the leathern bands of the harness, kicked his body heavily aside into the grass, and, groaning and muttering in savage wrath, pushed the cart lazily along the road up hill, and left the dying dog there for the ants to sting and for the crows to pick.

It was the last day before Kermesse away at Louvain, and the Brabantois was in haste to reach the fair and get a good place for his truck of brass wares.

He was in fierce wrath, because Patrasche had been a strong and much-enduring animal, and because he himself had now the hard task of pushing his charette all the way to Louvain. But to stay to look after Patrasche never entered his thoughts: the beast was dying and useless, and he would steal, to replace him, the first large dog that he found wandering alone out of sight of its master. Patrasche had cost him nothing, or next to nothing, and for two long, cruel years had been made to toil ceaselessly in his service from sunrise to sunset, through summer and winter, in fair weather and foul.

He had got a fair use and a good profit out of Patrasche: being human, he was wise, and left the dog to draw his last breath alone in the ditch, and have his bloodshot eyes plucked out as they might be by the birds, whilst he himself went on his way to beg and to steal, to eat and to drink, to dance and to sing, in the mirth at Louvain.

A dying dog, a dog of the cart—why should he waste hours over its agonies at peril of losing a handful of copper coins, at peril of a shout of laughter.

Patrasche lay there, flung in the grass-green ditch.

It was a busy road that day, and hundreds of people, on foot and on mules, in waggons or in carts, went by, tramping quickly and joyously on to Louvain. Some saw him, most did not even look: all passed on. A dead dog more or less—it was nothing in Brabant: it would be nothing anywhere in the world.

After a time, amongst the holiday-makers, there came a little old man who was bent and lame, and very feeble. He was in no guise for feasting: he was very poorly and miserably clad, and he dragged his silent way slowly through the dust amongst the pleasure-seekers.

He looked at Patrasche, paused, wondered, turned aside, then kneeled down in the rank grass and weeds of the ditch, and surveyed the dog with kindly eyes of pity.

There was with him a little rosy, fair-haired, dark-eyed child of a few years old, who pattered in amidst the bushes, that were for him breast-high, and stood gazing with a pretty seriousness upon the poor, great, quiet beast.

A Leaf in the Storm.

Thus it was that these two first met—the little Nello and the big Patrasche.

The upshot of that day was, that old Jehan Daas, with much laborious effort, drew the sufferer homeward to his own little hut, which was a stone's throw off amidst the fields, and there tended him with so much care that the sickness, which had been a brain-seizure, brought on by heat and thirst and exhaustion, with time and shade and rest passed away, and health and strength returned, and Patrasche staggered up again upon his four stout, tawny legs.

Now for many weeks he had been useless, powerless, sore, near to death; but all this time he had heard no rough word, had felt no harsh touch, but only the pitying murmurs of the little child's voice and the soothing caress of the old man's hand.

In his sickness they too had grown to care for him, this lonely old man and the little happy child.

He had a corner of the hut, with a heap of dry grass for his bed; and they had learned to listen eagerly for his breathing in the dark night, to tell them that he lived; and when he first was well enough to essay a loud, hollow, broken bay, they laughed aloud, and almost wept together for joy at such a sign of his sure restoration; and little Nello, in delighted glee, hung round his rugged neck with chains of marguerites, and kissed him with fresh and ruddy lips.

So then, when Patrasche arose, himself again, strong, big, gaunt, powerful, his great wistful eyes had a gentle astonishment in them that there were no curses to rouse him and no blows to drive him; and his heart awakened to a mighty love, which never wavered once in its fidelity whilst life abode with him.

But Patrasche, being a dog, was grateful. Patrasche lay pondering long with grave, tender, musing brown eyes, watching the movements of his friends.

Now, the old soldier, Jehan Daas, could do nothing for his living but limp about a little with a small cart, with which he carried daily the milk-cans of those happier neighbours who owned cattle away into the town of Antwerp.

The villagers gave him the employment a little out of charity—more because it suited them well to send their milk into the town by so honest a carrier, and bide at home themselves to look after their gardens, their cows, their poultry or their little fields. But it was becoming hard work for the old man. He was eighty-three, and Antwerp was a good league off, or more.

Patrasche watched the milk-cans come and go that first day when he had got well, and was lying in the sun with the wreath of marguerites round his tawny neck.

The next morning, Patrasche, before the old man had touched the cart, arose and walked to it, and placed himself betwixt its handles, and testified, as plainly as dumb show could do, his desire and his ability to work in return for the bread of charity that he had eaten. Jehan Daas resisted long, for the old man was one of those who thought it a foul shame to bind dogs to labour for which nature never formed them.

But Patrasche would not be gainsayed; finding they did not harness him, he tried to draw the cart onward with his teeth.

At length Jehan Daas gave way, vanquished by the persistence and the gratitude of this creature whom he had succoured. He fashioned his cart so that Patrasche could run in it, and this he did every morning of his life thenceforward.

When the winter came, Jehan Daas thanked the blessed fortune that had brought him to the dying dog in the ditch that fair-day of Louvain; for he was very old, and he grew feebler with each year, and he would ill have known how to pull his load of milk-cans over the snows and through the deep ruts in the mud if it had not been for the strength and the industry of the animal he had befriended.

As for Patrasche, it seemed heaven to him.

After the frightful burdens that his old master had compelled him to strain under, at the call of the whip at every step, it seemed nothing to him but amusement to step out with this little light green cart, with its bright brass cans, by the side of the gentle old man who always paid him with a tender caress and with a kindly word. Besides, his work was over by three or four in the day, and after that time he was free to do as he would—to stretch himself, to sleep in the sun, to wander in the fields, to romp with the young child, or to play with his fellow-dogs. Patrasche was very happy.

Fortunately for his peace, his former owner was killed in a drunken brawl at the kermesse of Mechlin, and so sought not after him nor disturbed him in his new and well-loved home.

A few years later, old Jehan Daas, who had always been a cripple, became so paralysed with rheumatism that it was impossible for him to go out with the cart any more.

Then little Nello, being now grown to his sixth year of age, and knowing the town well from having accompanied his grandfather so many times, took his place beside the cart, and sold the milk and received the coins in exchange, and brought them back to their respective owners with a pretty grace and seriousness which charmed all who beheld him.

The little Ardennois was a beautiful child, with dark, grave, tender eyes, and a lovely bloom upon his face, and fair locks that clustered to his throat; and many an artist sketched the group as they went by him—the green cart with the brass flagons of milk, and the great, tawny-coloured, massive dog, with his belled harness, that chimed cheerily as he went, and the small figure that ran beside him, which had little white feet in great wooden shoes, and a soft, grave, innocent, happy face like the little fair children of Rubens.

Nello and Patrasche did the work so well and so joyfully together that Jehan Daas himself, when the summer came and he was better again, had no need to stir out, but could sit in the doorway in the sun, and see them go forth through the garden wicket, and then doze, and dream, and pray a little, and then awake again as the clock tolled three, and watch for their return. And on their return Patrasche would shake himself free of his harness with a bay of glee, and Nello would recount with pride the doings of the day; and they would all go in together to their meal of rye bread and milk or soup, and would see the shadows lengthen over the plain, and see the twilight veil the fair cathedral spire; and then lie down together to sleep peacefully while the old man said a prayer.

So the days and the years went on, and the lives of Nello and Patrasche were happy, innocent, and healthful.

II.

IN the spring and summer especially were they glad. Flanders is not a lovely land, and around the burgh of Rubens it is perhaps least lovely of all.

Corn and colza, pasture and plough, succeed each other on the characterless plain in wearying repetition, and save by some gaunt gray tower, with its peal of pathetic bells, or some figure coming athwart the fields, made picturesque by a gleaner's bundle or a woodman's fagot, there is no change, no variety, no beauty anywhere; and he who has dwelt upon the mountains or amidst the forests feels oppressed as by imprisonment with the tedium and the endlessness of that vast and dreary level.

But it is green and very fertile, and it has wide horizons that have a certain charm of their own even in their dullness and monotony; and amongst the rushes by the water-side the flowers grow, and the trees rise tall and fresh where the barges glide with their great hulks black against the sun, and their little green barrels and vari-coloured flags gay against the leaves.

Anyway, there is a greenery and breadth of space enough to be as good as beauty to a child and a dog; and these two asked no better, when their work was done, than to lie buried in the lush grasses on the side of the canal, and watch the cumbrous vessels drifting by, and bringing the crisp salt smell of the sea amongst the blossoming scents of the country summer.

True, in the winter it was harder, and they had to rise in the darkness and the bitter cold, and they had seldom as much as they could have eaten any day, and the hut was scarce better than a shed when the nights were cold, although it looked so pretty in warm weather, buried in a great kindly-clambering vine, that never bore fruit, indeed, but which covered it with luxuriant green tracery all through the months of blossom and harvest.

In winter the winds found many holes in the walls of the poor little hut, and the vine was black and leafless, and the bare lands looked very bleak and drear without, and sometimes within the floor was flooded and then frozen. In winter it was hard, and the snow numbed the little white limbs of Nello, and the icicles cut the brave, untiring feet of Patrasche.

But even then they were never heard to lament, either of them. The child's wooden shoes and the dog's four legs would trot manfully together over the frozen fields to the chime of the bells on the harness; and then sometimes, in the streets of Antwerp, some housewife would bring them a bowl of soup and a handful of bread, or some kindly trader would throw some billets of fuel into the little cart as it went homeward, or some woman in their own village would bid them keep some share of the milk they carried for their own food; and they then would run over the white lands, through the early darkness, bright and happy, and burst with a shout of joy into their home.

So, on the whole, it was well with them, very well; and Patrasche, meeting on the highway or in the public streets the many dogs who toiled from daybreak into nightfall, paid only with blows and curses, and loosened from the shafts with a kick to starve and freeze as best they might,—Patrasche in his heart was very grateful to his fate, and thought it the fairest and the kindliest the world could hold. Though he was often very hungry indeed when he lay down at night; though he had to work in the heats of summer noons and the rasping chills of winter dawns; though his feet were often tender with wounds from the sharp edges of the jagged pavement; though he had to perform tasks beyond his strength and against his nature,—yet he was grateful and content: he did his duty with each day, and the eyes that he loved smiled down on him. It was sufficient for Patrasche.

There was only one thing which caused Patrasche any uneasiness in his life, and it was this. Antwerp, as all the world knows, is full at every turn of old piles of stones, dark and ancient and majestic, standing in crooked courts, jammed against gateways and taverns, rising by the water's edge, with bells ringing above them in the air, and ever and again out of their arched doors a swell of music pealing.

There they remain, the grand old sanctuaries of the past, shut in amidst the squalor, the hurry, the crowds, the unloveliness and the commerce of the modern world, and all day long the clouds drift and the birds circle, and the winds sigh around them, and beneath the earth at their feet there sleeps—RUBENS.

And the greatness of the mighty Master still rests upon Antwerp; wherever we turn in its narrow streets his glory lies therein, so that all mean things are thereby transfigured; and as we pace slowly through the winding ways, and by the edge of the stagnant water, and through the noisome courts, his spirit abides with us, and the heroic beauty of his visions is about us, and the stones that once felt his footsteps and bore his shadow seem to arise and speak of him with living voices. For the city which is the tomb of Rubens still lives to us through him, and him alone.

Without Rubens, what were Antwerp? A dirty, dusky, bustling mart, which no man would ever care to look upon save the traders who do business on its wharfes. With Rubens, to the whole world of men it is a sacred name, a sacred soil, a Bethlehem where a god of Art saw light, a Golgotha where a god of Art lies dead.

It is so quiet there by that great white sepulchre —so quiet, save only when the organ peals, and the choir cries aloud the Salve Regina or the Kyrie Eleison. Sure no artist ever had a greater gravestone than that pure marble sanctuary gives to him in the heart of his birth-place in the chancel of St. Jacques?

O nations! closely should you treasure your great men, for by them alone will the future know of you. Flanders in her generations has been wise. In his life she glorified this greatest of her sons, and in his death she magnifies his name. But her wisdom is very rare.

Now, the trouble of Patrasche was this.

Into these great sad piles of stones, that reared

their melancholy majesty above the crowded roofs, the child Nello would many and many a time enter, and disappear through their dark, arched portals, whilst Patrasche, left without upon the pavement, would wearily and vainly ponder on what could be the charm which thus allured from him his inseparable and beloved companion.

Once or twice he did essay to see for himself, clattering up the steps with his milk-cart behind him; but thereon he had been always sent back again summarily by a tall custodian in black clothes and silver chains of office; and fearful of bringing his little master into trouble, he desisted, and remained couched patiently before the churches until such time as the boy reappeared.

It was not the fact of his going into them which disturbed Patrasche: he knew that people went to church: all the village went to the small, tumble-down, gray pile opposite the red windmill. What troubled him was that little Nello always looked strangely when he came out, always very flushed or very pale; and whenever he returned home after such visitations would sit silent and dreaming, not caring to play, but gazing out at the evening skies beyond the line of the canal, very subdued and almost sad.

What was it? wondered Patrasche.

He thought it could not be good or natural for the little lad to be so grave, and, in his dumb fashion, he tried all he could to keep Nello by him in the sunny fields or in the busy market-place.

But to the churches Nello would not go: most often of all would he go to the great cathedral; and Patrasche, left without on the stones by the iron fragments of Quentin Matsys' gate, would stretch himself and yawn and sigh, and even howl now and then, all in vain, until the doors closed and the child perforce came forth again, and winding his arms about the dog's neck, would kiss him on his broad, tawny-coloured forehead, and murmur always the same words:—

"If I could only see them, Patrasche!—if I could only see them!"

What were they? pondered Patrasche, looking up with large, wistful, sympathetic eyes.

One day, when the custodian was out of the way and the doors left ajar, he got in for a moment after his little friend and saw. "They" were two great covered pictures on either side of the choir.

Nello was kneeling, wrapt as in an ecstasy, before the altar-picture of the Assumption, and when he noticed Patrasche, and rose and drew the dog gently out into the air, his face was wet with tears, and he looked up at the veiled places as he passed them, and murmured to his companion:—

"It is so terrible not to see them, Patrasche, just because one is poor and cannot pay! He never meant that the poor should not see them when he painted them, I am sure. He would have had us see them any day,— every day: that I am sure. And they keep them shrouded there,—shrouded in the dark, the beautiful things!—and they never feel the light, and no eyes look on them, unless rich people come and pay. If I could only see them, I would be content to die."

But he could not see them, and Patrasche could not help him, for to gain the silver piece that the Church exacts as the price for looking on the glories of the "Elevation of the Cross" and the "Descent of the Cross" was a thing as utterly beyond the powers of either of them as it would have been to scale the heights of the cathedral-spire.

They had never so much as a sou to spare: if they cleared enough to get a little wood for the stove, a little broth for the pot, it was the utmost they could do. And yet the heart of the child was set in sore and endless longing upon beholding the greatness of the two veiled Rubens.

The whole soul of the little Ardennois thrilled and stirred with an absorbing passion for art.

Going on his ways through the old city in the early daybreak before the sun or the people had seen them, Nello, who looked only a little peasant-boy, with a great dog drawing milk to sell from door to door, was in a heaven of dreams, whereof Rubens was the god. Nello, cold and hungry, with stockingless feet in wooden shoes, and the winter winds blowing amongst his curls and lifting his poor thin garments, was in a rapture of meditation, wherein all that he saw was the beautiful fair face of the Mary of "The Assumption," with the waves of her golden hair lying upon her shoulders, and the light of an eternal sun shining down upon her brow. Nello, reared in poverty, and buffetted by fortune, and untaught in letters, and unheeded by men, had the compensation or the curse which is called Genius.

No one knew it. He as little as any. No one knew it.

Only indeed Patrasche, who being with him always, saw him draw with chalk upon the stones any and every thing that grew or breathed, — heard him on his little bed of hay, murmur all manner of timid, pathetic prayers to the spirit of the great Master; watched his gaze darken and his face radiate at the evening glow of sunset or the rosy rising of the dawn; and felt, many and many a time, the tears of a strange, nameless pain and joy mingled together, fall hotly from the bright young eyes upon his own wrinkled, yellow forehead.

"I should go to my grave quite content if I thought, Nello, that when thou growest a man thou could'st own this hut and the little plot of ground, and labour for thyself, and be called Baas by thy neighbours," said the old man Jehan many an hour from his bed.

For to own a bit of soil, and to be called Baas—master—by the hamlet round, is to have achieved the highest ideal of a Flemish peasant; and the old soldier, who had wandered over all the earth in his youth, and had brought nothing back, deemed in his old age that to live and die on one spot in contented humility was the fairest fate he could desire for his darling.

But Nello said nothing.

The same leaven was working in him that in other times begat Rubens, and Jordaens and the Van Eycks, and all their wondrous tribe, and in times more recent begat—in the green country of the Ardennes, where the Meuse washes the old walls of Dijon—the great artist of the Patroclus, whose genius is too near us for us aright to measure its divinity.

Nello dreamed of other things in the future than of tilling the little rood of earth, and living under the wattle roof, and being called Baas by neighbours a little poorer or a little less poor than himself. The cathedral-spire, where it rose beyond the fields in the ruddy evening skies or in the dim, gray, misty mornings, said other things to him than this. But these he told only to Patrasche, whispering, child-like, his fancies in the dog's ear when they went together at their work through the fogs of the daybreak, or lay together at their rest amongst the rustling rushes by the water's side.

For such dreams are not easily shaped into speech to awake the slow sympathies of human auditors; and they would only have sorely perplexed and troubled the poor old man, bedridden in his corner, who, for his part, whenever he had trodden the streets of Antwerp, had thought the daub of blue and red that they called a Madonna, on the walls of the wine-shop where he drank his sou's worth of black beer, quite as good as any of the famous altar-pieces for which the stranger-folk travelled far and wide into Flanders from every land on which the good sun shone.

There was only one other beside Patrasche to

whom Nello could talk at all of his daring fantasies. This other was little Alois, who lived at the old red mill on the grassy mound, and whose father, the miller, was the best-to-do husbandman in all the village.

Little Alois was only a pretty baby, with soft, round, rosy features, made lovely by those sweet dark eyes that the Spanish rule has left in so many a Flemish face, in testimony of the Alvan dominion, as Spanish art has left, broadsown throughout the country, majestic palaces and stately courts, gilded house-fronts and sculptured lintels—histories in blazonry and poems in stone.

Little Alois was often with Nello and Patrasche. They played in the fields, they ran in the snow, they gathered the daisies and bilberries, they went up to the old gray church together, and they often sat together by the broad wood-fire in the mill-house.

Little Alois, indeed, was the richest child in the hamlet. She had neither brother nor sister; her blue serge dress had never a hole in it; at kermesse she had as many gilded nuts and Agni Dei in sugar as her hands could hold; and when she went up for her first communion, her flaxen curls were covered with a cap of richest Mechlin lace, which had been her mother's and her grandmother's before it came to her. Men spoke already, though she had but twelve years, of the good wife she would be for their sons to woo and win; but she herself was a little, gay, simple child, in nowise conscious of her heritage, and she loved no play-fellows so well as Jehan Daas' grandson, and his dog.

One day her father, Baas Cogez, a good man, but somewhat stern, came on a pretty group in the long meadow behind the mill, where the aftermath had that day been cut.

It was his little daughter sitting amidst the hay, with the great tawny head of Patrasche on her lap, and many wreaths of poppies and blue cornflowers round them both: on a clean smooth slab of pine wood the boy Nello drew their likeness with a stick of charcoal.

The miller stood and looked at the portrait with tears in his eyes, it was so strangely like, and he loved his only child closely and well. Then he roughly chid the little girl for idling there whilst her mother needed her within, and sent her indoors crying and afraid: then, turning, he snatched the wood from Nello's hands.

"Dost do much of such folly?" he asked, but there was a tremble in his voice.

Nello coloured and hung his head. "I draw everything I see," he murmured.

The miller was silent: then he stretched his hand out with a franc in it.

"It is folly, as I say, and evil waste of time: nevertheless, it is like Alois, and will please the house-mother. Take this silver bit for it and leave it for me."

The colour died out of the face of the young Ardennois: he lifted his head and put his hands behind his back.

"Keep your money and the portrait both, Baas Cogez," he said simply. "You have been often good to me."

Then he called Patrasche to him, and walked away across the fields.

"I could have seen *them* with that franc," he murmured to Patrasche, "but I could not sell her picture—not even for them."

Baas Cogez went into his mill-house sore troubled in his mind.

"That lad must not be so much with Alois," he said to his wife that night. "Trouble may come of it hereafter: he is fifteen now, and she is twelve; and the boy is comely of face and form."

"And he is a good lad and a loyal," said the housewife, feasting her eyes on the piece of pine wood where it was throned above the chimney with a cuckoo clock in oak and a Calvary in wax.

"Yea, I do not gainsay that," said the miller, draining his pewter flagon.

"Then, if what you think of were ever to come to pass," said the wife, hesitatingly, "would it be matter so much? She will have enough for both, and one cannot be better than happy."

"You are a woman, and therefore a fool," said the miller harshly, striking his pipe on the table. "The lad is nought but a beggar, and, with these painter's fancies, worse than a beggar. Have a care that they are not together in the future, or I will send the child to the surer keeping of the nuns of the Sacred Heart."

The poor mother was terrified, and promised humbly to do his will. Not that she could bring herself altogether to separate the child from her favourite playmate, nor did the miller even desire that extreme of cruelty to a young lad who was guilty of nothing except poverty. But there were many ways in which little Alois was kept away from her chosen companion; and Nello, being a boy, proud and quiet and sensitive, was quickly wounded, and ceased to turn his own steps and those of Patrasche, as he had been used to do with every moment of leisure, to the old red mill upon the slope.

What his offence was he did not know: he supposed he had in some manner angered Baas

Cogez by taking the portrait of Alois in the meadow; and when the child who loved him would run to him and nestle her hand in his, he would smile at her very sadly, and say with a tender concern for her before himself,—

"Nay, Alois, do not anger your father. He thinks that I make you idle, dear, and he is not pleased that you should be with me. He is a good man and loves you well: we will not anger him, Alois."

But it was with a sad heart that he said it, and the earth did not look so bright to him as it had used to do when he went out at sunrise under the poplars down the straight roads with Patrasche.

The old red mill had been a landmark to him, and he had been used to pause by it, going and coming, for a cheery greeting with its people as her little flaxen head had risen above the low mill-wicket, and her little rosy hands had held out a bone or a crust to Patrasche.

Now the dog looked wistfully at a closed door, and the boy went on without pausing, with a pang at his heart, and the child sat within with tears dropping slowly on the knitting to which she was set on her little stool by the stove; and Baas Cogez, working among his sacks and his mill-gear, would harden his will, and say to himself, "It is best so. The lad is all but a beggar, and full of idle, dreaming fooleries. Who knows what mischief might not come of it in the future?"

So he was wise in his generation, and would not have the door unbarred, except upon rare and formal occasions, which seemed to have neither warmth nor mirth in them to the two children, who had been accustomed so long to a daily, gleeful, careless, happy interchange of greeting, speech, and pastime, with no other watcher of their sports or auditor of their fancies than Patrasche, sagely shaking the brazen bells of his collar and responding with all a dog's swift sympathies to their every change of mood.

All this while the little panel of pine wood remained over the chimney in the mill-kitchen with the cuckoo clock and the waxen Calvary, and sometimes it seemed to Nello a little hard that whilst his gift was accepted he himself should be denied.

But he did not complain: it was his habit to be quiet: old Jehan Daas had said ever to him, "We are poor: we must take what God sends—the ill with the good: the poor cannot choose."

To which the boy had always listened in silence, being reverent of his old grandfather; but nevertheless a certain vague and sweet hope, such as beguiles the children of genius, had whispered in his heart, "Yet the poor do choose sometimes—choose to be great, so that men cannot say them nay."

And he thought so still in his innocence; and one day, when the little Alois, finding him by chance alone amongst the corn-fields by the canal, ran to him and held him close, and sobbed piteously because the morrow would be her saint's day, and for the first time in all her life her parents had failed to bid him to the little supper and romp in the great barns with which her feast-day was always celebrated, Nello had kissed her, and murmured to her in firm faith,—

"It shall be different one day, Alois. One day that little bit of pine wood that your father has of mine shall be worth its weight in silver; and he will not shut the door against me then. Only love me always, dear little Alois; only love me always, and I will be great."

"And if I do not love you?" the pretty child asked, pouting a little through her tears, and moved by the instinctive coquetries of her sex.

Nello's eyes left her face and wandered to the distance, where in the red-and-gold of the Flemish night the cathedral-spire rose.

There was a smile on his face so sweet and yet so sad that little Alois was awed by it.

"I will be great still," he said under his breath—"great still, or die, Alois."

"You do not love me, then!" said the little spoilt child, pushing him away; but the boy shook his head and smiled, and went on his way through the tall yellow corn, seeing as in a vision some day in a fair future when he should come into that old familiar land and ask Alois of her people, and be not refused nor denied, but received in honour, whilst the village folk should throng to look upon him, and say in one another's ears, "Dost see him? He is a king among men, for he is a great artist and the world speaks his name; and yet he was only our poor little Nello, who was a beggar, as one may say, and only got his bread by the help of his dog."

And he thought how he would fold his grandsire in furs and purples, and pourtray him as the old man is pourtrayed in the Family in the chapel of St. Jacques; and of how he would hang the throat of Patrasche with a collar of gold, and place him on his right hand, and say to the people, "This was once my only friend;" and of how he would build himself a great white marble palace, and make to himself luxuriant gardens of pleasure, on the slope looking outward to where the cathedral-spire rose, and not dwell in it himself, but summon to it, as to a home, all men young and poor and friendless, but of the will to do mighty things; and of how he would say to them always, if they sought to bless his name, "Nay, do not thank me—thank Rubens. Without him, what should I have been?"

These dreams, beautiful, impossible, innocent, free of all selfishness, full of heroical worship, were so closely about him as he went that he was happy —happy even on this sad anniversary of Alois' saint's day, when he and Patrasche went home by themselves to the little dark hut and the meal of black bread, whilst in the mill-house all the children of the village sang and laughed, and ate the big round cakes of Dijon and the almond gingerbread of Brabant, and danced in the great barn to the light of the stars and the music of flute and fiddle.

"Never mind, Patrasche," he said, with his arms round the dog's neck as they both sat in the door of the hut, where the sounds of the mirth at the mill came down to them on the night air—"never mind. It shall all be changed by and by."

He believed in the future: Patrasche, of more experience and of more philosophy, thought that the loss of the mill supper in the present was ill compensated by dreams of milk and honey in some vague hereafter.

And Patrasche growled whenever he passed by Baas Cogez.

III.

"This is Alois's name-day, is it not?" said the old man Daas that night from the corner where he was stretched upon his bed of sacking.

The boy gave a gesture of assent: he wished that the old man's memory had erred a little, instead of keeping such exact account.

"And why not there?" his grandfather pursued. "Thou hast never missed a year before, Nello."

"Thou art too sick to leave," murmured the lad, bending his handsome young head over the bed.

"Tut! tut! Mother Vulette would have come and sat with me, as she does scores of times. What is the cause, Nello?" the old man persisted. "Thou surely hast not had ill words with the little one?"

"Nay, grandfather—never," said the boy quickly, with a hot colour in his bent face. "Simply and truly, Baas Cogez did not have me asked this year. He has taken some whim against me."

"But thou hast done nothing wrong?"

"That I know—nothing. I took the portrait of Alois on a piece of pine: that is all."

"Ah!"

The old man was silent: the truth suggested itself to him with the boy's innocent answer. He was tied to a bed of dried leaves in the corner of a wattle hut, but he had not wholly forgotten what the ways of the world were like.

He drew Nello's fair head fondly to his breast with a tenderer gesture.

"Thou art very poor, my child," he said with a quiver the more in his aged trembling voice—"so poor! It is very hard for thee."

"Nay, I am rich," murmured Nello; and in his innocence he thought so—rich with the imperishable powers that are mightier than the might of kings. And he went and stood by the door of the hut in the quiet autumn night, and watched the stars troop by and the tall poplars bend and shiver in the wind.

All the casements of the mill-house were lighted, and every now and then the notes of the flute came to him. The tears fell down his cheeks, for he was but a child, yet he smiled, for he said to himself, "In the future!"

He stayed there until all was quite still and dark, then he and Patrasche went within and slept together, long and deeply, side by side.

Now he had a secret which only Patrasche knew. There was a little out-house to the hut, which no one entered but himself—a dreary place, but with abundant clear light from the north. Here he had fashioned himself rudely an easel in rough lumber, and here on a great gray sea of stretched paper he had given shape to one of the innumerable fancies which possessed his brain.

No one had ever taught him anything; colours he had no means to buy; he had gone without bread many a time to procure even the few rude vehicles that he had here; and it was only in black and white that he could fashion the things he saw. This great figure which he had drawn here in chalk was only an old man sitting on a fallen tree—only that. He had seen old Michel the woodman sitting so at evening many a time.

He had never had a soul to tell him of outline or perspective, of anatomy or of shadow, and yet he had given all the weary wornout age, all the sad, quiet patience, all the rugged, careworn pathos of his original, and given them so that the old lonely figure was a poem, sitting there, meditative and alone, on the dead tree, with the darkness of the descending night behind him.

It was rude, of course, in a way, and had many faults, no doubt; and yet it was real, true in Nature, true in Art, and very mournful, and in a manner beautiful.

Patrasche had lain quiet countless hours watching its gradual creation after the labour of each day was done, and he knew that Nello had a hope—

vain and wild perhaps, but strongly cherished—of sending this great drawing to compete for a prize of two hundred francs a year, which it was announced in Antwerp would be open to every lad of talent, scholar or peasant, under eighteen, who would attempt to win it with some unaided work of chalk or pencil. Three of the foremost artists in the town of Rubens were to be the judges and elect the victor according to his merits.

All the spring and summer and autumn Nello had been at work upon this treasure, which, if triumphant, would build him his first step toward independence, and the mysteries of the art which he blindly, ignorantly, and yet passionately adored.

He said nothing to any one: his grandfather would not have understood, and little Alois was lost to him. Only to Patrasche he told all, and whispered, "Rubens would give it me, I think, if he knew."

Patrasche thought so too, for he knew that Rubens had loved dogs or he had never painted them with such exquisite fidelity; and men who loved dogs were, as Patrasche knew, always pitiful.

The drawings were to go in on the first day of December, and the decision be given on the twenty-fourth, so that he who should win might rejoice with all his people at the Christmas season.

In the twilight of a bitter wintry day, and with a beating heart, now quick with hope, now faint with fear, Nello placed the great picture on his little green milk-cart, and took it, with the help of Patrasche, into the town, and there left it, as enjoined, at the doors of a public building.

"Perhaps it is worth nothing at all. How can I tell?" he thought, with the heart-sickness of a great timidity.

Now that he had left it there, it seemed to him so hazardous, so vain, so foolish, to dream that he, a little lad with bare feet, who barely knew his letters, could do anything at which great painters, real artists, could ever deign to look.

Yet he took heart as he went by the cathedral: the lordly form of Rubens seemed to rise from the fog and the darkness, and to loom in its magnificence before him, whilst the lips, with their kindly smile, seemed to him to murmur, "Nay, have courage! It was not by a weak heart and by faint fears that I wrote my name for all time upon Antwerp."

Nello ran home through the cold night, comforted.

He had done his best: the rest must be as God willed, he thought, in that innocent unquestioning faith which had been taught him in the little chapel amongst the willows and the poplar trees.

The winter was very sharp already. That night, after they reached the hut, snow fell; and fell for very many days after that, so that the paths and the divisions in the fields were all obliterated, and all the smaller streams were frozen over, and the cold was intense upon the plains. Then, indeed, it became hard work to go round for the milk, while the world was all dark, and carry it through the darkness to the silent town.

Hard work, especially for Patrasche, for the passage of the years, that were only bringing Nello a stronger youth, were bringing him old age, and his joints were stiff, and his bones ached often. But he would never give up his share of the labour. Nello would fain have spared him, and drawn the cart in himself, but Patrasche would never allow it. All he would ever permit or accept was the help of a thrust from behind to the truck as it lumbered along through the ice-ruts. Patrasche had lived in harness, and he was proud of it. He suffered a great deal sometimes from frost, and the terrible roads, and the rheumatic pains of his limbs, but he only drew his breath hard and bent his proud neck, and trod onward with steady patience.

"Rest thee at home, Patrasche—it is time thou didst rest—and I can quite well push in the cart by myself," urged Nello many a morning; but Patrasche, who understood him aright, would no more have consented to stay at home than a veteran soldier to shirk when the charge was sounding; and every day he would rise and place himself in the shafts, and plod along over the snow, through the fields that his four round feet had left their print upon so many, many years.

"One must never rest till one dies," thought Patrasche; and sometimes it seemed to him that that time of rest for him was not very far off. His sight was less clear than it had been, and it gave him pain to rise after the night's sleep, though he would never lie a moment in his straw when once the bell of the chapel tolling five, let him know that the daybreak of labour had begun.

"My poor Patrasche, we shall soon lie quiet together, you and I," said old Jehan Daas, stretching out to stroke the head of Patrasche with the old withered hand which had always shared with him its one poor crust of bread; and the hearts of the old man and the old dog ached together with one thought: When they were gone who would care for their darling?

One afternoon, as they came back from Antwerp, over the snow, which had become hard and smooth as marble over all the Flemish plains, they found dropped in the road a pretty little puppet—a tambourine-player, all scarlet and gold, about six inches high, and, unlike greater personages when Fortune lets them drop, quite unspoiled and unhurt by his fall. It was a pretty toy. Nello tried to find its owner, and, failing, thought that it was just the thing to please Alois.

It was quite night when he passed the mill-house: he knew the little window of her room. It could be no harm, he thought, if he gave her his little piece of treasure-trove, they had been play-fellows so long.

There was a shed with a sloping roof beneath her casement: he climbed and tapped softly at the lattice: there was a little light within.

The child opened it and looked out, half frightened.

Nello put the tambourine-player into her hands.

"Here is a doll I found in the snow, Alois. Take it," he whispered—"take it, and God bless thee, dear!"

He slid down from the shed-roof before she had time to thank him, and ran off through the darkness.

That night there was a fire at the mill. Out-buildings and much corn were destroyed, although the mill itself and the dwelling-house were unharmed. All the village was out in terror, and the engines came tearing through the snow from Antwerp. The miller was insured, and would lose nothing: nevertheless, he was in furious wrath, and declared aloud that the fire was due to no accident, but to some foul intent.

Nello, awakened from his sleep, ran to help with the rest; Baas Cogez thrust him angrily aside.

"Thou wert loitering here after dark," he said roughly. "I believe, on my soul, thou dost know more of the fire than anyone."

Nello heard him in silence, stupefied, not supposing that anyone could say such things except in jest, and not comprehending how anyone could pass a jest at such a time.

Nevertheless, the miller said the brutal thing openly to many of his neighbours in the day that followed; and though no serious charge was ever preferred against the lad, it got bruited about that Nello had been seen in the mill-yard after dark on some unspoken errand, and that he bore Baas Cogez a grudge for forbidding his intercourse with little Alois; and so the hamlet, which followed the sayings of its richest landowner, servilely, and whose families all hoped to secure the riches of Alois in some future time for their sons, took the hint to give grave looks and cold words to old Jehan Daas' grandson.

No one said anything to him openly, but all the village agreed together to humour the miller's prejudice, and at the cottages and farms where Nello and Patrasche called every morning for the milk for Antwerp, downcast glances and brief phrases replaced to them the broad smiles and cheerful greetings to which they had been always used. No one really credited the miller's absurd suspicion, nor the outrageous accusations born of them, but the people were all very poor and very ignorant, and the one rich man of the place had pronounced against him. Nello, in his innocence and his friendlessness, had no strength to stem the popular tide.

"Thou art very cruel to the lad," the miller's wife dared to say, weeping, to her lord. "Sure he is an innocent lad and a faithful, and would never dream of any such wickedness, however sore his heart might be."

But Baas Cogez, being an obstinate man, having once said a thing, held to it doggedly, though in his innermost soul he knew well the injustice that he was committing.

Meanwhile, Nello endured the injury done against him with a certain proud patience that disdained to disclaim: he only gave way a little when he was quite alone with Patrasche. Besides, he thought,

"If my picture should win! They will be sorry then, perhaps."

Still, to a boy not quite sixteen, and who had dwelt in one little world all his short life, and in his childhood had been caressed and applauded on all sides, it was a hard trial to have the whole of that little world turn against him for naught. Especially hard in that bleak, snow-bound, famine-stricken winter-time, when the only light and warmth there could be found abode beside the village hearths and in the kindly greetings of neighbours. In the winter-time all drew nearer to each other, all to all, except to Nello and Patrasche, with whom none now would have anything to do, and who were left to fare as they might with the old paralysed, bedridden man in the little cabin, whose fire was often cold, and whose board was often without bread, for there was a buyer from Antwerp who had taken to drive his mule in of a day for the milk of the various dairies, and there were only three or four of the people who had refused his terms of purchase and remained faithful to the little green cart. So that the burden which Patrasche drew had become very light, and the centime-pieces in Nello's pouch had become, alas! very small likewise.

The dog would stop, as usual, at all the familiar

gates, which were now closed to him, and look up at them with wistful, mute appeal; and it cost the neighbours a pang to shut their doors and their hearts, and let Patrasche draw his cart on again, empty. Nevertheless, they did it, for they desired to please Baas Cogez.

Noël drew close at hand.

The weather was very wild and cold. The snow was six feet deep, and the ice was firm enough to bear oxen and men upon it everywhere. At this season the little village was always gay and cheerful. At the poorest dwelling there were possets and cakes, joking and dancing, sugared saints and gilded Jésus. The merry Flemish bells jingled everywhere on the horses; everywhere within doors some well-filled soup-pot sang and smoked over the stove; and everywhere over the snow without laughing maidens pattered in bright kerchiefs and stout kirtles, going to and from the mass. Only in the little hut it was very dark and very cold.

Nello and Patrasche were left utterly alone, for one night in the week before the Christmas Day, Death entered there, and took away from life for ever old Jehan Daas, who had never known of life aught save its poverty and its pains. He had long been half dead, incapable of any movement except a feeble gesture, and powerless for anything beyond a gentle word; and yet his loss fell on them both with a great horror in it: they mourned him passionately. He had passed away from them in his sleep, and when in the gray dawn they learned their bereavement, unutterable solitude and desolation seemed to close around them. He had long been only a poor, feeble, paralysed old man, who could not raise a hand in their defence, but he had loved them well: his smile had always welcomed their return. They mourned for him unceasingly, refusing to be comforted, as in the white winter day they followed the deal shell that held his body to the nameless grave by the little church. They were his only mourners, these two whom he had left friendless upon earth—the young boy and the old dog.

"Surely, he will relent now and let the poor lad come hither?" thought the miller's wife, glancing at her husband where he smoked by the hearth.

Baas Cogez knew her thought, but he hardened his heart, and would not unbar his door as the little, humble funeral went by. "The boy is a beggar," he said to himself: "he shall not be about Alois."

The woman dared not say anything aloud, but when the grave was closed and the mourners had gone, she put a wreath of immortelles into Alois' hands and bade her go and lay it reverently on the dark unmarked mound where the snow was displaced.

Nello and Patrasche went home with broken hearts. But even of that poor, melancholy, cheerless home they were denied the consolation. There was a month's rental over-due for the little place, and when Nello had paid the last sad service to the dead he had not a coin left. He went and begged grace of the owner of the hut, a cobbler who went every Sunday night to drink his pint of wine and smoke with Baas Cogez. The cobbler would grant no mercy. He was a harsh, miserly man, and loved money. He claimed in default of his rent every stick and stone, every pot and pan, in the hut, and bade Nello and Patrasche to be out of it on the morrow.

Now, the cabin was lowly enough, and in some sense miserable enough, and yet their hearts clove to it with a great affection. They had been so happy there, and in the summer, with its clambering vine and its flowering beans, it was so pretty and bright in the midst of the sun-lighted fields! Their life in it had been full of labour and privation, and yet they had been so well content, so gay of heart, running together to meet the old man's neverfailing smile of welcome!

All night long the boy and the dog sat by the fireless hearth in the darkness, drawn close together for warmth and sorrow. Their bodies were insensible to the cold, but their hearts seemed frozen in them.

When the morning broke over the white chill earth it was the morning of Christmas Eve. With a shudder, Nello clasped close to him his only friend, while his tears fell hot and fast on the dog's frank forehead. "Let us go, Patrasche—dear, dear Patrasche," he murmured. "We will not wait to be kicked out: let us go."

Patrasche had no will but his, and they went sadly, side by side, out from the little home which was so dear to them, and in which every humble, homely thing was to them precious and beloved. Patrasche drooped his head wearily as he passed by his own green cart: it was no longer his—it had to go with the rest in the dues of debt, and his brass harness lay idle and glittering on the snow. The dog could have lain down beside it and died for very heart-sickness as he went, but whilst the lad lived and needed him Patrasche would not yield and give way.

They took the old accustomed road into Antwerp. The day was yet scarce more than dawned, most of the shutters were still closed, but some of the villagers were about. They took no notice whilst the dog and the boy passed by them. At one door Nello paused and looked wistfully within: his grandfather had done many a kindly turn in neighbour's service to the people who dwelt there.

"Would you give Patrasche a crust?" he said, timidly. "He is old, and he has had nothing since last forenoon."

The woman shut the door hastily, murmuring some vague saying that wheat and rye were very dear that season. The boy and the dog went on again wearily: they asked no more.

By slow and painful ways they reached Antwerp as the chimes tolled ten.

"If I had anything about me I could sell to get him bread!" thought Nello, but he had nothing except the wisp of linen and serge that covered him, and his pair of wooden shoes.

Patrasche understood, and nestled his nose into the lad's hand, as though to pray him not to be disquieted for any woe or want of his.

The winner of the drawing-prize was to be proclaimed at noon, and to the public building where he had left his treasure Nello made his way. On the steps and in the entrance-hall there was a crowd of youths—some of his age, some older, all with parents or relatives or friends. His heart was sick with fear as he went amongst them, holding Patrasche close to him. The great bells of the city clashed out the hour of noon with brazen clamour. The doors of the inner hall were opened; the eager, panting throng rushed in: it was known that the selected picture would be raised above the rest upon a wooden daïs.

A mist obscured Nello's sight, his head swam, his limbs almost failed him. When his vision cleared he saw the drawing raised on high: it was not his own! A slow sonorous voice was proclaiming aloud that victory had been adjudged to Stephan Kiesslinger, born in the burgh of Antwerp, son of a wharfinger in that town.

When Nello recovered his consciousness he was lying on the stones without, and Patrasche was trying with every art he knew to call him back to life. In the distance a throng of the youths of Antwerp were shouting around their successful comrade, and escorting him with acclamations to his home upon the quay.

The boy staggered to his feet and drew the dog into his embrace. "It is all over, dear Patrasche," he murmured—"all over!"

He rallied himself as best he could, for he was weak from fasting, and retraced his steps to the village. Patrasche paced by his side with his head drooping and his old strong limbs feeble under him from hunger and sorrow.

The snow was falling fast: a keen hurricane blew from the north: it was bitter as death on the plains. It took them long to traverse the familiar path, and the bells were sounding four of the clock as they approached the hamlet. Suddenly Patrasche paused, arrested by a scent in the snow, scratched, whined, and drew out with his teeth a small case of brown leather. He held it up to Nello in the darkness. Where they were there stood a little Calvary, and a lamp burned dully under the cross: the boy mechanically turned the bag to the light: on it was the name of Baas Cogez, and within it were notes for six thousand francs.

The sight roused the lad a little from his stupor. He thrust it in his shirt, and stroked Patrasche and drew him onward. The dog looked up wistfully in his face.

Nello made straight for the mill-house, and went to the house-door and struck on its panels. The miller's wife opened it weeping, with little Alois clinging close to her skirts.

"Is it thee, thou poor lad?" she asked kindly through her tears. "Get thee gone ere the Baas see thee. We are in sore trouble to-night. He is out seeking for a power of money that he has let fall riding homeward, and in this snow he never will find it; and God knows it will go nigh to ruin us. It is heaven's own judgment for the things we have done to thee."

Nello put the note-case in her hand and signed Patrasche within the house.

"Patrasche found the money to-night," he said quickly. "Tell Baas Cogez so: I think he will not deny the dog shelter and food in his old age. Keep him from pursuing me, and I pray of you to be good to him."

Ere either woman or dog knew what he did, he had stooped and kissed Patrasche: then had closed the door hurriedly on him, and had disappeared in the gloom of the fast-falling night.

The woman and the child stood speechless with joy and fear: Patrasche vainly spent the fury of his anguish against the iron-bound oak of the barred house-door. They did not dare unbar the door and let him forth: they tried all that they knew how to solace him. They brought him sweet cakes and juicy meats; they tempted him with the best they had; they tried to lure him to abide by the warmth of the hearth; but it was of no avail. Patrasche refused to be comforted or to stir from the barred portal.

It was six at night when, from an opposite entrance, the miller at last came, jaded and broken, into his wife's presence. "It is lost for ever," he said, with an ashen cheek and a quiver in his stern voice. "We have looked with lanterns everywhere: it is gone—the little maiden's portion and all!"

His wife put the money into his hold, and told him how it had come back to her. The strong man sank trembling into a seat and covered his face with his hands, ashamed and almost afraid.

"I have been cruel to the lad," he muttered at length: "I deserved not to have good at his hands."

Little Alois, taking courage, crept close to her father and nestled against him her curly fair head.

"Nello may come here again, father?" she whispered. "He may come to-morrow as he used to do?"

The miller pressed her in his arms: his hard, sunburned face was very pale and his mouth trembled. "Surely, surely," he answered his child. "He shall bide here on Christmas Day, and any other day he will. In my greed I sinned, and the Lord chastened me gently: God helping me, I will make amends to the boy—I will make amends."

Little Alois kissed him in gratitude and joy, then slid from his knees and ran to where the dog kept watch by the door.

"And to-night I may feast Patrasche?" she cried in a child's thoughtless glee.

Her father bent his head gravely: "Ay, ay; let the dog have the best;" for the stern old man was moved and shaken to his heart's depths.

It was Christmas Eve, and the mill-house was filled with oak-logs and squares of turf, with cream and honey, with meat and bread, and the rafters were hung with wreaths of evergreen, and the Calvary and the cuckoo-clock looked out from a red mass of holly. There were little paper-lanterns, too, for Alois, and toys of various fashions, and sweetmeats in bright-pictured papers. There were light and warmth and abundance everywhere, and in it the child would fain have made the dog a guest honoured and feasted.

But Patrasche would neither lie in the warmth nor share in the cheer. Famished he was and very cold, but without Nello he would partake neither of comfort nor food. Against all temptation he was proof, and close against the door he leaned always, watching only for a means of escape.

"He wants the lad," said Baas Cogez. "Good dog! good dog! I will go over to the lad the first thing at day-dawn."

For no one but Patrasche knew that Nello had left the hut, and no one but Patrasche divined that Nello had left him there, to face starvation and misery alone.

The mill-kitchen was very warm; great logs crackled and flamed on the hearth; neighbours came in for a glass of wine and a slice of the fat goose baking for supper. Alois, gleeful and sure of her playmate back on the morrow, bounded and sang, and tossed back her yellow hair. Baas Cogez, in the fullness of his heart, smiled on her through moistened eyes, and spoke of the way in which he would befriend her favourite companion; the housemother sat with calm contented face at the spinning-wheel; the cuckoo in the clock chirped mirthful hours. Amidst it all Patrasche was bidden with a thousand words of welcome to tarry there a cherished guest, and he would not. Neither peace nor plenty could allure him where Nello was not.

When the supper smoked on the board, and the voices were loudest and gladdest, and the Christchild brought choicest gifts to Alois, Patrasche, watching always an occasion, glided out when the door was unlatched by a careless new-comer, and as swiftly as his weak and tired limbs would bear him sped over the snow in the bitter, black night. He had only one thought—to follow Nello. A human friend might have paused for the pleasant meal, the cheery warmth, the cozy slumber; but that was not the friendship of Patrasche. He remembered a bygone time, when an old man and a little child had found him sick unto death in the wayside ditch.

Snow had fallen freshly all the evening long; it was now nearly ten; the trail of the boy's footsteps was almost obliterated. It took Patrasche long and arduous labour to discover any scent by which to guide him in pursuit. When at last he found it, it was lost again quickly, and lost and recovered, and again lost and again recovered, a hundred times, and more.

The night was very wild. The lamps under the wayside crosses were blown out: the roads were sheets of ice; the impenetrable darkness hid every trace of habitations; there was no living thing abroad. All the cattle were housed, and in all the huts and homesteads men and women rejoiced and feasted. There was only Patrasche out in the cruel cold—old and famished and full of pain, but with the strength and the patience of a great love to sustain him in his search.

The trail of Nello's steps, faint and obscure as it was under the new snow, went straightly along the accustomed tracks into Antwerp. It was past midnight when Patrasche traced it over the boundaries of the town and into the narrow, tortuous, gloomy streets. It was all quite dark in the town. Now and then some light gleamed ruddily through the crevices of house-shutters, or some group went homeward with lanterns chanting drinking-songs. The streets were all white with ice: the high walls and roofs loomed black against them. There was scarce a sound save the riot of the winds down the passages as they tossed the creaking signs and shook the tall lamp-irons.

So many passers-by had trodden through and through the snow, so many divers paths had crossed and recrossed each other, that the dog had a hard task to retain any hold on the track he followed. But he kept on his way, though the cold pierced him to the bone, and the jagged ice cut his feet, and the hunger in his body gnawed like a rat's teeth. But he kept on his way—a poor gaunt, shivering, drooping thing in the frozen darkness, that no one pitied as he went—and by long patience traced the steps he loved into the very heart of the burgh and up to the steps of the great cathedral.

"He is gone to the things that he loved," thought Patrasche; he could not understand, but he was full of sorrow and of pity for the art-passion that to him was so incomprehensible and yet so sacred.

The portals of the cathedral were unclosed after the midnight mass. Some heedlessness in the custodians, too eager to go home and feast or sleep, or too drowsy to know whether they turned the keys aright, had left one of the doors unlocked. By that accident the footfalls Patrasche sought had passed through into the building, leaving the white marks of snow upon the dark stone floor. By that slender white thread, frozen as it fell, he was guided through the intense silence, through the immensity of the vaulted space—guided straight to the gates of the chancel, and stretched there upon the stones, he found Nello. He crept up noiselessly, and touched the face of the boy. "Didst thou dream that I should be faithless and forsake thee? I—a dog?" said that mute caress.

The lad raised himself with a low cry and clasped him close.

"Let us lie down and die together," he murmured. "Men have no need of us, and we are all alone."

In answer, Patrasche crept closer yet, and laid his head upon the young boy's breast. The great tears stood in his brown sad eyes: not for himself —for himself he was happy.

They lay close together in the piercing cold. The blasts that blew over the Flemish dykes from the northern seas were like waves of ice, which froze every living thing they touched. The interior of the immense vault of stone in which they were

5*

was even more bitterly chill than the snow-covered plains without. Now and then a bat moved in the shadows—now and then a gleam of light came to the ranks of carven figures. Under the Rubens they lay together, quite still, and soothed almost into a dreaming slumber by the numbing narcotic of the cold. Together they dreamed of the old glad days when they had chased each other through the flowering grasses of the summer meadows, or sat hidden in the tall bulrushes by the water's side, watching the boats go seaward in the sun.

No anger had ever separated them; no cloud had ever come between them; no roughness on the one side, no faithlessness on the other, had ever obscured their perfect love and trust. All through their short lives they had done their duty as it had come to them, and had been happy in the mere sense of living, and had begrudged nothing to any man or beast, and had been quite content because quite innocent. And in the faintness of famine and of the frozen blood that stole dully and slowly through their veins, it was of the days they had spent together that they dreamed, lying there in the long watches of the night of Noël.

Suddenly through the darkness a great white radiance streamed through the vastness of the aisles; the moon, that was at her height, had broken through the clouds; the snow had ceased to fall;

the light reflected from the snow without was clear as the light of dawn. It fell through the arches full upon the two pictures above, from which the boy on his entrance had flung back the veil: the Elevation and the Descent of the Cross were for one instant visible as by day.

Nello rose to his feet and stretched his arms to them: the tears of a passionate ecstasy glistened on the paleness of his face.

"I have seen them at last!" he cried aloud. "O God, it is enough!"

His limbs failed under him, and he sank upon his knees, still gazing upward at the majesty that he adored. For a few brief moments the light illumined the divine visions that had been denied to him so long—light, clear, and sweet and strong as though it streamed from the throne of Heaven.

Then suddenly it passed away: once more a great darkness covered the face of Christ.

The arms of the boy drew close again the body of the dog.

"We shall see His face—*there*," he murmured; "and He will not part us, I think; He will have mercy."

IV.

ON the morrow, by the chancel of the cathedral, the people of Antwerp found them both. They were both dead: the cold of the night had frozen into stillness alike the young life and the old. When the Christmas morning broke and the priests came to the temple, they saw them lying thus on the stones together. Above, the veils were drawn back from the great visions of Rubens, and the fresh rays of the sunrise touched the thorn-crowned head of the God.

As the day grew on there came an old, hard-featured man, who wept as women weep.

"I was cruel to the lad," he muttered, "and now I would have made amends—yea, to the half of my substance—and he should have been to me as a son."

There came also, as the day grew apace, a painter who had fame in the world, and who was liberal of hand and of spirit.

"I seek one who should have had the prize yesterday had worth won," he said to the people,— "A boy of rare promise and genius. An old woodcutter on a fallen tree at eventide—that was all his theme. But there was greatness for the future in it. I would fain find him, and take him with me and teach him art."

And a little child with curling fair hair, sobbing bitterly as she clung to her father's arm, cried aloud, "Oh, Nello, come! We have all ready for thee. The Christ-child's hands are full of gifts, and the old piper will play for us; and the mother says thou shalt stay by the hearth and burn nuts with us all the Noël week long—yes, even to the Feast of the Kings! And Patrasche will be so happy! Oh, Nello, wake and come!"

But the young pale face, turned upward to the light of the great Rubens with a smile upon its mouth, answered them all, "It is too late."

For the sweet, sonorous bells went ringing through the frost, and the sunlight shone upon the plains of snow, and the populace trooped gay and glad through the streets, but Nello and Patrasche no more asked charity at their hands. All they needed now Antwerp gave unbidden.

Death had been more pitiful to them than longer life would have been. It had taken the one in the loyalty of love, and the other in the innocence of faith, from a world which for love has no recompense, and for faith no fulfilment.

All their lives they had been together, and in their deaths they were not divided; for when they were found the arms of the boy were folded too closely around the dog to be severed without violence, and the people of their little village, contrite and ashamed, implored a special grace for them, and, making them one grave, laid them to rest there side by side—for ever.

A BRANCH OF LILAC.

I.

Yes, I shall be shot at dawn. So they say.

All for a branch of lilac. You do not believe? Chut! Men have been shot many a time for as little. A glance, a smile, a tear, a withered flower. So little. And yet so much when they are a woman's. So much. All one's present, all one's past, all one's future.

There is the lilac—look! There is no colour, no fragrance, no loveliness in it now. It is so pale, so faded, so scentless. So faded—just like a love that is dead.

People say that men cannot love in these days. It is a lie. Rich men—perhaps not. But the poor!—Then, women do not care for that.

You asked me my story. Why? To have a history is a luxury for the rich. What use can one be to the poor? If they tell it, who listens? And I have been very poor, always. Yet I was happy till that lilac blossomed one fair spring day.

I am a comedian. My mother was one before me. My father—oh, ta-ta-ta! That is another luxury for the wealthy.

My mother was quite obscure always. A little, humble player. She passed with a little wandering troupe, at certain seasons, from town to town, from province to province.

I remember, when I was very small, being carried on her shoulders or about her waist along the dusty roads, and catching at the butterflies in the sunshine as we went.

I was a little, round, brown, mischievous child—very ugly, I am sure, as I am now and have ever been. But to her, no doubt—dear soul!—I had beauty.

I must have plagued her sorely, always on the move as she was; but she never made me think myself a nuisance. However tired she might be, she was never too tired to romp and gambol with me. Poor little white, bright, thin-cheeked mother! I see her now, dancing in her spangles with the red paint on, and the bird-like eyes of her always seeking the plump, rough boy who only pulled her dress to pieces when he was hungry, or pommeled her with his sunburnt fists when he was cross and tired. And he was often both tired and hungry: that I remember also. But it was not her fault. Poor little mother! She would have danced her feet to the bone to keep me like a baby prince, if it had been possible for dancing to have brought in wealth.

Poor little mother! She had a heavy fall from some scaffolding when I was five years old; but I can see her now, as though it were yesterday, in her scarlet bodice and her silvered skirts, running off the stage the moment she was free to take me in her arms and cover me with kisses.

And, as I remember her, I think she must have been full of grace—such grace as a bird's is on a bough full of summer leaf; but if I am right, the people whom she danced for were wrong, for the public never saw anything particular in her, and she died as she had lived—a strolling player to the last.

"Piccinino" was the last word she spoke; Piccinino was the name she always called me; Piccinino I remained. I must have had some other name, of course, that the law gave me. But the law and I were never close friends, and I never asked my debts to it.

The little troupe of comedians whom my mother had been associated with were very good to me. There is so very much goodness in all Bohemians. They are always kindly, generous, sympathetic, compassionate. I was a little motherless, penniless, desolate wretch of five years old; ugly, too—brown and ugly, as you see me now, very much. I have had a face too good for comedy, too good to make the people laugh, for it ever to have been anything except grotesque and unlovely. But they were as good to me as though I had been beautiful to the sight and had inherited a patrimony.

The old men and the young, the beldames and the pretty women of the little company, vied with each other in charity and hospitality. True, they were all very poor, but what they had they never grudged to me. They took me with them everywhere, and never even dreamed of turning off the cost and trouble of me upon that bitter stepmother—the state.

As I grew older I took to the stage myself. I could not have imagined life lived to any other music than that of the little shrill reed-pipe and deep-rolling drum, that had drowned my first cries at my birth; and had awakened my laughter so many and many a time later on, that it seemed to me that their cheery sounds were as needful to all sense of existence as was the very light of the sun itself.

There were little things that a child could do, little parts that a child could play, and these I had and these I did almost from the time my mother left me alone in the world. They said I did them well. I do not know about that. I only know that the boards of our little travelling theatre always seemed the natural home to me, and that I was never afraid of the innumerable eyes of the largest audience: they always seemed to me the eyes of friends—of the only friends that I had upon earth.

It was so pleasant, too, to make them laugh. I, a little child, a little ugly fellow, whom the children of the towns and villages hooted as I passed up their streets, could hold all these mature men and women, all these fathers of families and grandsires and granddames, shaking and shouting with laughter at the pranks of my mirth and my talent. It was my revenge, and it was sweet to me. Those children who hooted me, who sometimes stoned me, who called me "mountebank," and yelled at me for my ugliness,—they could not make their elders laugh at will. But I could.

I did not bear the children, my foes, any malice. I was what they called good-tempered, and whether I were on or off the stage I was gay at heart almost always at that time, and every other time indeed till that lilac blossomed two years ago.

It was a merry life we led. Very poor, oh yes, and hard in many ways. We had to tramp in all weathers from place to place, timing ourselves to reach this hamlet or that town by such and such a saint's day or festivity. We had to sleep very often in haylofts or even in cattle-sheds, for usually such taverns as we alone could afford to go to were full to overflowing at any feast-time or market-season. At other periods, too, we did not always make enough to leave anything to be divided amongst ourselves after all expenses of setting up and lighting our little portable playhouse were paid; and old Vico Mathurin, our head and chief, was as honest as the day, and would cheat no man of a sou though he starved for it.

But what did that matter? We were a cheerful little fraternity, loving one another, only vying with each other in good-natured rivalry; and always ready, each of us, to make the best of all chances and all circumstances. We often thought, as we went through the towns, how much happier and freer we were than those were who dwelt in them, bound to one spot, mewed under one roof, seeing one landscape always, looking always to find a grave in the self-same place where they were born, whilst we went and came as we chose, never tarried long enough in one place to grow weary of it, seldom saw the fruit ripen on the same trees where we saw it blossom, and had nothing between us and the width of the skies.

I dare say the townspeople pitied us as homeless vagrants. No doubt. But we never pitied ourselves. So we must have been happy. Wisely or unwisely?

I was but a little creature when I went first on the stage, but I was born a Bohemian, and I was content—more than content, full of joy—as I pattered along by Vico Mathurin's side, my little bare feet deep in the summer dust or splashing into puddles of the autumn rain.

Full of joy, for Mathurin would pat me on the head and prophesy wondrous things of my talent; and then pretty, blue-eyed Euphrasie would kiss me and weave the roadside grasses into crowns for me, and big Francisque, her lover, would raise me for a ride on his stout shoulder; and ever and again a lark would sing, or a rabbit would scud across the path, or an old peasant would drop me a handful of mulberries or a clump of honeycomb wrapped in a green leaf; or some other little homely, innocent, simple pleasure would blossom in my way as the country wild-flowers sprang up beneath my steps.

In the winter, it is true, it was more severe. Winter tries hardly all the wandering races: if the year were all summer, all the world would be Bohemians.

But even in the winter there was so much that

was mirthful and pleasant one could not be sad or despondent. Usually in the winter we tarried in some southerly town; and if one were cold, some good creature sitting at her chestnut-stall in the street would be sure to thrust some fine nuts smoking into my hands with a smile, or pretty Euphrasie would catch me in her arms and warm my cheek upon her beating heart; and then big Francisque would pretend a ferocious jealousy, and take a terrible vengeance by pelting me with gilded gingerbreads from the fairy booths until I cried for quarter, while Vico Mathurin, the gentle good old man, would, if he had a chance to do so unperceived, slip his share of the frugal meal into my plate, and make believe that some friend at a wineshop had so feasted him at breakfast that he had no appetite nor power left for more. Ah, dear people, dear people! are you with the dead? I wonder. I shall know soon.

So my childhood and boyhood went away very happily. Poverty I did not mind, for it was a poverty so contented and mirthful, and I had never known anything else; and ugliness I did not regret, for they all told me that my physiognomy was the most ductile and expressive for the comic mummeries which were the special vein of my stage-talent.

Only now and then, when the little dark-eyed

girls of some religious procession with their white lilies and their upraised crosses shrank a little from me under their white clouds of muslin,—only then did I wish that I were straight of feature and comely to the eye, as most lads were.

"It is stupid to be as ugly as that," said one little pretty, fair creature to me once on a confirmation-day, pushing me aside in the street on to the sharp-set stones of the roadway. I stumbled and I winced, she was so fair and angel-like.

But that night she came, my little angel, still with her white rosebuds on her yellow curls, to the theatre which we had set up in the market-place—came with her parents, who were rich tanners in the town. I saw her; I saw nothing but her: she laughed, she cried, she applauded: she was scarlet with wonder, beside herself with glee.

They told me—Mathurin and Francisque, my teachers and masters—that I had never played so well, so wonderfully for my years, as I played that night. I laughed as I heard them, an hysterical, choking laugh, I remember, not seeing them, only seeing in the sea of faces one little golden head crowned with white rosebuds.

"Ask her *now* if it be stupid to be ugly," I said to them; then I fainted.

You do not care to hear all this. What does

it matter? Whether I suffered or enjoyed, loved or hated, is of no consequence to any one. The dancing-dog suffers intensely beneath the scourge of the stick, and is capable of intense attachment to any one who is merciful enough not to beat him; but the dancing-dog and his woe and his love are nothing to the world: I was as little.

There is nothing more terrible, nothing more cruel, than the waste of emotion, the profuse expenditure of fruitless pain, which every hour, every moment, as it passes, causes to millions of living creatures. If it were of any use who would mind? But it is all waste, frightful waste, to no end, to no end.

I wander: I cannot help it. I must tell of myself in my own way, or not at all.

Thus I grew up with these gay, kindly, tender-souled people, who were outcasts in the sight of most men. When I was about fifteen years of age the old man died—died of cold, I believe. He gave his little *scaldino* and his one thick cloak to warm the feet of a poor young creature who had hardly recovered from child-birth, and who lay shivering on a bed of straw in a wayside hut; and having done this, saying nothing to any one, he lay shivering all night in his garret in a bitter frost, till his heart ceased its slow gentle beating for ever.

His loss broke up the little troop. Its members held loosely together for a while, but the keystone which had united the whole had fallen when Mathurin died, and the several pieces of the little structure dropped asunder one by one. Francisque and Euphrasie bethought themselves late in the day of getting the sanction of priests on their love, and wedded one another and went somewhere southward, I forget whither, and together opened a café and flower-shop, thinking it time to get a roof over their heads and a place in the reputable world as middle age crept upon them. The others all went right and left, east and west, as they would. I went first with some, then with others.

Euphrasie would have had me go to live with them and help to plant her flower seeds and bind up her carnations, but I would not leave the old ways of the old life. A roof!—what could that matter to me, young and strong and gifted with one talent, as all people said?

Besides, I had been born a Bohemian: the wanderer's, the stroller's blood was in me strong and ardent. I loved the freedom and the change—ay, I loved the very risks and deprivations—of the career I had always followed, and I was resolved that there should never be any music sweeter in my ear than the sounds of the old reed-pipe and the brazen drum which had greeted my young senses in my cradle. I was eighteen: I was full of health and strength. I had a talent that at least was good for this—to make the people laugh. I do not need to say I had no fear of the future: I loved the career of a comedian, and I would not have exchanged its gayety and carelessness and freedom for anything—nay, not for an empire.

My early instructor, Mathurin, although he had remained an obscure stroller to the last, had been a man of accurate judgment and of genuine taste. He had reared me to discern the difference between a graceful fooling and a witless buffoonery: he had taught me to aim always at raising the pure mirth and the happy glee of the populace by legitimate means, and not by the vile medium of obscene jests and of lascivious side-play. I was a comic actor, as he had been: yes, but this I can say, as he did before me—that never by me were the people the worse for the laughter I raised.

What does that matter, either? you say. Not much to any one; only, when one is to die at break of day, it is not unpleasant to remember that no girl's mind was the baser, no man's impulses were the lewder, for the way one has followed one's art.

I joined various troops of wandering players

after the old band broke up at Mathurin's death. I was successful, in my way, with the people. I never attracted notice enough to be called to any city or sought by any impresario.

I do not think I was ever coarse enough for the famous theatres. Nay, I speak in sober earnest, not in any irony. The taste of cities requires indecent gesture, and sees no point in a jest unless it have some foul meaning hidden in its *équivoque*. Now, my fooling was cleanly and honest in its mirth—simple, I dare say, but, as far as I could make it, harmless. When the tired hordes of the labouring classes and the stupid, open-mouthed peasantry crammed the wooden booth to overflowing, and laughed at me till they lifted the canvas roofing with the loud gusts of their expanding lungs, they were never the worse for that momentary oblivion of their hunger and travail—never:—that I know.

So I spent my life for ten years—spent it till that lilac bloomed.

Oh, do not think I was a saint. I had plenty of follies, plenty of sins. I loved a draught of wine, a fling at dominoes, a kiss of ripe lips, a dance with limber limbs: I loved all these as well as any man, and had my share of them. But what I would say is, that in my art I always tried to do good. Vico Mathurin had always led me to see that any career may be ennobled by the leading of it, and he had always held that though the world may rate it low, the art of the comic player may have a noble aim if it aspire ever to make the weary and overtasked multitude forget for a little season the gall of heavy harness and the toil of flinty roads.

"See you here," he would say to me many a time when I was a boy. "These people come and look at us and hearken to us, and laugh and are glad for a little space: then, when they go back into their cabins or their attics, some little trill of our song will stay on their famished lips, some little bubble of laughter at the memory of one of our jokes will remain with them amidst their poverty and their hard work; and these will be like a stray sunbeam in a cellar in the darkness of their lot. Think of that, think of that, Piccinino, and it will not hurt you when any scoffer casts at you, as a term of scorn, your title of strolling player."

And these words of my dear old master abode with me always, and as far as I could I trod closely in his footsteps; and in many places where he had been known the people welcomed me and loved me a little for his sake.

I never left France: we who speak only to the

populace cannot go where the populace have another tongue than ours. But France is so wide, and I was for ever on the move—in the north for the harvest, in the centre for the vintage, in the south for the winter season; going whithersoever there was a festival or a bridal or a great market, or a holiday of any sort that made the townsfolk or the villagers in festal trim and in the mood to smile.

When I sit in the gloom here I see all the scenes of that pleasant life pass like pictures before me.

No doubt I was often hot, often cold, often footsore, often ahungered and athirst: no doubt; but all that has faded now. I only see the old, lost, unforgotten brightness; the sunny roads, with the wild poppies blowing in the wayside grass; the quaint little red roofs and peaked towers that were thrust upward out of the rolling woods; the clear blue skies, with the larks singing against the sun; the quiet, cool, moss-grown towns, with old dreamy bells ringing sleepily above them; the dull casements opening here and there to show a rose like a girl's cheek, and a girl's face like the rose; the little wineshops buried in their climbing vines and their tall, many-coloured hollyhocks, from which sometimes a cheery voice would cry, "Come, stay for a stoup of wine, and pay us with a song."

Then, the nights when the people flocked to us, and the little tent was lighted, and the women's and the children's mirth rang out in peals of music; and the men vied with each other as to which should bear each of us off to have bed and board under the cottage roof, or in the old mill-house, or in the weaver's garret; the nights when the homely supper-board was brightened and thought honoured by our presence; when we told the black-eyed daughter's fortunes, and kept the children round-eyed and flushing red with wonder at strange tales, and smoked within the leaf-hung window with the father and his sons; and then went out, quietly, alone in the moonlight, and saw the old cathedral white and black in the shadows and the light; and strayed a little into its dim aisles, and watched the thorn-crowned God upon the cross, and in the cool, fruit-scented air, in the sweet silent dusk, moved softly with noiseless footfall and bent head, as though the dead were there.

Ah, well! they are all gone, those days and nights. Begrudge me not their memory. I am ugly, and very poor, and of no account; and I die at sunrise, so they say. Let me remember whilst I can: it is all oblivion *there*. So they say.

II.

I LED this life for ten years after the death of Vico Mathurin—led it happily, yes, very happily in the main, although at no time in it did I ever make money enough to pay for more than the simplest fare, the hardest couch, the thinnest draught of wine.

But happiness depends so much upon one's self. That is a threadbare saying of the preachers. Yes, I know. But it is true, for all that.

So long as one has no regret, one can be happy; and as for me, I envied no man. This was ignorance, no doubt. If I had ever known what wealth and its powers and its pleasures were like, no doubt I should have hungered for them like the rest of men. But I had never known, and it was not in my nature merely to be jealous of possession. If I had been crippled, I should have passionately envied those who still walked at will straightly and swiftly whither they would. But it was not in me, whilst I could march as I pleased, strongly and fast, through the seeding grasses, over the sun-swept plains, amongst the red and gold leaves of autumn, and over the white fields of the midwinter snows, —it was not in me then, I say, to envy the men who rolled on wheels or were borne by horses. It was not in me: it would have seemed to me peevish, childish, ingrate, mean.

This was my ignorance, no doubt. Men, I have noticed, knowing much, do envy much—almost always.

One day in the early spring-time, I came with my troop into a little town that stood on the Loire River—a little old, gray town, high on a rock, circled by crumbling walls, all blossoming everywhere just then with bud and leaf, all over its moat and its ramparts, in its streets and its casements: its very ditches were white with lilies-of-the-valley, and its very roofs were yellow with flowering houseleeks, while at every nook and corner over the walls of its gardens the lilacs, white and purple, were in bloom. I can smell them now: in the ditch that they will bury me in, I shall smell them still, I think.

We entered the gates at high noon, and set up our play-house in the market-square.

The morrow would be a fête-day, and the town was stirred from the gray torpor and stillness of its extreme old age, and was alive and gay with country-people and its own small population, all afoot and thronging the wooden stalls of the fair, and the crooked steep alleys that crossed and recrossed each other up the slope of the place.

As I went up one of these, bearing my share of the framework and the canvas of our play-house, with the reed-pipe and the old drum sounding merrily as ever before our tired steps, I heard a voice above me, the clear, high voice of a woman.

"How ugly he is, that one!" it cried with a laugh. "His face alone is a burlesque. He will make the very dogs in the streets die of laughter."

"Hush!" said a voice that was lower in tone and fuller. "Who knows? He may hear. And he looks so weary and so tired!"

The other voice laughed on in its cruel and saucy glee:

"Pooh! He is too ugly to live! Why does God make such creatures?"

And across the eyes the fragrance of lilac in full blossom struck me a cool, refreshing blow.

She who spoke last had broken a branch of the sweet spring flower and cast it down to me in merry scorn, so that it fell across the timber on which my hands were clasped. There was a little saffron-hued butterfly upon it, I remember, and one golden-brown bee. The bee paused a moment upon my wrist and then flew from me; the butterfly remained upon the blossoms.

I looked up. An old man, a gardener, who had chidden her and the bright creature who had thrown the sweet blossom and the harsh words at me, leaned over the old gray, moss-grown wall. The lilac boughs were all about her—above, beneath, around. Her golden head glistened in the sunlight. She had a knot of lilacs in her breast.

Can I describe her? No: think of the woman who to you, above all others of her sex, has meant —Love.

She was but a young girl of the people, the orphan daughter of a poor wood-carver, simply clad in the garb of her province, spending a momentary rest from her daily labour in leaning over the old garden wall to watch the strange strollers pass by with pipe and beat of drum; but to me she became the world.

It is so strange! We see a million faces, we hear a million voices, we meet a million women with flowers in their breasts and light in their fair eyes, and they do not touch us. Then we see one, and she holds for us life or death, and plays with them idly so often—as idly as a child with toys. She is not nobler, better or more beautiful than were all those we passed, and yet the world is empty to us without her.

I went on up the street. I held the bough of lilac in my hand.

Yes: this bough, poor faded, scentless thing!

And that morning it was so bright, so full of odour, so eagerly kissed by the butterfly and the bee. Two years ago, just two years ago! Are the lilacs in flower there, I wonder, now? Surely; and she gathers them and throws them to her lover. Why not?

Shall she think of the bough that is dead—of the bough that blossomed last season—so long ago, so long ago? No. The lilac flowers live but a day. But that brief day is longer than a woman's memory, I think.

I went on up the street.

That night!—how I played I cannot tell. I did not know what I did. All about me was the smell of the lilac trees, and in the sea of faces below I looked only for hers. She was not there.

When the stage wanted me no longer, and the audience had flocked out, loud in eager praises of us, I shook myself free of all my comrades and of the hearty townsfolk, and went back to that little steep street full of the smell of the lilacs.

There was a clear, full moon. The lilacs were all colourless in it, and their scent was heavy on the wind. Some rill of water within the garden walls was falling with musical and even measure. An owl flew by me with swift white wing gleaming silver-bright in the lustre of the stars. Why do I speak of these things? They are nothing now. And yet they are with me always.

I walked there to and fro all night. At sunrise I went away ashamed.

What was a bough of lilac to make me a fool, thus?

At daybreak I asked a stone-cutter, as he went by me to his work, who dwelt behind those old crumbling walls. He told me no one. They were the walls of an old monastic garden, into which any one might stray at pleasure. I asked him no more. I felt a strange silence and shyness upon me.

I went home to the little miserable tavern where my people had found lodging, and went up to my garret there, and looked at the lilac bough, and bent my head and kissed it foolishly. I felt as though it were my fate in some way.

I had placed it in water, and kept it in the shade, but already it had withered, and the yellow butterfly was dead.

All that day through I endeavoured to find the woman who had dropped it into my hands, but I had no success. It was a festal day, and the streets were full of people, bright with banners and streamers, crucifixes and images, white-robed singing-boys and gay little children with their heads crowned with spring flowers. But I did not light, amongst all the faces, on the face for which I sought. She must have been there, but in some way or other she had escaped me.

Night came, and I went again upon the stage. I was still incessantly pursued by one image.

"What are you looking for, Piccinino?" my companions asked me.

I laughed stupidly, and answered them, "A bough of lilac."

They stared, and thought me out of my wits, for all over the town, in the little gardens and in the shrubberies on the ramparts, and against the old stone gateways, the lilacs, white and purple, were in bloom, and amongst their tender green leafage the mated birds were nestling.

I went on the boards as usual. I remember well the little piece we performed that evening. It was a very simple little scene of humour, wherein I played the chief part—a part which always suited me—a poor cobbler, who, old and ugly and crippled, loves a young girl of his village, and is the butt and laughing-stock of all the village youth for his misplaced and despised passion.

The part was a very droll one, and I was always accustomed to play it amidst shrieks of laughter from my audiences at the follies and presumptions of the old, crippled, ugly, withered shoemaker, who had dared to lift his eyes and his thoughts to the loveliest and most mischievous maiden in his village.

This night, however, I played it in a different spirit. The sounds of those words, "How ugly he is!" were ringing in my ears, and my brain was giddy with them.

They shouted me a vociferous welcome when I appeared. I was popular in the place, and the piece was popular likewise. The presumption of emotion in any creature unlovely and aged has always been a favourite theme with the populace for gibes and mockery. It must seem very ridiculous, no doubt. And yet it is not the young, not the handsome, who feel most.

This night I played the part differently.

I did not know what possessed me. It had been a comic part always: I had always been a comic actor. Neither in the part nor in me had ever any one seen on the stage aught except farcical drolleries, absurd situations, ludicrous aspects. And yet that night suddenly I changed, and the part with me, and I was powerless to help it.

I was compelled by an impulse stronger than myself to transform the character into something higher, nobler, infinitely sadder than the poor old fool whom it had been my amusement to portray and theirs to applaud. I cannot tell how it was.

I changed no action, altered no single word, and yet the part I played ceased to be contemptible, farcical, absurd: it became full of pathos, dignity almost—I might say, of heroism. That poor old, feeble, ill-favoured, poverty-stricken man, had a heart that could love infinitely and infinitely despair —a heart which knew itself deeper and truer and keener in loyalty and suffering than any heart that beat around him with the joyous, vain throbs of an exultant youth, and yet which only made him the standing jest of all his little world, the jeered-at dotard mocked by the gay lips of the very creature for whom he would have died a thousand deaths.

That was how I read the character now: this was how I played it; and when my last words were spoken, I, looking for the first time that night on the crowd before me, saw that they were breathless, tremulous, very still—saw that I, their paid buffoon, their hired jester, had not made them laugh, but made them weep.

They did not know what ailed them, but by that strange tie which unites the actor with his audience, the vague and bitter pain in me communicated itself to them, and they wept where they had mocked, they sorrowed where they had scoffed.

"What possessed you, Piccinino?" my comrades said to me, clustering around when the piece was over. "Who could have thought you had it in you? A part like that, too! Why, the people cried like children—all of them, old and young. What could possess you, eh?"

I laughed foolishly again, I know, for my own throat was husky and my own eyes were dim.

"It is all the fault of a branch of lilac," I muttered to them, laughing off my folly. They must have thought me mad, I suppose: I thought myself so.

My chief came and stared at me curiously, then struck me a kindly blow upon the shoulders.

"Peste, Piccinino!" he swore with a good-humoured oath of wonder, "you will be a tragic actor, after all, I should not be surprised. But another time do not make my whole house cry like women when we advertise a comic entertainment. Our trade is to make folk laugh: do not forget that, my friend, again."

I was silent. I could not offer any explanation of what had so strangely and so unwontedly moved me.

It had all come of a branch of lilac. But then who would believe that? People never will believe what is true.

Well, it appeared later on that, although the impresario of our troupe of jesters had feared the anger of the audience for being mournful when we had promised to be gay, he had feared it needlessly. This little piece, which my change of mood had changed from farce to poetry, pleased them none the less in its altered aspect. They knew me well, had known me when I was a little round, sunburnt child; and it was wonderful to these simple people that their odd, ugly old friend Piccinino should have any such powers in him.

"We knew he could always make us laugh, but he makes us weep too, the droll one! Who knows! He may be great one day. He may even go to Paris," they said to one another as they left the theatre.

And they clustered round me and embraced me, and pressed me to go drink and smoke with them; but seeing that I was silent and in no mood for boisterous company, forbore to solicit me, and went away shaking their heads sadly, and yet proudly withal; for I was their old friend Piccinino: their graybeards had given me pears and peaches when I was a little lad; their elders had all seen me toddle by my poor mother's side, holding on to her spangled skirts; and now I had genius, their wiseacres said, and genius was something very vague in their minds, very audacious, very terrible—an honour and yet a plague.

The next time we were to play that piece I would fain have had it changed and have gone back to my old fooling; but I was not master of the troupe, and the townspeople, it seemed, clamoured for me, Piccinino, to play the part a second time with that new talent which time or chance, as they thought, had developed in me. So we played it.

Genius can do as it likes with its world, but we poor folk, who had only a little trifle of talent, for which we could not always even find any market at all,—we could only obey our little shred of the public obediently, and give it what it asked.

That night, when I went on the stage, I felt that she was there before I saw her—there amidst the populace, with that bright golden head of hers rising out from the sea of the swarthy peasant faces, and the sweet, saucy child's eyes laughing upon me across the yellow smoky flicker of the dull oil lamps.

I saw her: I stammered, I stumbled, I felt blind and dizzy. My comrades playing with me hissed sharply in my ear, "What ails thee, Piccinino? Art mad, or drunk, or ill, or what?" They did not rouse me. I stood staring dully across the little play-house.

The people grew angry at the pause and at the silence. Their favour was my daily bread; their wrath would be my ruin. Yet they did not stir me. I did not see them; I only saw the face that had laughed on me from the lilacs.

Across the rising uproar in the tent there came to me a small, soft, silvery sound. It was the sound of her voice, and it murmured with a cruel glee,—

"So ugly and so stupid, too! That is surely too much in one creature!"

And then she laughed again, the pretty, babyish, mutinous laugh with which she had tossed me the lilac-bough.

That one sound roused me, like a thorn thrust in an open wound. I rallied; I forced myself into the part I played; I knew little, nothing, all the time, of where I was or of what I did, and the audience was gone to me: I only saw one face. But to this one I played with all the soul that was in me; and they told me that I eclipsed myself,— that I held the people breathless and almost afraid. This, from my own knowledge, I cannot say, of course. I only know that they shouted for me, at the end, again and again; that, in their rude fashion, they did me all the homage they could; that they waved their kerchiefs and their caps at me; that they screamed their vivas at me until their lungs were weary; and that they clutched at me with a hundred eager hands, to lead me out amidst them to the noisy honours of the tavern. But I shook myself free of them—churlishly, I fear—upon some plea of sickness, and got out alone, and hid myself and watched the women depart from the wooden booth of the play-house.

But I was too late. My kindly tormentors had robbed me of the only recompense I cared for. She was gone, and I could not tell whether or no I had gained my triumph there,—whether or no the sunny, cruel eyes had moistened into tears as the eyes of all the other women had done that night.

I went away sick at heart, despite that victory on which my old companions so generously felicitated me. A victory over these poor boors who knew not one letter from another! What was it worth?

In the great cities, no doubt, they would have hissed down my acting. For the first time, my career seemed miserable, and any successes in it seemed ridiculous either to seek or to prize. For, in imagination, I followed the bright creature to her home, and saw her unloose her thick light hair before her mirror, and heard her laugh in her solitude as she thought of me, an ugly wretch who fancied if ploughmen laughed at him, or kitchen-wenches wept, that he had fame!

For the first time since I had awakened in my poor mother's arms to the summons of the pipe and the drum, the life I had led seemed vile to me,—foolish and wretched, and of no result.

As I went home in the darkness, her laughter seemed all about me,—in the leaves, in the fountains, in the little low winds, in the tremulous singing of the grass-hidden insects.

All of them seemed to laugh at me with her laughter, and shout in chorus with all their tiny, tender voices, in a derision the more cruel because coming from things so slight and fair. "So ugly and so stupid too! Why does God make such creatures?"

Ah, why indeed? Often have I asked that also.

My story is nothing new, you see. It is such a common one. I was a fool.

That night my chief followed me up into the garret where I slept, and told me that he would give me some increase of payment, and that he thought that we might tarry full a month in this small town, since I was so popular with the people, and the district was in a manner rich; its tanners, its vine-dressers, its husbandmen were well to do, and, for our country, it was populous, and from the many hamlets round there would be, most likely, audience for us all the summer season through.

I did not question his judgment. I caught eagerly at his will to stay. For me, I knew the whole earth now only held one road worth the treading—the road where the lilacs blossomed.

Well, we stayed on till the lilacs faded, as he had said, and long ere the month was out I had found her name and her dwelling. I do not care to say her name: let it die with me. After I saw her that first day it was always "She" in my thoughts. The world held for me only one woman.

She lived in a high old house, in a gray, dusky street, in the topmost corner of it, close against the sky. The old garden was near, and she went thither often. She had no friends. She got her bread by making lace. She sat at her lattice, with her golden hair bound up in the gold-coloured kerchief, with her small rosy hands flying in and out among the bobbins, and the senseless pillow close-pressed against the white warmth of her breast.

I have often watched her so, hidden myself in some old dark doorway or some crumbling arch opposite and far below. And all the time the lilacs were in blossom. She always had a great sweet cluster of them set in a brown, broken jar upon the stone sill of her window. And while I watched there below, the winds would shake some breath of their fragrance out to me, and the little blue butterflies would fly to and fro betwixt me and the lattice; and, like a fool, I would tell myself that she would hardly, sure, have flung me a bough of her favourite flower if she had thought me so utterly hideous and ridiculous as her words had said.

I was very shy and silent. I had been bold enough in my day. I had never cared what audacious jest I passed, what careless impudence I attempted, with any woman. My very knowledge of how absolutely I, poor and ill-favoured, was nothing to all their sex, had made me reckless and dauntless in my ways with them.

Such kisses as I had ever tasted had all been bought; such lips as had smiled on me had only smiled because even my small guerdon was the only thing which stood between them and starvation: and although my memory of my mother had kept me less vicious than my mode of life might have made me, yet I had never been over-modest where female creatures were in question. But with her,—I did not know what ailed me, I was so timid, so dumb-stricken, so unlike what I had ever been.

Partly, no doubt, it was the knowledge of her scorn that silenced me. But chiefly it was that she had been to me, from the first instant I had seen her, a creature inexpressibly beautiful and full of sanctity, as far above me as though she had been a sovereign in her palace and amidst her guards, instead of a girl of the populace weaving lace at her casement in an attic.

All her people were dead. She was sixteen years old, and she was poor. So much I learned. I had not courage to speak her name, or to ask much of her. I fancied every one must see the blood coming and going in my foolish face if I but spoke of her by chance to any neighbour.

One old woman, who had a fruit-stall in the street, shrugged her shoulders and thrust out her mouth, and muttered some evil words against her, and would have told me something, I remember now, one day. But I knew what the venom of women was: I would not hear; I could not bear to look to play the spy on her. Otherwise, perhaps—— But it was not to be.

Men, when they stumble to their fate, are blind and deaf: it is the will of God.

She seemed to me to live quite innocently and most simply, for she, too, was very poor. Poverty for myself I had never esteemed as any sort of ill: I thought that in it men were healthy, strong, untempted, and most manlike. But it made my heart ache to watch that little bare chamber which was all her home.

She was so infinitely lovely, so golden-bright, so rose-like, so dainty in hue and shape, that it seemed to me she ought to be housed as graciously as a butterfly in a lily cup, as a little blue warbler in a summer nest of leaves.

She soon espied me where I kept my vigil. She would laugh a little and glance at me with her sweet mischievous eyes, and now and then would nod her head with some charming little gesture, half of invitation, half of derision and disdain. And yet she was coy too.

She would take her way to mass in early morning, with a string of red dried berries round her throat for rosary, and would go counting them, with her white lids and her long dark eyelashes cast downward, nor look to right or left of her, seeming ever absorbed in earnest prayer.

God in heaven! who teaches women? This one had not fully spent her seventeenth year; she had been the child of poor labouring people, her father a hewer of wood, her mother a weaver of lace; she had seen naught of any world except this little one of the gray, quiet old town set on the river-rock; and yet who could have taught her any wile which she had not by nature of her sex's science? No one —not even him by whom the mother of Cain was tempted, as priests say.

It is strange—strange and most terrible. And still I think they know not what they do. They are subtle for very play; they are cruel for mere sport; they devour what loves them by their simple instinct, as the young kitten dallies with its mouse.

Others have said this all much better than I say it? Oh yes, no doubt—only to every man, when he suffers, it seems new, and he thinks no wound was ever yet so deep, or dealt in such utter wantonness, as his has been.

III.

WELL, we tarried in that place until all the blossoms of the lilacs had died off, and above the low stone walls, and between the gables of the streets, and in the gardens slanting to the water's edge, there flowered in their stead the tall silver lilies and the radiant roses of the summer-time.

My lilac bough was withered and colourless as dust, but in its stead there budded for me the wonder-flower of a supreme happiness. She came oftentimes to our play-house with some of the townspeople, and I thought, or cheated myself into thinking, that after she had seen me act she grew to despise me less.

The nights she was not there I played ill, very ill, I know: our chief rated me gravely many a time. But when she was there, though I saw nothing of any audience, save only the bright ring of her hair in the lamplight, that glistened like the nimbus about the heads of saints, I know that I performed my part with a fire and a soul in me which were wholly inspired by her.

"If he were not so uncertain he would be an artist fit even for Paris," I heard the folk say round me; and my old chief said so likewise.

I laughed to myself and felt heartsick; it was horrible to have one's skill, one's brain, one's strength, one's life, all ruled by the presence or absence of one human creature.

And yet so it was. If I could make her mouth part with mirth or fill her eyes with wondering concern at the humour or the pathos of my representation, I became for the time a great artist. If she were not before me, the whole place was empty; I was dull, lifeless, stupid, and I dragged my limbs with effort through the allotted part until the play was over.

But she was often there. In common with the other players, I had a right to admit some one when I would to the theatre free, and every morning she found a pass upon her little deal table, with some simple gift of flowers or fruit or other trifles, such as I could afford to get with the poor pittance which was all to which my share in the profits of our representations ever amounted.

She took all I offered, and I was more than repaid whenever she gave me in return a saucy nod, a sunny smile. Sometimes she would deny me these, and pass me by with a little shudder of aversion, or affect not even to see me standing in her path.

I could not resent it; I had no title; I knew full well she thought me too grotesque and ugly for any female thing to smile on twice in the same day. I was content if she would let me follow her without rebuke, or gaze at her without her putting her hands before her eyes, as though to screen them from some sight repulsive to her. For this she did often, and then would laugh with sauciest merriment at my misery, so that I never rightly knew whether she hated me or no.

Until one day. It had been very warm. There was no wind to cool the air. The yellow sun scorched that old dark, cool street into an amber glare, and turned the dusky, sombre shadows to a russet gold.

The little sad caged birds opened their bills thirstily and gasped. The red carnations in the window embrasures drooped sadly, and the dogs crept faint and fevered into the shelter of every jutting doorway or projecting gallery of the ancient houses. Between the roofs shone the blue cloudless sky. I can see the quiver of the white dusty trees against it. I can hear the slow, indolent murmur of the unseen river far below. I can smell the sickly heavy odour of the parched lilies in the heat. All the blinds and shutters were closed. No one was astir. The whole place seemed to sleep.

I only was awake and out—I only, who felt neither heat nor cold, knew neither day nor night, but only looked up at that one little casement in the roof to see the sunbeams illumine a girl's hand passing amidst the threads, or to watch the moonbeams slanting in their purity upon the dark closed lattice where she slept.

I was out in the burning noontide, pacing to and fro on the stony way, lest by any chance she might be there, at the window, at her work. Long I stayed in vain, moving up and down in the shadowless heat on the other side of the street, as my custom was.

The garret window was empty, and the flowers in it, my flowers, were dead. I had others in my hand, screened with wet leaves from the searching sun-rays. I waited for her to come to the lattice ere I should lay them down, as my wont was, in the entrance, upon the basin scooped above the bench in the stone wall to hold the holy water.

But instead of leaning above there, high up against the heavens, she came toward me—came down the street, drooping in the heat as the roses drooped.

She had been out with some lace to the marketsquare.

She and I were all alone, facing one another suddenly in the silent, sultry, sleepy noon beneath the eaves of the old houses. She had a kirtle of green, I remember, and a bodice of white; and she had sheltered her bright hair and her little yellow kerchief with some broad woven green leaves. She looked herself like a flower blossoming out from the gray wrinkled square stones of the pavement.

It might be the heat, it might be her fatigue, it might be—I know not. Her face was paler than its wont, and her eyes were softer. I cannot tell what it was: something gave me voice, and I spoke —spoke as I gave her my poor little gift.

I knew how foolish it was: I knew how mad it was. I knew no woman could ever ook on me with any sentiment perhaps except disgust—with nothing more than pity at the most. I knew a man's heart might break for ever and no creature see aught except a jest in his despair if he were vilely-featured and poor of habit and estate, as I was.

And yet I spoke, borne out of myself and swept away upon a flood of words, irresistibly, senselessly, I know not how, as some impulse would impel me on the stage sometimes, so that in the torrent of my speech the hearers would be carried away, and forget that he who moved them was but an ugly, poor, and nameless comic player. I could not hope to move her thus, and yet I spoke. It would end all, I thought. I must do so, I knew. And yet I spoke in the old dim, quiet street, with no listeners anywhere except the dusky carnations drooping in the heat.

What I said I cannot tell, but I prayed to her as men should only pray to their God, they say. I did not ask her for any love in answer: I might as soon have dreamed of asking for the sun in heaven. But I begged for a little pity, for a little patience: it was a crime, I knew, for any creature ugly and poor as I to speak of love at all to any woman.

When my heart had spent itself and my voice had died on my parched dry lips, I grew cold with deadly fear. I listened for her laughter, her cruel, sweet, merciless, childlike, mocking laughter.

Instead, she was quite silent. Then suddenly she trembled and grew pale, and was so still—so still. I heard the loud heavy beating of my own heart in the silence: that was all the sound there was.

Suddenly she looked at me, and her mouth quivered, and she drew her breath with a little, low, quick sob.

"I am all alone," she murmured, half with laughter, half with tears—"I am all alone!"

What could I think?

I was so ugly, so grotesque, so poor, so utterly deserted by all fortune; and yet the gray street, the yellow light, the red carnations nodding at the window, the hard blue sky, with the white, thirsty leaves painted on it, all went round with me in a blind, sickly whirl. It was impossible!—and yet she looked at me and laughed a little, with her own old, sweet scorn at my madness, though her tears were falling.

"Yes, do you hear?" she said low in her throat, so softly, and yet with such a pretty petulance. "Do you hear? You are so ugly, so absurd: you have a mouth like a frog and eyes like a fish, and yet you are good—you can say beautiful things, and—I am all alone!"

And then I knew her meaning. Ah, God! If only I could have died that day, when heaven itself seemed open to me!

Was it all a lie, then? I often wonder.

Nay, not all, I think. Perhaps not any of it. She was very young, and she was very poor, and she was weary of her life; and even such a one as I was welcome to her, since I loved her with such utter passion, and could give her freedom, as she thought. Nay, I would not think it a lie—then.

She never loved me. But she knew that I loved her, and perhaps the woe of my words had moved her to compassion; and perhaps she thought, "Better go with this poor fool and roam the world, and be a little glad, than waste all my fair years in loneliness, losing my sight over the cobwebs of laces that I only weave for other women's wear."

Perhaps, too, she had heard the people say that I had genius, and might make a name for myself in the great cities of the earth some day; and so it seemed to her that even my poor life might become worth the sharing; and she surely knew that any harvest it might ever reap upon the fields of wealth and fame would be garnered for her only, and into her lap only poured.

Or perhaps she did not reason at all, did not at all reflect, but only felt—felt some new impulse, vague and childish, stir at her heart on hearing how I loved her—as never surely woman yet was loved by man—and so leaned toward me and took the gift I gave, and wept a little, and then softly laughed, not rightly knowing what she wished, nor looking to the future.

Yes, that is likeliest. Yes, I would not think all was a lie—then.

Well, I married her. Do you know what life was to me then? A paradise—a fool's paradise, doubtless, but one without cloud, or stain, or fear, or regret upon it whilst it lasted.

She loved me!

So she had said, so she had proved. It seemed so marvellous to me! Day and night I thanked Heaven for it, for in Heaven I believed — now. What but a God—pure and perfect as the priests said—could create such a creature as this?

She seemed so wonderful to me, this white and golden thing, with her snowy limbs, and rosy lips, and her smile like the sunlight, which yet were all *mine*—only mine. When I looked at her in the first faint morning light and watched her soft still slumber, I used to think that this must be a dream—this wondrous ecstasy of mine, this intoxication of possession.

What was I, a man so poor, so ill-favoured, so grotesque, so destitute of any charm or grace which could win love, that I should have been able to touch and gather such a rare blossom as this was to bloom upon my heart?

With every night that fell, with every day that dawned, I blessed the sacred chances which had led my footsteps thither in the month of lilacs.

All the while I kept the dear branch by me, dead and scentless and without colour as it was.

It would have seemed no miracle to me if any morning I had found it bloom with fresh bud and leaf, for that would have been not more miraculous than was the beauty and the joy into which my life had suddenly burst forth.

I do not know if ever she quite knew how much I loved her.

Poor men cannot show their love in those symbols of rich gifts which women most value and most easily read. No doubt it seems hard and cold in us that we do not lavish on our best beloved all that her heart craves: no doubt it seems to a young, thoughtless female creature that it is not so much the power lacking as the will when we forbear to hang her neck with gems and fill her hand with gold. And when not only do we fail in that, but when we are even powerless to feed the bright lips we kiss with any save the scantiest fare, and stretch the fair limbs we cherish on any save the poorest bed of straw,—then,

I dare say, it seems to her that if we truly loved we should discover some means, by some periling of our body or our soul, to bestow on her the luxuries she craves.

No doubt it seems so. And I was very poor. I could not change the manner of my life. The only talent that I had was my talent on the stage, and though I had some true dramatic power in me, I was obscure and nameless, and could not, in a day nor in a year, change my estate. The simple folk of the provinces applauded me, it is true, but to win applause in Paris!—one must be very great for that.

I had always loved the old life, as I say.

It had always seemed to me the freest and the gladdest that a man born of the people could enjoy or could desire. But now it seemed to me to alter, some way. It was not fit for her, and it would not give me what I wished for her.

To tramp all along the sun-baked roads had been for me no hardship; to be hungry and suffer thirst had been to me small pain; to go to roost in some straw-yard or cattle-shed no difficult matter when the taverns were all full. The rough jests, the rude revelries, the drinking bouts, and the wine-shop supper-tables,—these had all been welcome enough to me at the end of a long day's travel afoot.

But now—she was so young, so fair to see, so delicate of frame, so precious to me, that it was horrible to me to make her toil along the stony shadowless highways, to lay down her dainty body on a truss of hay, to see the glances of my comrades light on her, and to hear the jests of the drunkards soil her ear. It poisoned the old life to me.

I had never wanted anything easier, choicer, better in any manner, for myself; but for her—for her, for the first time, I envied others; for her I looked with jealousy on the snow-white villas set within their gardens, and the gilded balconies of the pretty houses in the streets, and the silken standards fluttering from the gray towers of the nobles' châteaux, as we passed by them in our route.

Perhaps I should not have felt this had she herself been contented with the life. But she was not.

When we give a woman a great love she so often repays us by teaching us discontent!

Nay, I do not blame the woman. A man should not take his heart in his hand to her, unless in the other hand he can take also idols of gold and silver.

Before the lilac had dropped across the path I had only noticed the different way of life of the rich to draw pleasure from it.

It had afforded me many pretty pictures as I had looked at it from the outside, and I had never felt any desire to look at it more closely, or to be angered with it because I stood without. When I had looked through the gilt gateways into some rose-pleasaunce, where the great ladies sauntered and pretty children played, I had always felt glad that there were people so happy as that, and had passed on the better for the sight. But now, when I saw such things, I only felt, "Why has my darling not such rose-gardens as these, and why should her children be born and nurtured in poverty instead of wealth?"

I did what I could to soften what seemed for such a one as she the hardness and privations of our lot.

I was able to hire an old mule, which I could lead across the fields and along the highlands where the stones and the sun had so sorely tried her. By doing some turn at hand-labour in the towns where we tarried, such as hewing wood or weeding garden-plats, or fetching heavy weights, I was able also to get a little chamber for her in some quiet place away from the boisterous life of the taverns. Sometimes some one among the audiences would take some special interest in my performance, and ask me what I would choose that he should give me—a bottle of wine, a supper at the restaurant, a bundle of cigars?—and then I would thank him and decline them all, and in their stead select some basket of rich fruit or some cluster of rare flowers, and depart with it gratefully, and take it home to her and enjoy her innocent surprise.

I did what I could—indeed I did what I could—but then that uttermost was so little.

The love-gifts of one who is poor must always seem so small. How can it be otherwise?

What a rich man can do every hour with a mere sign of the hand, a mere stroke of the pen, a poor man can only do so slowly, so laboriously—in such niggardly, foolish fashion, no doubt it seems—once a year maybe, on a fête-day. And that only by sore hard work of body and of mind; for when it is difficult to get enough even to live on, look you, how can one have surplus to spare for roses, and trinkets, and all pretty trifles such as pretty women love?

It is impossible. But then that very impossibility looks so harsh, so narrow, so miserly, beside the easy lavishness of love that has gold at its call. A woman can hardly believe that you care for her unless, at her bidding, you know how to make all impossibilities possible.

And how can one be a magician without gold? I have heard that in old times there were men who spent their years and lost their wits trying always to transmute base metals, by fire and chemistry, into gold. I am very sure that they would never have thought of it unless some woman whom they loved had first wailed in their ear for some jewel they were too poor to be able to gain for her.

I do not know what she could have expected in my life. I had never, from the first, disguised to her how poor and often hard it was. But she had seen it from the outside, and, I suppose, she had anticipated more merriment and variety from it. At any rate, she was disappointed, and nothing I could do would avail to render her content. One thing, indeed, she was very restless for, which I denied,—the sole denial I ever gave her of any wish she had. She desired to go upon the boards herself. Some of my comrades told her, thoughtlessly, that it was a sin, with such a face as hers, to sit behind the scenes in lieu of passing before them to delight an audience. And she would fain have gone. But I—I told her bitterly, the only time that ever I spoke violently to her, that I would sooner slay her with my own hand than see her give her loveliness to the lewd public gaze.

Ay, so I felt. For I loathed to see even

the passers-by on the high-road glance freely at her. I could have struck to earth even my best friend amongst our own company when over-easily he parried jests and exchanged gay phrases with her.

"You are a simpleton, Piccinino," the chief of my troop said to me. "Chance has given you, in your wife, a lantern of Aladdin. But in lieu of using the brightness of your lamp to get you gold, you hide it and bury it in your bosom."

I understood him: he never said it twice to me. Nor were we ever after friends.

My comrades did not regard me with all their old careless amity,—any one of them.

"Have a care!" I heard them say one to another. "Our old dancing-dog, Piccinino, can growl—ay, and bite, too, it seems. One used to be able to plague him on all sides: he never turned; but now——"

And yet I do not think that I was jealous of her in any foolish or barbarous manner then. I begrudged her no pleasure that came through others. I would have had her happy at any privation to me of body or of mind. I loved her to trick out her delicate beauty in all the fantasies she would, and make it radiant in the eyes of all men. But when a man is as ugly as I am, and regards the creature that he loves as I regarded her, with breathless adoration, as a thing sent by Heaven and too perfect to tarry long with him on earth, he cannot choose but bitterly resent any glance or any phrase which would seem to treat a possession so sacred as though it were a thing of mere beauty or rarity, to be admired and coveted by any chance observer. There are countries, I have heard, where women go always thickly veiled, hiding their beauty from all men's eyes save those of husband or father. I do not wish that it were so in France: I would not desire that the loveliness God has given to be the delight of his creatures should be secreted from view, casting none of its light or glory on surrounding objects. But, surely, if a man may not gaze at the stars without a reverent awe, much less should he be permitted to examine with a curious stare, or accost with familiar speech, one of those beings whose outward beauty was meant as the reflection of an inward purity and sacredness. Therefore it was that I watched closely all who came near her, seeking to shield her from all obtrusive looks or words, even such as she herself might not have noticed or understood. And sometimes, not knowing why I so acted, she would be impatient or angry, and perhaps go away and be silent or petulant, like a spoiled child when it is denied. But then she had so many other moods, when she would sing and laugh and be gay! Yes, I think she was not otherwise than happy then.

It was midwinter when a great thing happened to me,—a wonder which I had all my life dreamed of as a glory quite impossible to ever fall to such a one as myself. Whilst we were in the central provinces, playing in a little town at the Noël season, a man from Paris, owning a theatre there,—it was the theatre of the Folies-Marigny,—saw me act in our wooden booth, and thought so much of it, that he sought me out at the close of the performance.

"You are a fine actor," he said. "Has no one ever found that out before now, that you stroll about with a wooden show? Come with me and I will make you known in Paris."

I could not believe my ears. Yet he was quite serious, and had meant every word he had said. I closed with his offer, dizzy with astonishment at such fulfilment of my most golden dream; and then I went and told her.

She threw her arms round my throat and kissed me many times.

"Ah, now I shall be very happy!" she cried. "To be in the world at last!"

And then she fell to a thousand pretty schemes for feasts and ornaments and all sorts of brilliancies, as though I had become possessor of some vast estate. But I had no thought to check her ecstasies or teach her reason. I was too full of triumph, for her sake, myself.

I was so proud and glad that night! My head was so light that I was in amity with all creation.

I bought a simple little supper and a stoup of Burgundy, and called my comrades in to rejoice with us; and I purchased for her some bright gilded papers of sugared meats, and a stove-forced rose, and a thread of amber beads, for she was a very child in all these things; and my new chief joined with us, and we kept the night right joyously.

It was the old Nuit des Rois I knew, and all the town was dancing and feasting, and there were not beneath its many roofs any group gladder or gayer than the light-hearted people who gathered in my attic under the eaves, by the light of one little lamp.

The Burgundy wine was good, and she looked so fair with the snow-born rose red in her breast, and I knew that all men envied me; and we laughed long and lightly, and my heart was fearless and content as we drank our pledge to the Future.

Ah, Heaven! the old saw may well say that the gods make us blind ere they drive our stumbling fools' feet to our bitter fools' end.

Well, that same week we went to Paris. There I played under my new master: there I won success—in a humble manner.

It was a little theatre, of no great account, and its patrons came chiefly from students and artists and sewing-girls, and their like,—merry people and poor. Still, it was a theatre of Paris, a public of Paris: it was a theatre, too, of fixed position and name, builded of wood and stone and iron; and such a change was in itself eminence for me, Piccinino, a strolling droll, who had never played under any better roof than a sheet of canvas, which blew to and fro as it would in all the four winds of the air.

It was eminence for me, and might lead—who could say?—to great things—to the greatest, perhaps. It was so much to have one's foot planted at all, one's voice at all heard, amidst the busy throng and the loud clamours of the capital.

Certes, the theatre was every night filled from floor to roof, so I cannot doubt that I did, in a measure, stand well with this volatile, critical, hard-to-win public of Paris. They applauded me to the echo, and for a season I dreamed golden dreams. Truly, I was not myself altogether so much at ease as I had been under the old, malleable, mutable roof, which had often, indeed, been in holes, through which the rains had dropped, but which also had been so easily taken down, folded up, and borne whithersoever one would, where the life of the hour might promise the best.

I had been a country stroller always. I knew nothing of the great city: the streets seemed to pen me in a prison, and the sea of gas to suffocate me. But, still, I was making money: I was making also —in a minor way, indeed, but still surely—a histrionic repute. I had ambition,—for her,—and so, when I drank a pint of red wine, I still pledged, with firm heart, my future.

She was so well content too.

We had a little bright rose-and-white room, gilded like a sweetmeat-box, set very high under the glittering zinc roof of a house of many stories, shut in a narrow passage-way amongst many other buildings, close against the theatre.

It was terribly dear, and no bigger than a hazelnut, and hot and stifling always, being so near the roof.

But she thought it a paradise—a paradise, because above the stove there was a mirror, and opposite in the street, far down below, there was a busy café that was thronged the whole day long; and beneath, on the ground-floor, was a great magazine of laces and shawls and such-like fineries, into which the keepers thereof let her peep from time to time, and even handle the precious stuffs, for sake of her fair eyes.

She thought it a paradise, I say; but I—I thought wistfully, many and many a time, of our old clean, bare, wind-swept attics, with their empty walls, and their quaint lattices, and their shadowy eaves, and the little ancient towns where the old belfry bells were ringing in the quiet provinces far away.

I had always been in the air, you see—in the sun and the rain, and the open weather: even when I had played, it had been under a tent, where every breeze that blew stirred the awning above my head, and made the little round coloured lamps flicker and grow brighter and duller by turns. I had led a hardy, free, open-air life, and the imprisonment of a city—even of such a city as Paris—was, in a manner, grievous to me.

Not that I ever let her think so. Oh no: it would have been very selfish. She was so content!

When I came home from the day-business of the stage at noon, I would find her always looking down into the street below, leaning her little soft face on her hands, and watching the tide of life in the café opposite. It was always full, as I said: there was a barrack hard by, and the place was always gay with uniforms and noisy with the clatter and clash of steel, as the officers ate and drank at the tables in front of the doors, under the gilded scrollwork and the green shutters.

It was a pretty scene: it was no wonder that she watched it; and no doubt I seemed to her a brute, and a fool to boot, when I pulled her, one day, from her favourite seat and drew the sun-blinds sharply. I could not bear the lewd bold looks those soldiers cast up at her.

She broke out into a low piteous sobbing, and wailed wearily to know what had she done. I kissed her, and knelt to her, and besought her pardon, and blamed my jealous passion, and cursed the world which was not worthy of a look from her.

And then she laughed—no doubt I seemed a fool to her—such a fool, good God!—and shut her hands upon my mouth to silence me, and broke from me and threw the shutter open wide again, laughing still, to get her way thus wilfully.

The cuirassiers in the courtyard of the café down beneath laughed too. A man poor and ugly and jealous—jealous of his wife—is a thing ridiculous to all, no doubt.

They thought me jealous, and they laughed, those handsome, careless, gay youngsters, drinking their breakfast wines under the green vine-leaves and the gold scrollwork; but their thought did me wrong. I was never jealous then: jealousy can only be born of suspicion, and I had in her a spotless, implicit, perfect faith, to which suspicion was impossible.

But she was to me so sacred and so precious, that a light look or a loose word cast at her cut me like a sword. The face that had first looked on me amidst the lilac-blossoms always seemed to me a thing of sanctity, a gift of Heaven. I would fain have had the city crowds bend before it as reverently as the poor peasants bend before the images of Mary.

I was never jealous. It had seemed wonderful to me that she could give her beauty to any creature so ungainly in person and so ill-favoured by fortune as myself—a miracle, indeed, for which I thanked Heaven daily. But that, having thus bestowed herself, she would be faithless, was a thought against her of which I never once was guilty. I am thankful to remember that—now.

Thankful to have been a dolt, a fool, a madman? you will say. Ah, well! it is our moments of blindness and of folly that are the sole ones of happiness for all of us on earth. We only see clearly, I think, when we have reached the depths of woe.

The time went by in Paris, and I was successful

in my own small way, and she was happy. I am sure she was happy—then. She was very young and very ignorant, and the little suppers at some cheap restaurant in the woods, the simple ornaments and dresses I could alone afford her, the mere sense of the stir and glow and glitter and change that were all around, sufficed to amuse her and keep her contented—then.

Besides, she had also what is very dear to every female thing—she had admiration everywhere, from the errand boys who cried aloud her praises in street slang, to the titled soldiers who doffed their caps to her from the café-court below, and would, no doubt, have heaped upon her flowers and bonbons, and jewels and rare gifts, had I not stood betwixt her and their smiles.

They jeered at me and jested about me many a time I knew, but I turned a deaf ear: for her sake I would not be embroiled; and though very surely they despised me—me, the poor, ugly comedian who owned a thing so fair—yet they did not openly provoke me.

The grief I had—and it was one I could not change—was that I was compelled to leave her so often in solitude.

With rehearsal and performance the theatre usurped almost all the hours. But I made her chamber as bright as it was possible, and bands played and troops passed by, and showmen exhibited their tricks, and churchmen defiled with banners and crucifixes all day long through the busy street below: she said it was amusement enough to watch it all, and she told me she was content, and I had no suspicion. She said she was so well pleased sitting there at the little window among the plants of musk and the red geranium blossoms, watching that stream of street-life, which seemed to me so tawdry, so dusty, so deafening, but which, I know well, almost always seems paradise to women, who are seldom poets, and who are almost never, one may say, artists.

All this while I gave offence and even, in some sense, lost friends in many quarters, because I kept her thus sacredly and would have none of the women of our stage associate with her. I have often thought since that this was wrong and harsh in me.

What right had I to judge? Priestly benison had never hallowed my poor mother's loves, and yet a gentler and truer little soul never dwelt in human body. What right had I to judge?

This poor, gay, frail, light-hearted sisterhood, which had been about me always—had I not seen in it sacrifice, tenderness, generosity, even heroism, many and many a time, from the first days of my orphanage, when the blue-eyed Euphrasie had sold her necklace of beads to get my motherless mouth bread by the weary wayside?

Had I not beheld, time out of mind, a stanch patience under poverty and ill-usage, a cheery contentment under all the evils of adversity, a genuine mirth that laughed through tears, a tender goodness to all comrades in misfortune,—all these virtues and others likewise in those dear friends of my childhood and manhood whom I banned from her because their life was defiled by one frailty?

Yes: it was harsh in me, and presumptuous and ungrateful: that I knew too late; and yet it was because I held my lustre lily so soilless that I could not bear a profane breath to stir the air it dwelt in.

Well, if this were sin in me—sin of ingratitude and of pharisaism,—it has been punished.

So our life in Paris went by until the weeks grew into months, and in all the gardens of the city, and all about the palaces, and in the parks and woods, the lilac-trees were blossoming with the sweet odours that seemed born to me of paradise.

It might be foolish,—for I was quite poor still, since the expenses of my new and greater life were more than equal to its profits,—but I spent many silver pieces to fill her little chamber every day freshly with endless masses, white and purple, of those flowers all the while they lasted. They were to me the symbol of the greatest happiness that ever man had known on earth.

I loved them so well that I was almost superstitious about them; and when they were faded and had lost their colour, I hardly liked to cast them aside to go into the dust-cart; and when their fallen petals strewed by millions the green paths through the woods and on the edge of the river, I could never crush them as I passed along without regret.

When the last lilac-blossom had died that spring, the troop with which I was associated had offers made to it which its leader deemed too advantageous to reject. His lease of the theatre in Paris had expired in the first days of May, and with the beginning of the month he changed his quarters and took us eastward to the little town of Spa, where lucrative promises had tempted him to pass the season.

I knew it well. In the old times, with my dear old Mathurin, we had often passed through it on our way from Lorraine and Luxembourg to play at the various kermesses of the pretty hill hamlets of the Meuse district and the villages and bourgs of the wide Flemish plains farther northward.

But that had been many years before, and then

we had set up our little wooden and leathern booth humbly in some retired quarter, where the poor people of the place could come to us, for we had no means or hopes of attracting the rich, gay crowd of foreign residents. The wood-carvers and wood-cutters from all the villages round about had used to throng to us; but the mass of fashion and frivolity that scattered its gold in the town we had never approached in any way, we, simple strollers, playing in a tent which any one might enter for a few centimes a head.

But now it was all different.

I had an established repute, if not a very great one: I belonged to a settled management; I had the aroma of Paris upon my name; I played at the theatre which all the fashionable guests frequented; and I could afford to dwell, no longer at some miserable tavern in a stifling lane, half stable and half wine-shop, but in a cheery and sunshiny little apartment that looked out upon the trees of the avenue of Marteau.

My spirits rose as I came once more amongst the woods and fields, and heard the waters brawl and murmur their pleasant song over the stones. The unaccustomed life of the great city had stifled and depressed me, but in this mountain air I could breathe again.

I was even childishly happy: I could have sung aloud in very gaiety of heart to the chiming bells of the Flemish teams and the carillons of the churches. The leaves, the streams, the hills, the skies, all seemed to sparkle and to smile. It was warm and light and fresh: the woods were full of wild flowers, the fields were green with the long hay-grasses, the sweet smell of the firs came into the valley on every breath that blew. Ah God! how happy I felt!

In the oldest part of the little place there lived an old man and his wife, who maintained themselves by painting fans and silk-reels and bonbon-boxes and the like toys, such as are made in that neighbourhood.

They had been good to me when I had come thither, a mere lad, with Mathurin. I went to see them, and took her with me. They would scarce believe that the boy Piccinino whom they had known, could be an artist great enough to be playing to all the nobles and gentry in the theatre in the town, which, to them, appeared the grandest building of the sort that any kingdom in the universe could hold.

These old people looked long and with devout eyes of wonder at the young beauty of my wife.

"Thou art a happy soul, Piccinino," said the old

man, heartily; and would make a present to her—though I knew he could ill afford it—of a little black fan on which he had just painted with much grace and truthfulness a group of white and purple violets.

The old woman looked up sharply through her spectacles, and said nothing.

"What will she care for it?—it is not jewelled and gilded," she muttered, as she went on with her spinning in the doorway in the sun.

I have often wondered since how it is that the eyes of women at a glance read the souls of other women, so cruelly, as it seems to us, and yet so surely.

It was a pretty little fan: it had cost him much labour, though it could only have sold for a franc or two. It was a plaything as graceful as if it had been encrusted with diamonds—more so, I think, for the old man had studied the forest flowers till he could portray them to the very life.

But a few days later the kindly little gift was lost: she dropped it from the balcony, and it fell shivered to atoms on the ground.

I reproached her gently for her carelessness.

"To give thee the fan," I urged, "he will, I know well, have to go for many a day without a bit of meat to boil with his beans and lentils in the soup-pot."

She only laughed.

"It was worth nothing," she answered me.

I picked up the poor little broken plaything in the street below, and put the pieces aside and kept them. It was only the carelessness of her youth and of her sex, I told myself. But for the first time that day there seemed to me a dissonance in the chiming bells and the murmuring streams, a shadow on the sparkling sunshine, a taint in the sweet young summer odours of the wood-clothed hills.

Why should she value my love, I thought, more than the little broken fan? It was hardly worth more to her in any sense of wealth.

IV.

We were to stay in the town whilst its season lasted. This had scarcely begun when we entered it. There were very few persons arrived then, and I had plenty of leisure time, in which I took her to spend the hours in the shady alleys of the hills and under the deep foliage of the winding woodland roads, taking our noonday meal most often under the trees of Géronstère.

There were two or three of the artists of my

company who used generally to go with us: one of them sang well—he was of the South. There were two young painters, brothers, poor but full of talent, and full of mirth and hope: these would accompany us also. We were a gay, light-hearted, merry little group enough, and raised the echoes of the rocks many a time with our part-singing, and many a time brought some great, white, mild-eyed bull from out the woods to gaze at us with grave eyes in amazement at our laughter.

They were happy times, full of harmless gaiety and blissful belief in the fortunes of the future, in that pleasantest season of the earliest summer, when the first dog-roses were budding on the briers, and the abundant dews of the morning silvered every blade of grass, and were shaken off in a million drops from every stem of cowslip or bough of hawthorn that one gathered. This was yet in earliest summer, whilst the visitors were still few in numbers, and all the green alleys and pretty promenades and shadowy bridle-paths seemed almost all our own, and the fresh mountain air blew through the place cool and strong, untainted by the perfumes and the powders and the bouquets and the wine-odours of fashion.

But very soon this changed. Very soon the avenue grew gay with equipages and riding-parties.

Very soon the nobles and the idlers flocked into the little valley-town, and all was movement and colour and change from noon to midnight. Of course for the theatre I was glad: the house filled nightly; our bright little comic pieces charmed an idle audience of fainéants. I was well received and became popular, and disputed with the Redoute in power of attraction. Of course I was glad of this.

My impressario was well pleased with me, and offered me an increase of salary from midsummer. I even came to be noted enough for people to point me out when I passed into the paths or lingered to hear the music in the pretty Promenade des Sept Heures.

"There!" they would say to one another, "do you see him that quaint, misshapen, ugly fellow? That is Piccinino, the French player. Have you seen him in *Le Chevreuil?* Myself, I like him better than Ravel."

Then would the other answer.

"Yes, he is clever, no doubt; but what an ugly beast! And that pretty creature—she is his wife they say."

And then they would laugh, and the music would seem all discord to me.

Not that I heeded the taunt about my ill looks: I had become long used to that. I knew so well that I was ugly: that could not wound me. It was the way in which they spoke of her, as if, because I was not handsome, I had no title to her. And indeed it seemed so to myself sometimes.

When I moved in the crowded alleys amidst those *beaux messieurs dorés*, it seemed to me that such a homely, ill-favoured brown bird as I was had no right to mate with that beautiful young golden oriole.

I knew they thought so: I wondered often if she did likewise.

So, though I had success and fair promise of the future from my present popularity, I was ill at ease now that the world had come about us, and that we could no more go and laugh and sing and drink our little cheap wine in the green woods by ourselves without meeting scores of brilliant, languid, graceful people, who stared at us coldly, and then turned aside and laughed.

Amongst these—we met him often—was a young noble of the southern provinces, the Marquis de Carolyié, a cavalry soldier and a man of wealth. He was as beautiful as a woman: he was beautiful living—and dead. I see his face now, there where the lilac flowers are.

What? I am alone in my cell, you say, and it is late in the autumn, and the lilac trees are all torn with shot and ploughed up with cannon-balls all over

France, and will blossom no more this year, nor any other year, but are all killed—for ever, for ever!

You think that my brain wanders? It is not so. You cannot see the dead man's face, you cannot smell the lilac flowers, but I can. No, I am not mad. I am quite calm. I will tell you how it all happened. Let me go on in my own way.

This young Marquis de Carolyié came into the Ardennes with the midsummer. We saw him very often, a dozen times a day. Every one is always seeing every one else in Spa.

I held aloof as much as I could from the gay world. I had nothing in common with it, and no means to shine amidst it. Besides, every evening I was playing at the theatre; and as I knew no woman with whom to leave my wife, I took her with me to the playhouse, and whilst I was upon the stage she stayed in my dressing-chamber.

It was dull, I knew, very dull for her: she wanted to be at the Kursaal and at the balls, I knew, but none of the women there of any fair repute would have associated with her, a girl of the populace, the wife of a comic actor; and with those of light fame I would never let her exchange a word. So we went hardly at all into any of the resorts of the idle people, yet we saw them and they saw us in the promenades, by the bands of music and in the woods; and so we came a dozen times a day by chance across Carolyié's path, or he, by design, across ours.

He lodged at the D'Orange, and could have had no call to pass and repass, as he did, down our avenue; but this he would do, either riding or on foot, continually.

I noticed him at first for his great beauty: people as ugly as I am are sure to note any singular physical perfection. He rode in the steeple-chases too, and won; he played recklessly at the tables, and won there also, because he could so well afford to lose; he was sought and adored by many of the elegant and weary women there; he was very rich and very attractive: he was a man, in a word, of whom the world always talked.

I ought to have said ere now that she had her first anger against me — or at least the first she showed — on the score of the gaming-tables. She had urged me with the prettiest and most passionate insistence to try and make my fortune in a night at the roulette-ball. And I had refused always.

I was no better than other men; I did not condemn what they did; but gaming had no charm for me, and it seemed to me that in one who had so little as I it would be utter madness to court ruin by staking that little on the chance of an ivory ball. And my resolve on this point was very bitter to her.

It seemed to her so cruel in me, when by one lucky hazard I might make in an hour as much as it took me years to earn. She wanted dresses, cachemires, laces, jewels, like those of the great ladies that she saw; she wanted to sweep along the grassy roads with carriage-horses in gilded harness and with chiming bells, like the aristocratic teams that trotted by; she wanted to go to the Redoute of an evening in trailing trains of velvet and of satin: she wanted, in a word, to be entirely other than she was. It is a disease, very common, no doubt, but it is mortal always.

She was a soft, dainty, mignonne thing, full of natural grace, though she had been but a little Loirais peasant-girl making lace in a garret: she would have taken kindly to affluence and luxury, and would have looked at home in them, no doubt. But how could I give her them? It was impossible.

I could not run the chance of fortune at the roulette-wheel when, if I had lost my little all, she would have been cast a beggar on the world.

So this was a difference and a barrier between us.

She would not pardon me, and I could not alter my resolve against my reason and my conscience.

But I think her thoughts were first drawn to

Carolyié because she heard from some of our people how recklessly he played at nights, and how continually he won.

Well, one evening he came behind the scenes at our theatre. He knew our chief, it seemed, and was made welcome. He paid me many courteous compliments. He was so frank, so easy, so kindly in his ways, I could not choose but like him. Still, I shut the door of my dressing-room in his face.

She was there, making lace for herself, as her habit was, but whilst her hands moved with their old skill, the tears dropped on the network.

"It is so dull!" she murmured piteously. "It is so dull! You do not think of that, you! You are on the stage there, in the light, with all the people before you applauding you, and calling you on; but here! It is miserable, miserable! I can hear them laugh and shout and clap their hands, while I am all alone!"

I could not bear to see her so. I took blame to myself for my cruel carelessness. The next night I asked for a stage-box for her, and she passed the hours that I played in front. Whilst I was acting I saw Carolyié with her. It seemed that he had requested my chief to take him thither, which had been done. I joined them between the acts.

He told us that he was very weary of the daily

round of gaieties, as they were called. He begged us to let him join us in our little breakfast parties in the woods. He had heard us singing often, he had said, and had longed to get away from his friends and join us and laugh with us. I assented willingly.

I liked the young man, and his gallant, gracious ways and candid eyes, that were blue as the cornflowers. I had no thought of any evil, and I had a perfect faith in her.

So the next day he went with us. But our breakfast parties were not the same—never quite the same.

He brought his carriage, with its four black horses with their Flemish collars and silver bells, and he would have us drive with him; and when the others came on foot, heated and dusty, and joined us at Géronstère, it was not quite the same. My comrades were never quite so merrily absurd in their vagaries, nor did the buffo songs sound ever quite so joyously as they had done when we had all walked up the hilly road together, shouting and rallying one another, and gathering ferns and foxgloves for our caps, like children out of school.

It was no fault of the Marquis de Carolyié; he was cordial and gay and familiar, as though he were a Bohemian like ourselves; but yet, with those horses champing in the background in their silver harness, with the champagne that he had brought superseding our cheap little thin wine, with the bearskins and tigerskins that his servants spread for our seats over the green hill-mosses;—with all this some subtle charm of mirth had fled, some sense of inequality, of difference, had arisen.

I think he must have found us nearly as dull as he said that his own great world was.

He took greatly to our company, however; he would forsake his own people for us always, whenever he could. He would fain have had us go in return to brilliant suppers and the like that he gave in his rooms at the D'Orange, and at which they said that he was accustomed to spare no extravagance. My fellow-artists went to them, but not I: I had no means to return such costly courtesies, and it had always been my habit to refuse what I could not repay.

They thought, no doubt, that I kept her away from jealous fear, but I had no feeling of the kind: that I swear. I liked the young man, and I had no suspicion of evil. It was only that I had always been in a manner proud amongst those whom birth and wealth made my superiors in station, and I could not become a debtor.

It seemed to me that it would have a very ill look if I, a man ugly and poor, and struggling in my first efforts after fame, should accept the gifts and banquets of this rich young aristocrat. I knew well how my companions would all laugh and sneer and shrug their shoulders, and mutter, "They ask Peccinino because his wife has a fair face; and the fool goes. Oh ho! he knows how his bread is buttered!"

I knew the sort of scoffs that they would surely cast; and I thought it worthy neither of her innocence nor of my honesty to incur them; so that I never broke bread with Carolyié once. But it was not because I ever had an evil thought of him.

Here again there arose matter of difference betwixt her and myself. She thought me harsh and cruel and tyrannous that I would not accept for myself or her the many brilliant offers of the young Marquis; and I—I could not tell her the real reasons which influenced me; I could not soil her ear with the things that mean, vile tongues would say; and so my motives doubtless seemed to her but poor ones, and perhaps she fancied that I crossed her will and denied her pleasure from sheer caprice or hardness.

For a while she reproached me bitterly; for many days she would upbraid me in her pretty and impetuous manner, with her petulant, childlike anger continually; she would take no enjoyment in any scheme that I proposed nor any toy I bought for her; she would tell me always that I hated to see her happy.

It was a cruel saying, for she knew, as God knew, that I would have laid down my life any day to give her joy. But she was disappointed, and blind to justice, and angered like a spoilt child that is denied a plaything; the glitter of the young man's gay and gracious life had dazzled her.

After a week or two had lapsed, however, she ceased to reproach me aloud.

She grew very silent, and seemed strangely softened into obedience to my desires on all subjects. She did not care to go out nearly so much as she used to do. It was with some trouble that I prevailed on her to go forth at the hours when the bands played.

She would sit all day long by the window of our little chalet in the Marteau Road, working at her lace, with a cluster of flowers on the table before her. She talked little; she did everything I asked her; she was often in reverie, musing, with a smile upon her lips, and when I spoke to her after some minutes' silence, she would start up as if awaking suddenly from a dream.

I thought she was not well, and grew anxious, but she assured me that she ailed nothing; and indeed I had never seen her sweet eyes clearer or the rose bloom brighter on her cheeks. I thought it was the mountain air perhaps which was too strong, and made her listless.

Of course I had to leave her very often. I could not anyway avoid it. We were the only company at Spa: and to amuse the fastidious audience for which we played, we were obliged to change our little pieces almost every night.

This entailed on us great fatigue, and most of all on me, because the kind of pieces that we now performed were not such as I had acted in when I had gone about with my little wooden theatre; which, indeed, I had written chiefly myself. The studying so many new characters, and the rehearsal of them, occupied much of my day-time, and left me but little leisure as the season advanced.

Of an evening she would always go with me to the theatre, and sit in the little *baignoire* which they assigned her: occasionally, when I joined her in the entr'actes, I found Carolyié there, but not very often. He somewhat avoided me. I supposed that I might have given him some cause for offence in my persistent refusal of the many invitations which he had pressed upon me in the beginning of the summer.

Once, too, in quite the earliest days of his

appearance there, he had sent her a magnificent bouquet of rare flowers; and I had taken him aside, and spoken to him frankly.

"You mean well and in all kindness, I know," I said to him, "but do nothing of this sort with us. Remember that what is a mere pretty grace of courtesy amongst your equals is to people poor and obscure as we are a debt that we can ill carry without losing the only honour that we have—our title to respect ourselves."

He had seemed moved, and had coloured a little, and had shaken my hand with cordiality. And from that time he had sent no gifts to her. But I fancied that to me he, on afterthought, resented the words I had spoken.

One night, when the summer was well advanced, I was to play in a quite new piece, in which it was thought that I should achieve a signal success.

There were some very great people at that time in Spa; for want of something to do they came to our little entertainments. The favour with which they received and spoke of me was something very promising, and made me more and more valued by my chief. On the whole, life was very good and pleasant to me at that time, and many whose words were of weight said that I should become with time and practice one of the best comedians of the country.

That night she pleaded that she was not quite well—she had a headache from the heat of the past day, and feared the suffocating atmosphere of the theatre.

She smiled and sang a little to herself, and told me she would sit by the open window in the little alcove which she had made peculiarly her own, and wait for me and hear the tidings of the night's triumphs when I returned.

I knew the theatre was oppressive at this season of the year, crowded nightly as it was, and I did not attempt to press her to accompany me.

I took her an immense knot of white roses which I had bought in the town. She set them in a large blue jar, and said their fragrance and freshness had already done her good. She kissed me, and threw her arms about my neck, and murmured, with a little tender laugh, "Au revoir, au revoir!" and then bade me go or I should be late.

I left her sitting in the window, the unlit lamp, with a small crucifix against it, on the table by her, with the jar of roses.

She had her frame and bobbins, and was working at her lace. She looked at me from the open lattice, and waved me a second adieu.

I had no thought, no suspicion. I only said to

myself, "Surely she has learned to love me a little now."

It is an old old story, you will say. Yes, very old.

I left her, and went to the theatre. I remember walking down the avenue in the brilliant sunlight. It had rained at noonday. It was a red and golden evening, very beautiful. The band was playing in the Place Royale. Every one was out. From the little gardens there were all sorts of sweet scents from roses and mignonettes and carnations, and all fragrant midsummer things that were growing in the warmth and the moisture. Clouds in all manner of lovely shapes swept above the green hills, and seemed to rest on them.

I saw the people go in and out of the gaming-rooms. I pitied them for wasting this divine weather, which they were all free to enjoy as they would, in that feverish atmosphere. Amongst them there came out Carolyié. He appeared to avoid or not to see me; he passed by on the other side, and went on to dine at Baas-Cogez.

Some one near me said,

"What good-fortune that young man has! He wins every day. If he goes on like that one week more, he will break the bank."

Another added,

"Because he wants nothing, he gets everything."

I heard, but I did not envy him: I envied no one. I would not have changed places with a king, though I was but a poor actor going to his work, to be shut up in a steaming theatre to amuse others with the tricks of gesture and of language. I would not have exchanged my lot for that of an emperor.

I was so happy that night, as I went on through the town, away from the smell of the gardens and woods, and the sounds of the music and the falling waters, and the singing of many little birds, into the dusky den where I dressed for my part in the playhouse!

The new piece was called *Le Pot de Vin de Thibautin*. It was very absurd and humorous, and yet graceful. I have never played in it since, and yet every line of it is burnt into my mind.

I had a fresh and genuine success in the part of Thibautin.

I was recalled five times, and the house, which was a full one, applauded me to the echo. A great duke who was there, a foreigner, came behind the scenes and gave me a gold snuff-box of his own, and spoke very high words of praise. I knew my future was sure: I had a reputation which would grow with every year in France. I went from the theatre a happy man.

It was still very warm—a beautiful dark, starless night. The clouds were heavy: there was a sort of hush in the air. There was only just light enough in the little town to make deeper by contrast the circle of the hills. The flowers scented the air more strongly still than at sunset: they were heavy with great dews.

All was so quiet. Everyone was in the ball-room or the card-room. The casements stood wide open in the deserted houses. Here and there the little coloured lamps glimmered. Here and there a woman leaned from a balcony.

I went on down the avenue of Marteau.

In the stillness I could hear the brook running over the stones, and the rustle of the leaves in the water as the wind stirred them.

I looked up at the windows of my little rooms. The light shone through their green shutters. The vine that climbed around them was dark against the reflection. I looked up, and, though I had known little of God in the life that I had led, I blessed Him.

Yes, I blessed God that night.

I opened the door, and went up the stairs, and entered my own chamber. I looked for her in her accustomed place, near the lamp, in the alcove, where the great jar of white roses stood. She was not there.

I need not tell you any more, the story is so old, so old.

For many weeks after that night I knew nothing. I was mad, I believe. They say so. I cannot tell; I remember nothing; only that blank deserted room, and the great mass of white roses, and the lamp with the little crucifix under it, and the empty chair with the lace-work that had fallen beside it, all unfinished and untangled. I can see that always, always.

She had gone without any word or any sign; and yet it was all so plain. Everyone had foreseen it, so they said—everyone except myself.

From that night nothing more was ever seen or heard in that place of him or of her: the people of the house knew nothing; so at least they said. But on the floor, under the mirror, there was a torn letter, which had been forgotten or mislaid.

Not many words were in it, but they were words enough to tell me that when she had kissed me on the mouth, and smiled, and sent me on my way to play in my new part that evening at sunset, she had known that when the night fell she would betray me.

It is a woman's way, they say.

I might be really mad: they told me that I was; it may be so. I think it was quite late in autumn when I had any sense or consciousness of what I did or what I spoke. The place was all deserted, the woods were brown, the music was silent, the flowers were dead.

I awoke stupidly, as it were, but yet I was quite calm, and I knew what had chanced to me. It seemed to me that I had lived many years since that horrible night. My hair was gray. I felt feeble and grown old.

Life was ended for me, you know. I wondered why I was not dead as others were, and quiet in my grave.

When they let me go I walked out into the forsaken streets: they looked so strange—there was scarcely a soul in them, and the shutters of the houses were closed. I had only one idea—to follow them, to find them. And I had lost so much time: it was now nearly winter.

My chief and his troop had all gone, of course. What little money I had had people had taken whilst I was unconscious. They told me I owed my life to charity. My life! I laughed aloud in their faces.

They were afraid of me: they thought I was mad still. But I was not. I knew what I did, and I had one fixed purpose left, which was quite clear to me, and for which alone I endured to live an hour.

I was a fool—oh yes!—and she was worthless. No doubt, no doubt. But then—I loved her.

Not that I ever dreamed of winning her back. Nay, do not think so base a thought of me. My life had been upright and without shame in the sight of men: I would not have stained it with any weakness so unmanly and so foul. But I had a purpose, and that one purpose gave me nerve and strength.

In the gray of the morning I left the town. I had not a coin in the world. My one little talent was killed in me. My career was gone. My dawning repute was already a thing of the past, forgotten by all men. You see she had destroyed all for me—utterly.

But no doubt she never counted the cost. They do not think, those fair, soft, smiling things.

When I had come into that valley I had had an honest past, a precious present, a hopeful future. When I left it——

Well, it matters not now. I died then. The bullets to-morrow for me can have no pain.

It signifies little to tell you how I have subsisted betwixt the time that I quitted the little town in the mountains, and this day when I lie under sentence of death.

My old career had become to me abhorrent, impossible. Such skill as I had been master of had perished out of me. If I had gone upon the stage, I could not have said a word nor moved a limb. The old pursuit, the old pleasure, familiar and dear to me from my childhood, was all withered up for ever.

Men have played—and women too, I know—a thousand times with hearts broken and bleeding, and the world has applauded them. But with me any talent I had ever possessed was gone for ever: to have passed within a playhouse would have made me mad, I think. That last night I had been so happy—that last night, in the fulness of my joy, I had blessed God!

I lived—no matter how. The life of a very wretched creature, but still not the life of a beggar. The manner of my existence from my birth up had taught me to live almost upon nothing, and had taught me also many ways of providing for myself such scanty daily bread as I was forced to eat.

All the winter long I sought for tidings of her—and him. But the land was wide, and months had gone by, and I had no knowledge of where he dwelt, and I gleaned nothing that was of any service to me.

When I reached Paris I abode there for a while.

I reasoned that soon or late—being of fair fortune and of lofty rank—he would of a surety come thither. So I waited.

I waited all through the winter, but he did not come. I worked my way into his own south-country, and tried to find traces of him. I saw his great palace amongst pine forests, the palace as of a prince, but I learned that he had not been there for several seasons. He had deserted it almost utterly for the world of cities.

They said that he was in Italy.

I travelled thither, but there I was always too late: he had left each city before I entered it. It is no use to tell of all these wanderings, none of which bore any fruit.

Once, in Venice, I only missed him by a day: a gondolier told me that he had a woman with him fair as a rose.

Ah, God! that was in the sweet time of spring. Everywhere the lilacs were in flower.

I lived to hear that and to see the trees blossom. How can the bullets hurt *me* to-morrow?

Let me make an end quickly. I lived, wretchedly, indeed, but still I lived on: I would not lie down and die without my vengeance.

The summer came, and with summer, war. When it was declared I was on the frontier. I hastened into my own country as well as I could, being on foot always, and having to work my way from village to village, day by day.

I had lost everything. I had become feeble, stupid, dull: I was what they call a monomaniac, I think. I thought always I saw her face looking toward me amidst the lilac clusters. I never spoke to anyone of her, but that was what I saw, always.

I had lost all the mind I had ever had, and when I met any of my old comrades I shunned them.

Some of them wanted to pity me, to assist me. They meant well, no doubt, but I would sooner that they should have stabbed me. I avoided everyone and everything which could remind me of what I had been, and I was morose, and perhaps in a manner mad; I do not know.

But when I heard of war I seemed to myself to awake. It seemed to call to me like a living creature. I was good for nothing else, but I could still strike, I thought. Besides, I knew he was a soldier. It would go hard if I found him not somewhere in the mêlée.

And indeed I loved France: still, in the misery of my life, I loved her for all that I had had from her.

I loved her for her sunny roads, for her

cheery laughter, for her vine-hung hamlets, for her contented poverty, for her gay sweet mirth, for her pleasant days, for her starry nights, for her little bright groups at the village fountain, for her old brown, humble peasants at her wayside crosses, for her wide, wind-swept plains all red with her radiant sunsets. She had given me beautiful hours; she is the mother of the poor, who sings to them so that they forget their hunger and their nakedness; she had made me happy in my youth. I was not ungrateful.

It was in the heats of September that I reached my country. It was just after the day of Sedan. I heard all along the roads, as I went, sad, sullen murmurs of our bitter disasters. It was not the truth exactly that was ever told at the poor wine-shops and about the harvest-fields, but it was near enough to the truth to be horrible.

The blood-thirst which had been upon me ever since that night when I found her chair empty seemed to burn and seethe, till I saw nothing but blood—in the air, in the sun, in the water.

I had always been of a peaceful temper enough. I had always abhorred contention. I had lived quietly, in amity and agreement at all times with my fellow-creatures. It had used even to be a jest against me that if any man were to rob me I should only think of how best I could shield him from justice. But all that was changed.

I had become, as it were, a beast of prey. I wanted to *kill*, to appease the sickly hot thirst always in me. You do not know? Well, pray to God, if you have one, that you may never know.

No man, I think, is ever safe from coming to know it, if Fate so wills. A day can change us so that the very mother who bore us would not recognise her sons.

I hated myself, and yet I could not alter what I had become. If we are held accountable hereafter for such changes in us, it will be very unjust. We cannot escape from them.

By the time I reached the centre of France, they were everywhere forming new corps and bands of francs-tireurs. In one of these latter I enrolled myself. I was strong of body and of good height, though somewhat misshapen: they were glad of me. For me, I had only one idea—to strike for the country, and, soon or late, to reach *him*.

I fought several times, they said—well, I do not know. Probably I did, for I flew on them like a tiger—that I can remember—and of personal pain or peril I had never any consciousness.

We lived in the woods. We hid by day: by night we scoured the country. We made fierce raids, we stopped convoys, we cut telegraph wires, we intercepted orderlies, we attacked and often routed the invaders' cavalry. We knew that if taken we should be hanged like common murderers for the guilt of patriotism, but I do not think any one of us ever paused for that: we only attacked them with the greater desperation.

Sometimes, in the forests or on the highway we would find the body of some of our comrades hung by the neck to a straight tree, though he had been taken fighting fairly for his country's sake: such a sight did not make us gentler. We poured out blood like water, and much of it was the proud blue blood of the old nobility. We should have saved France, I am sure, if there had been any one who had known how to consolidate and lead us. No one did; so it was all of no use.

Guerillas like us can do much, very much, but to do so much that it is victory we must have a genius amidst us. And we had none. If the First Bonaparte had been alive and with us, we should have chased the foe as Marius the Cimbri.

I think other nations will say so in the future: at the present they are all dazzled, they do not see clearly—they are all worshipping the rising sun. It is blood-red, and it blinds them.

In time it became known that I fought, they

said, like ten men in one. They gave me an officer's grade in the real army. It was the doing of Gambetta, I believe.

For me it made no difference. Place, name, repute,—what could these be to me? I was dead—dead with my old life: it was a devil, I thought, that inhabited my body, and drank himself with blood into a likeness of humanity—as humanity is in war.

I was drafted from the free corps into the battalions of Bourbaki. I saw more service, hard service, and the Republic said that I did well. By my side there often fought, and often fell, old comrades of my own. The comedians and the artists did their full duty by France: the derided kingdom of Bohemia sent hundreds of its brightest leaders in loyal answer to the call of Death.

Well, all this while I never saw his face, though continually I searched for it, and for it alone, in the tempest of a charge and in the slaughter-heaps after battle.

"Is it a brother you seek always?" men asked me often, seeing how I would lift up face after face from amongst the dead upon a battle-field, and let each one drop, and go on again upon my quest. And I answered them always, "One closer than a brother."

For was he not?

But all this while I never saw his face.

France was a great sea in storm, on which the lives of all men were as frail boats tossing to their graves: some were blown east, some west: they passed each other in the endless night, and never knew, the tempest blew so strong.

One day there was a bitter strife. It was in the time of our last struggle. We were trying to cut our way through the iron wall that had raised itself round Paris.

We failed, as the world knows, but we strove hard that day. At least all those around me did, and for a little space we saw the granite mass roll back from us, and we thought that we had won.

In that moment, in the white thick shroud of smoke where I pressed forward on foot with my comrades of the line, there came on with us, in a beautiful fierce sweep, like lightning, a troop of horse half cut to pieces, with many of its chargers riderless, and with its thinned ranks hidden in clouds of blinding dust.

But shattered though it was, it charged for us: it was one of the southern nobles' free corps of cavalry, the Cuirassiers of Corrèze.

Close against me a grey horse, shot through

the body, reeled and fell: the rider of it sank an instant, then shook himself free and rose.

It was he—at last!

He knew me, and I him, even in that mad moment.

I sprang upon him like a beast; my sword was at his throat; the smoke was all around us; no one saw; he was disarmed and in my power.

My men shouted together, "En avant! en avant!" They thought they were victorious.

I heard, I remembered: he too fought for France. I dared not slay him. I let him go.

"Afterwards! afterwards!" I said in his ear. He knew well what I meant.

He caught a loose charger that galloped snorting by; he seized his fallen sabre; he swept onward with his troops; I charged in line with my own men. With the roar of the firing in my ear, and the shouts of our fancied triumph, I pressed onward and downward into the ranks of the enemy: then I dropped senseless.

When the surgeon found me at dawn the next day, I had no wound on me.

For the victory—it had lived only in vanquished soldiers' dreams, as all the victories of France have lived in this bitter season.

I woke to consciousness and to remembrance,

saying again and again in my heart, "Afterwards! afterwards!"

The time soon came.

I saw him no more then. The Cuirassiers of Corrèze passed eastward. Those whom I served sent me into the capital. It was now the beginning of the new year.

There soon came to us that deadliest hour when all we had done and endured received as recompense the shame of the capitulation.

How long is it ago?—a day, a year?

I cannot tell. I was amongst those who held it a crime, an outrage, a betrayal. I did not pretend to have any knowledge, any statecraft, but I knew that, had I been a man in power there, sooner than sign the surrender I would have burned Paris as the Russians did Moscow.

There were many who thought as I did, but we were not asked, were not counted. We had but to hold our tongues, and stand quiet and see the Germans enter Paris.

Then you know this other war came, the civil war. I was in the capital still. It seemed to me that the people were in the right. I cannot argue, but I think so still. They might go ill to work unwisely perhaps, but they asked nothing unreasonable, and they were not at fault—in the commencement, at least.

When the strife and carnage had ceased, I felt very strange. I felt as men do who have been long in the great roar of a cataract, and who come suddenly again where all is quiet. The calm seems to daze them. So the stillness bewildered me.

I began to think that it had all been a dream, a nightmare; only I remembered so well the look of his eyes into mine when my steel was at his throat, and if I dropped asleep a while I always awoke muttering, "Afterwards! afterwards!"

At this time I often went and looked at the house where I had dwelt with her in Paris.

A shell had laid open the little rose-and-white room under the roof; the front and back walls had been torn away; I saw the day through them; some of the gilding of the mirror still clung there.

Another shell had struck the little gay theatre where I had played for the first and last time in Paris: it was now a blank and smoking ruin. And it had been such a little while ago!—Great Heaven!

At such times I asked myself why I had spared him.

I was dull and silent, and lived wholly to myself: all the people I had known were slain or had perished of want.

I made no new friends, I dwelt aloof. Nevertheless, the day came when I had to choose sides: whilst one lives at all on earth one cannot be a coward.

I chose the side of the people; I cast in my lot with them; I remained in Paris. They might be right, they might be wrong—I do not say; I knew they were my class, my kind, my brethren. I abided by their election.

The world will always say they were wrong because they failed: of course; but I think they were only wrong in this—that they tried a mighty experiment before the earth was ripe for it. It is fatal to be before your time—always.

But it was not because I thought them very right that I joined with them. I was no politician: I hardly asked them what they meant. I cast in my lot with theirs because I was of them, and because it would have seemed to me a cowardice to desert them.

All that horrible season went by slowly, slowly. It was but yesterday, you say: it seems a thousand years ago.

I was cooped up in the city: it was much worse than the first siege. I went out in many sorties. I made no doubt he was at Versailles, and every day that I arose and went into the air I said in my soul, "There will be no need to spare him—now."

On the bastions where the red flag was set, through the smoke of guns, I used to stand hour after hour, and look across at the woods of Versailles, and think to myself.

"If only we might meet once more—only once more!"

For I was free now: his brethren fought against mine. It was the thought that nerved my arm for the Commune.

I think it was with many as with me; or something like it.

I remember in that ghastly time seeing a woman put the match to a piece whose gunner had just dropped dead. She fired with sure aim: her shot swept straight into a knot of horsemen on the Neuilly road, and emptied more than one saddle.

"You have a good sight," I said to her.

She smiled.

"This winter," she said slowly, "my children have all died for want of food—one by one, the youngest first. Ever since then I want to hurt something—always. Do you understand?"

I did understand: I do not know if you do. It is just these things that make revolutions.

This is only away from us by a day or so, you say? It is strange: it seems to me half a lifetime.

It was a horrible season. The streets ran wine and blood. The populace was drunk, and savage in its drunkenness. The palaces were pillaged, the churches reeked with filth. I fought without the gates when I could: when I could not, I shut myself in my garret, so that I should not see or hear. So far as I had sense to feel, my heart was sick for France.

One day, when I was going from the fortifications through the by-streets to the place that sheltered me, I passed through a street which had been almost utterly destroyed by shell and fire.

The buildings were mere skeletons, the hearths and homes mere heaps of calcined dust. The rafters, the bricks, the iron girders, the rubble and the rubbish had fallen pell-mell amidst the broken mirrors, the shattered gilding, the scorched pictures: perhaps under the mountains of cinders and of ruin the charred bodies of the dwellers and the owners might be lying: no one knew.

It was all desolate, dark, unutterably miserable.

Yet amidst it all there was one lovely living thing, surrounded everywhere by devastation, but uncrushed, unharmed, untouched. In what had once been a green and cherished little garden there sprang upward a young lilac tree in full flower, fragrant, erect, wet with sweet dews, covered with blossoms—alone amidst the wreck.

For the first time since she had left me I fell on my knees and hid my face in my hands, and wept —as women weep.

Soon after that the end came.

Paris was on fire in a thousand places. They slew the hostages: they did strange and fearful things. You have seen them more clearly than I. I was in the midst of the smoke, of the violence, of the flames, of the bloodshed, of the ignorance, of the ferocity: I was too close to it all to judge any of it aright.

Evil had become their good; and yet in the beginning of the time the people had not been to blame.

From the day they put the old priests to death I would fight no more for the Commune.

But I knew that the Commune would fall, and so I would not forsake them. I think many felt as I did—detested the acts into which the people had plunged, but would not forsake them on the edge of ruin.

I would not fight again for them, but neither would I fight against them: I went forth into the streets and stood and looked.

It seemed hell itself. The sky was black: everything else was illumined by the fires.

The Versaillais were pouring in: I do not know how many hours or days had gone. It seemed to me all night—all one endless night that the endless flames illumined.

Little children ran past me with lighted brands in their hands, which they flung into houses or cellars, laughing all the while. Women, black with powder, with their hair loose and their breasts bare, streamed by me like furies, shrieking curses till the shot struck them and they dropped upon the stones.

From the windows, from the roofs, from the trees, the people fired upon the soldiery: the soldiery raked the streets with their fire in return, and stormed the dwellings, and threw the dead bodies out of the casements. The roads were wet everywhere with a tide of blood, always rising higher and higher: the corpses were strewn in all directions. Some lay in the aisles of the churches, some on the steps of the high altars. You know, you know: I need not tell it.

It will seem strange to you, but in all that horror I thought of the lilac tree: I went and looked for it.

The street behind, the street before, were both burning. In the little garden there had been a bitter strife: the dead lay there in pools of blood by scores.

But the little lilac was still erect, its green boughs and its sweet blossoms blowing in the wind.

There were some little birds that had their young in a nest in the lilac boughs. They were uneasy; they twittered and fluttered about amongst the leaves. It was so dark they thought that it was night. But the church chimes were tolling noon.

I sat down on a pile of timber that had crushed the grasses at the roots of the tree. I sat still there and waited. I could do nothing. I could not fight for them: I would not fight against them.

Down the ruined, smoking street, as I sat thus, there came a soldier hastily, with his sword drawn, glancing hither and thither rapidly, as one who had lost his way or missed his men. His dress was splashed, torn, covered with dust, and here and there with blood, but it was the dress of a soldier of rank. As he came the glare of the fires in front shone full on his face—his beautiful face: I knew it in an instant.

God had delivered him into my hands. So I said in my soul, exultant. We always charge our crimes upon God.

I sprang up and stood in his way.

"At last! at last!" I cried to him.

He wavered, paused, and looked at me bewildered: no doubt I was greatly changed, and in the horrid scorching gloom he did not recognise my features.

I gave him no breathing-space, but drew my sword and rushed on him.

"Defend yourself!" I said in his ear ere I touched him. We would fight until death—that I swore in my heart—but we would fight fairly, man to man.

When I spoke he knew me. He was a brave man and loyal. He raised no shout to rally his comrades. He took my challenge as I gave it. He threw himself in a second into position.

"I am ready," he said, simply.

We were all alone. The fire was around us on all sides. The dead alone were our spectators. The little lilac tree waved in the wind.

Our swords crossed a score of times swift as the lightning: then, in a moment as it seemed, he fell forward on my blade: his body drooped and doubled like a broken bough.

The steel had passed through his breast-bone. I had my vengeance.

It was a fair fight, man to man.

He looked up at me as he sank down dying on the stones.

A strange shadowy smile flickered over his mouth.

"You were revenged—before," he said slowly, each word drawn feebly with his breath. "Did you not know? She betrayed me last autumn to the Prussians; she had a lover amongst them greater than I."

A rush of blood choked his voice: he lay silent, leaning upon one hand. The flames shone upon his face, the smoke drove over us, the little lilac tree blew in the breeze, the birds murmured to their young ones.

Then all at once the street grew full of men. They were his own soldiery. They rushed on me to avenge his death. With the last effort of life in him he raised himself and signed them back.

"Do not touch him," he cried aloud to them. "It was I who injured him: I fall in fair fight."

Even as he spoke a shudder shook him, and he died.

His head was on the stones; his hair was soaked with the blood that had already been shed there; a grey pallor stole over his face; and yet even then he was still beautiful.

The lilac blossoms, loosened by the driving

wind and by the fire's heat, fell softly on him, one by one, like tears.

I did not stir; I stood there looking down at him. My hate of him had died away with his young life: I only pitied him with an intense passion of pity.

We both perished for a thing so vile.

His comrades and men heeded nothing of his words; they arrested me as they would have done a common felon. I did not attempt to resist them. I had broken my sword and cast it down by his body: its end was accomplished, its fate was fulfilled: I had no further use for it.

They have brought me hither; they have given me a full trial, so they say, and to-morrow they will kill me.

What is the charge against me? That I, a soldier of the Commune, slew a soldier of Versailles. It is enough, more than enough, in these days. I say nothing. I am glad there should be an end.

If you ask any grace for me, ask only this— that the men who fire on me shall not be the same men by whose side I fought so long for France.

And when they throw my body in the ditch— see here!—let them bury this branch of lilac with me.

It is of no value—it is dead.

A PROVENCE ROSE.

I.

I WAS a Provence rose.

A little slender rose, with leaves of shining green and blossoms of purest white—a little fragile thing, but fair, they said, growing in the casement in a chamber in a street.

I remember my birth-country well. A great wild garden, where roses grew together by millions and tens of millions, all tossing our bright heads in the light of a southern sun on the edge of an old, old city—old as Rome—whose ruins were clothed with the wild fig-tree, and the scarlet blossom of the climbing creepers growing tall and free in our glad air of France.

I remember how the ruined aqueduct went like a dark shadow straight across the plains; how the green and golden lizards crept in and out and about amongst the grasses; how the cicala sang her song in the moist, sultry eves; how the women from the wells came trooping by, stately as monarchs, with their water-jars upon their heads; how the hot hush of the burning noons would fall, and all things droop and sleep except ourselves; how swift amongst us would dart the little blue-winged birds, and hide their heads in our white breasts and drink from our hearts the dew, and then hover above us in their gratitude, with sweet faint music of their wings, till sunset came.

I remember— But what is the use? I am only a rose; a thing born for a day, to bloom and be gathered, and die. So you say: you must know. God gave you all created things for your pleasure and use. So you say.

There my birth was; there I lived—in the wide south, with its strong, quivering light, its radiant skies, its purple plains, its fruits of gourd and vine. I was young; I was happy; I lived: it was enough.

One day a rough hand tore me from my parent stem and took me, bleeding and drooping, from my birth-place, with a thousand other captives of my kind. They bound a score of us up together, and made us a cruel substitute for our cool, glad garden-home with poor leaves, all wet from their own tears, and mosses torn as we were from their birth-nests under the great cedars that rose against the radiant native skies.

Then we were shut in darkness for I know not how long a space; and when we saw the light of day again we were lying with our dear dead friends, the leaves, with many flowers of various kinds, and foliage and ferns and shrubs and creeping plants, in a place quite strange to us—a place filled with other roses and with all things that bloom and bear in the rich days of midsummer; a place which I heard them call the market of the Madeleine. And when I heard that name I knew that I was in Paris.

For many a time, when the dread hand of the reaper had descended upon us, and we had beheld our fairest and most fragrant relatives borne away from us to death, a shiver that was not of the wind had run through all our boughs and blossoms, and all the roses had murmured in sadness and in terror, "Better the worm or the drought, the blight or the fly, the whirlwind that scatters us as chaff, or the waterspout that levels our proudest with the earth—better any of these than the long-lingering death by famine and faintness and thirst that awaits every flower which goes to the Madeleine."

It was an honour, no doubt, to be so chosen. A rose was the purest, the sweetest, the haughtiest of all her sisterhood ere she went thither. But, though honour is well, no doubt, yet it surely is better to blow free in the breeze and to live one's life out, and to be, if forgotten by glory, yet also forgotten by pain. Nay, yet: I have known a rose, even a rose who had but one little short life of a summer day to live through and to lose, perish glad and triumphant in its prime because it died on a woman's breast and of a woman's kiss. You see there are roses as weak as men are.

I awoke, I say, from my misery and my long night of travel, with my kindred beside me in exile, on a flower-stall of the Madeleine.

It was noon—the pretty place was full of people; it was June, and the day was brilliant. A woman of Picardy sat with us on the board before her—a woman with blue eyes and ear-rings of silver, who bound us together in fifties and hundreds into those sad gatherings of our pale ghosts which in your human language you have called "bouquets."

The loveliest and greatest amongst us suffered decapitation, as your Marie Stuarts and Marie Antoinettes did, and died at once to have their beautiful bright heads impaled—a thing of death, a mere mockery of a flower—on slender spears of wire.

I, a little white and fragile thing, and very young, was in no way eminent enough amongst my kind to find that martyrdom which as surely awaits the loveliest of our roses as it awaits the highest fame of your humanity.

I was bound up amongst a score of others with ropes of gardener's bass to chain me amidst my fellow-prisoners, and handed over by my jailer with the silver ear-rings to a youth who paid for us with a piece of gold—whether of great or little value I know not now. None of my own roses were with me: all were strangers. You never think, of course, that a little rose can care for its birth-place or its kindred; but you err.

O fool! Shall we not care for one another?— we who have so divine a life in common, who together sleep beneath the stars, and together sport in the summer wind, and together listen to the daybreak singing of the birds, whilst the world is dark and deaf in slumber—we who know that we are all of heaven that God, when He called away His angels, bade them leave on the sin-stained, weary, sickly earth to now and then make man remember Him!

You err. We love one another well; and if we may not live in union, we crave at least in union to droop and die. It is seldom that we have this boon. Wild flowers can live and die together; so can the poor amongst you; but we of the cultivated garden needs must part and die alone.

All the captives with me were strangers: haughty, scentless pelargoniums; gardenias, arrogant even in their woe; a knot of little, humble forget-me-nots, ashamed in the grand company of patrician prisoners; a stephanotis, virginal and pure, whose dying breath was peace and sweetness; and many sprays of myrtle born in Rome, whose classic leaves wailed Tasso's lamentation as they went.

I must have been more loosely fettered than the rest were, for in the rough, swift motion of the youth who bore us my bonds gave way, and I fell through the silver transparency of our prison-house, and dropped stunned upon the stone pavement of a street.

There I lay long, half senseless, praying, so far as I had consciousness, that some pitying wind would rise and waft me on his wings away to some shadow, some rest, some fresh, cool place of silence.

I was tortured with thirst; I was choked with dust; I was parched with heat.

The sky was as brass, the stones as red-hot metal; the sun scorched like flame on the glare of the staring walls; the heavy feet of the hurrying crowd tramped past me black and ponderous: with every step I thought my death would come under the crushing weight of those clanging heels.

It was five seconds, five hours—which I know not. The torture was too horrible to be measured by time.

I must have been already dead, or at the very gasp of death, when a cool, soft touch was laid on me: I was gently lifted, raised to tender lips, and fanned with a gentle, cooling breath—breath from the lips that had kissed me.

A young girl had found and rescued me—a girl of the people, poor enough to deem a trampled flower a treasure-trove.

She carried me very gently, carefully veiling me from sun and dust as we went; and when I recovered perception I was floating in a porcelain bath on the surface of cool, fresh water, from which I drank eagerly as soon as my sickly sense of faintness passed away.

My bath stood on the lattice-sill of a small chamber; it was, I knew afterward, but a white pan of common earthenware, such as you buy for two sous and put in your birdcages. But no bath of ivory and pearl and silver was ever more refreshing to imperial or patrician limbs than was that little clean and snowy pattypan to me.

Under its reviving influences I became able to lift my head and raise my leaves and spread myself to the sunlight, and look round me.

The chamber was in the roof, high above the traffic of the passage-way beneath; it was very poor, very simple, furnished with few and homely things.

True, to all our nation of flowers it matters little, when we are borne into captivity, whether the prison-house which receives us be palace or garret.

Not to us can it signify whether we perish in Sèvres vase of royal blue or in kitchen pipkin of brown ware. Your lordliest halls can seem but dark, pent, noisome dungeons to creatures born to live on the wide plain, by the sunlit meadow, in the hedgerow, or the forest, or the green, leafy garden way; tossing always in the joyous winds, and looking always upward to the open sky.

But it is of little use to dwell on this. You think that flowers, like animals, were only created to be used and abused by you, and that we, like your horse and dog, should be grateful when you honour us by slaughter or starvation at your hands.

To be brief, this room was very humble, a mere attic, with one smaller still opening from it; but I scarcely thought of its size or aspect. I looked at nothing but the woman who had saved me.

She was quite young; not very beautiful, perhaps, except for wonderful soft azure eyes and a mouth smiling and glad, with lovely curves to the lips, and hair dark as a raven's wing, which was braided and bound close to her head. She was clad very poorly, yet with an exquisite neatness and even grace; for she was of the people no doubt, but of the people of

France. Her voice was very melodious; she had a silver cross on her bosom; and though her face was pale, it had health.

She was my friend, I felt sure. Yes, even when she held me and pierced me with steel, and murmured over me,—

"They say roses are so hard to rear thus, and you are such a little thing; but do grow to a tree and live with me. Surely you can, if you try."

She had wounded me sharply and thrust me into a tomb of baked red clay filled with black and heavy mould. But I knew that I was pierced to the heart that I might—though only a little offshoot gathered to die in a day—strike root of my own and be strong, and carry a crown of fresh blossoms.

For she but dealt with me as your world deals with you, when your heart aches and your brain burns, and Fate stabs you, and says in your ear, "O fool! to be great you must suffer."

You to your fate are thankless, being human; but I, a rose, was not.

I tried to feel not utterly wretched in that little dull clay cell: I tried to forget my sweet glad southern birth-place, and not to sicken and swoon in the noxious gases of the city air.

I did my best not to shudder in the vapour of the stove, and not to grow pale in the clammy heats of the street, and not to die of useless lamentation for all that I had lost—for the noble tawny sunsets, and the sapphire blue skies, and the winds all fragrant with the almond tree flowers, and the sunlight in which the yellow orioles flashed like gold.

I did my best to be content and show my gratitude all through a parching autumn and a hateful winter; and with the spring a wandering wind came and wooed me with low, amorous whispers—came from the south, he said; and I learned that, even in exile in an attic window, love may find us out and make for us a country and a home.

So I lived and grew and was happy there, against the small, dim garret panes, and my lover from the south came, still faithful, year by year; and all the voices round me said that I was fair—pale indeed, and fragile of strength, as a creature torn from its own land and all its friends must be; but contented and glad, and grateful to the God who made me, because I had not lived in vain, but often saw sad eyes, half blinded with toil and tears, smile at me when they had no other cause for smiles.

"It is bitter to be mewed in a city," said once to me an old, old vine who had been thrust into the stones below and had climbed the house wall, heaven knew how, and had lived for half a century jammed between buildings, catching a gleam of sunshine on his dusty leaves once perhaps in a whole summer. "It is bitter for us. I would rather have had the axe at my root and been burned. But perhaps without us the poorest of people would never remember the look of the fields. When they see a green leaf they laugh a little, and then weep —some of them. We, the trees and the flowers, live in the cities as those souls amongst them whom they call poets live in the world—exiled from heaven that by them the world may now and then bethink itself of God."

And I believe that the vine spoke truly. Surely, he who plants a green tree in a city way plants a thought of God in many a human heart arid with the dust of travail and clogged with the greeds of gold.

So, with my lover the wind and my neighbour the vine, I was content and patient, and gave many hours of pleasure to many hard lives, and brought forth many a blossom of sweetness in that little nook under the roof.

Had my brothers and sisters done better, I wonder, living in gilded balconies or dying in jewelled hands?

I cannot say: I can only tell of myself.

The attic in which I found it my fate to dwell was very high in the air, set in one of the peaked roofs of the quarter of the Luxembourg, in a very narrow street, populous and full of noise, in which people of all classes, except the rich, were to be found—in a medley of artists, students, fruit-sellers, workers in bronze and ivory, seamstresses, obscure actresses, and all the creators, male and female, of the thousand and one airy arts of elegant nothingness which a world of pleasure demands as imperatively as a world of labour demands its bread.

It would have been a street horrible and hideous in any city save Florence or Paris: in Florence it would have been saved by colour and antiquity—in Paris it was saved by colour and grace. Just a flash of a bright drapery, just a gleam of a gay hue, just some tender pink head of a hydrangea, just some quaint curl of some gilded woodwork, just the green glimmer of my friend the vine, just the snowy sparkle of his neighbour the water-spout,—just these, so little and yet so much, made the crooked passage a bearable home, and gave it a kinship with the glimpse of the blue sky above its pent roofs.

O wise and true wisdom! to redeem poverty with the charms of outline and of colour, with the green bough and the song of running water, and the artistic harmony which is as possible to the rough-hewn pine-wood as in the polished ebony. "It is of no *use!*" you cry. O fools! which gives you perfume—we, the roses, whose rich hues and matchless grace no human artist can imitate, or the rose-trémière, which mocks us, standing stiff and gaudy and scentless and erect?

Grace and pure colour and cleanliness are the divinities that redeem the foulness and the ignorance and the slavery of your crushed, coarse lives when you have sight enough to see that they are divine. But that is so seldom—so seldom.

In my little attic, in whose window I have passed my life, they were known gods and honoured; so that, despite the stovepipe and the poverty, and the little ill-smelling candle, and the close staircase without, with the rancid oil in its lamps and its fœtid faint odours, and the refuse, and the gutters, and the gas in the street below, it was possible for me, though a rose of Provence and a rose of the open air freeborn, to draw my breath in it and to bear my blossoms, and to smile when my lover the wind roused me from sleep with each spring, and said in my ear, "Arise! for a new year is come."

Now, to greet a new year with a smile, and not a sigh, one must be tranquil, at least, if not happy.

Well, I and the lattice, and a few homely plants of saxafrage and musk and balsam who bloomed there with me, and a canary who hung in a cage amongst us, and a rustic creeper who clung to a few strands of strained string and climbed to the roof and there talked all day to the pigeons,—we all belonged to the girl with the candid sweet eyes, and by name she was called Lili Kerrouel, and for her bread she gilded and coloured those little cheap boxes for sweetmeats that they sell in the wooden booths at the fairs on the boulevards, while the mirlitons whirl in their giddy go-rounds and the merry horns of the charlatans challenge the populace.

She was a girl of the people: she could read, but I doubt if she could write. She had been born of peasant parents in a Breton hamlet, and they had come to Paris to seek work, and had found it for a while and prospered; and then had fallen sick and lost it, and struggled for a while, and then died, running the common course of so many lives amongst you. They had left Lili alone at sixteen, or rather worse than alone—with an old grandam, deaf and quite blind, who could do nothing for her own support, but sat all day in a wicker chair by the lattice or the stove, according as the season was hot or cold, and mumbled a little inarticulately over her worn wooden beads.

Her employers allowed Lili to bring these boxes to decorate at home, and she painted at them almost from dawn to night. She swept, she washed, she stewed, she fried, she dusted; she did all the housework of her two little rooms; she tended the old woman in all ways; and she did all these things with such cleanliness and deftness that the attics were wholesome as a palace; and though her pay was very small, she yet found means and time to have her linen spotless, and make her pots and pans shine like silver and gold, and to give a grace to all the place, with the song of a happy bird and the fragrance of flowers that blossomed their best and their sweetest for her sake, when they would fain have withered to the root and died in their vain longing for the pure breath of the fields and the cool of a green woodland world.

It was a little, simple, hard life, no doubt—a life one would have said scarce worth all the trouble it took to get bread enough to keep it going. A hard life, colouring always the same eternal little prints all day long, no matter how sweet the summer day might be, or how hot the tired eyes.

A hard life, with all the wondrous, glorious, wasteful, splendid life of the beautiful city around it in so terrible a contrast; with the roll of the carriages day and night on the stones beneath, and the pattering of the innumerable feet below, all hurrying to some pleasure, and every moment some burst of music or some chime of bells or some ripple of laughter on the air.

A hard life, sitting by one's self in a little dusky garret in the roof, and straining one's sight for two sous an hour, and listening to an old woman's childish mutterings and reproaches, and having always to shake the head in refusal of the neighbour's invitations to a day in the woods or a sail on the river. A hard life, no doubt, when one is young and a woman, and has soft shining eyes and a red curling mouth.

And yet Lili was content.

Content, because she was a French girl; because she had always been poor, and thought two sous an hour, riches; because she loved the helpless old creature whose senses had all died while her body lived on; because she was an artist at heart, and saw beautiful things round her even when she scoured her brasses and washed down her bare floor.

Content, because with it all she managed to gather a certain "sweetness and light" into her youth of toil; and when she could give herself a few hours' holiday, and could go beyond the barriers, and roam a little in the wooded places, and come home with a knot of primroses or a plume of lilac in her hands, she was glad and grateful as though she had been given gold and gems.

Ah! In the lives of you who have wealth and leisure we, the flowers, are but one thing among many: we have a thousand rivals in your porcelains, your jewels, your luxuries, your intaglios, your mosaics, all your treasures of art, all your baubles of fancy. But in the lives of the poor we are alone: we are all the art, all the treasure, all the grace, all the beauty of outline, all the purity of hue that they possess: often we are all their innocence and all their religion too.

Why do you not set yourselves to make us more abundant in those joyless homes, in those sunless windows?

Now, this street of hers was very narrow, it was full of old houses, that nodded their heads close together as they talked, like your old crones over their fireside gossip.

I could, from my place in the window, see right into the opposite garret window. It had nothing of my floral nation in it, save a poor colourless stone-wort, who got a dismal living in the gutter of the roof, yet who too, in his humble way, did good and had his friends, and paid the sun and the dew for calling him into being.

For on that rainpipe the little dusty thirsty

sparrows would rest and bathe and plume themselves, and bury their beaks in the pale stone-crop, and twitter with one another joyfully, and make believe that they were in some green and amber meadow in the country in the cowslip time.

I did not care much for the stone-crop or the sparrows; but in the third summer of my captivity there with Lili the garret casement opposite stood always open, as ours did, and I could watch its tenant night and day as I chose.

He had an interest for me.

He was handsome, and about thirty years old; with a sad and noble face, and dark eyes full of dreams, and cheeks terribly hollow, and clothes terribly threadbare.

He thought no eyes were on him when my lattice looked dark, for his garret, like ours, was so high that no glance from the street ever went to it. Indeed, when does a crowd ever pause to look at a garret, unless by chance a man have hanged himself out of its window? That in thousands of garrets men may be dying by inches for lack of bread, lack of hope, lack of justice, is not enough to draw any eyes upward to them from the pavement.

He thought himself unseen, and I watched him many a long hour of the summer night when I sighed at my square open pane in the hot, sulphurous mists of the street, and tried to see the stars and could not. For, between me and the one small breadth of sky which alone the innumerable roofs left visible, a vintner had hung out a huge gilded imperial crown as a sign on his roof-tree; and the crown, with its sham gold turning black in the shadow, hung between me and the planets.

I knew that there must be many human souls in a like plight with myself, with the light of heaven blocked from them by a gilded tyranny, and yet I sighed, and sighed, and sighed, thinking of the white pure stars of Provence throbbing in the violet skies.

A rose is hardly wiser than a poet, you see: neither rose nor poet will be comforted, and be content to dwell in darkness because a crown of tinsel swings on high.

II.

WELL, not seeing the stars as I strove to do, I took refuge in sorrow for my neighbour. It is well for your poet when he turns to a like resource. Too often I hear he takes, instead, to the wine-cellar which yawns under the crown that he curses.

My neighbour, I soon saw, was poorer even than we were. He was a painter, and he painted beautiful things. But his canvases and the necessaries of his art were nearly all that his empty attic had in it; and when, after working many hours with a wretched glimmer of oil, he would come to his lattice and lean out, and try as I had tried to see the stars, and fail as I had failed, I saw that he was haggard, pallid, and weary unto death with two dire diseases—hunger and ambition.

He could not see the stars because of the crown, but in time, in those long midsummer nights, he came to see a little glow-worm amongst my blossoms, which in a manner, perhaps, did nearly as well.

He came to notice Lili at her work.

Often she had to sit up half the night to get enough colouring done to make up the due amount of labour; and she sat at her little deal table, with her little feeble lamp, with her beautiful hair coiled up in a great knot and her pretty head drooping so wearily—as we do in the long days of drought —but never once looking off, nor giving way to rebellion or fatigue, though from the whole city without there came one ceaseless sound, like the sound of an endless sea; which truly it was—the sea of pleasure.

Not for want of coaxings, not for want of tempters, various and subtle, and dangers often and perilously sweet, did Lili sit there in her solitude earning two sous an hour with straining sight and aching nerves that the old paralytic creature within might have bed and board without alms.

Lili had been sore beset in a thousand ways, for she was very fair to see; but she was proud and she was innocent, and she kept her courage and her honour; yea, though you smile—though she dwelt under an attic roof, and that roof a roof of Paris.

My neighbour, in the old gabled window over the way, leaning above his stone-wort, saw her one night thus at work by her lamp, with the silver ear-rings, that were her sole heirloom and her sole wealth, drooped against the soft hues and curves of her graceful throat.

And when he had looked once, he looked every night, and found her there; and I, who could see straight into his chamber, saw that he went and made a picture of it all—of me, and the bird in the cage, and the little old dusky lamp, and Lili with her silver ear-rings and her pretty drooping head.

Every day he worked at the picture, and every night he put his light out and came and sat in the dark square of his lattice, and gazed across the street through my leaves and my blossoms at my mistress. Lili knew nothing of this watch which he kept on her: she had put up a little blind of white network, and she fancied that it kept out every eye when it was up; and often she took even that away, because she had not the heart to deprive me of the few faint breezes which the sultry weather gave us.

She never saw him in his dark hole in the old gable there, and I never betrayed him—not I. Roses have been the flowers of silence ever since the world began. Are we not the flowers of love?

"Who is he?" I asked of my gossip the vine. The vine had lived fifty years in the street, and knew the stories and sorrows of all the human bees in the hive.

"He is called René Claude," said the vine. "He is a man of genius. He is very poor."

"You use synonyms," murmured the old balsam who heard.

"He is an artist," the vine continued. "He is young. He comes from the south. His people are guides in the Pyrenees. He is a dreamer of dreams. He has taught himself many things. He has eloquence too. There is a little club at the back of the house which I climb over. I throw a tendril or two in at the crevices and listen. The shutters are closed. It is forbidden by law for men to meet so. There René speaks by the hour, superbly. Such a rush of words, such a glance, such a voice, like the roll of musketry in anger, like the sigh of music in sadness! Though I am old, it makes the little sap there is left in me thrill and grow warm. He paints beautiful things too; so the two swallows say who build under his eaves; but I suppose it is not of much use: no one believes in him, and he almost starves. He is young yet, and feels the strength in him, and still strives to do great things for the world that does not care a jot whether he lives or dies. He will go on so a little longer. Then he will end like me. I used to try and bring forth the best grapes I could, though they had shut me away from any sun to ripen them and any dews to cleanse the dust from them. But no one cared. No one gave me a drop of water to still my thirst, nor pushed away a brick to give me a ray more of light. So I ceased to try and produce for their good; and I only took just so much trouble as would keep life in me myself. It will be the same with this man."

I, being young and a rose, the flower loved of the poets, thought the vine was a cynic, as many of you human creatures grow to be in the years of your age when the leaves of your life fall sere.

I watched René long and often. He was handsome, he suffered much; and when the night was far spent he would come to his hole in the gable and gaze with tender, dreaming eyes, my pale foliage to the face of Lili. I grew to care for him, and I disbelieved the prophecy of the vine; and I promised myself that one summer or another, near or far, the swallows, when they came from the tawny African world to build in the eaves of the city, would find their old friend flown and living no more in a garret, but in some art-palace where men knew his fame.

So I dreamed—I, a little white rose, exiled in the passage of a city, seeing the pale moonlight reflected on the gray walls and the dark windows, and trying to cheat myself by a thousand fancies into the faith that I once more blossomed in the old sweet leafy garden-ways in Provence.

One night—the hottest night of the year—Lili came to my side by the open lattice. It was very late: her work was done for the night. She stood a moment, with her lips rested softly on me, looking down on the pavement that glistened like silver in the sleeping rays of the moon.

For the first time she saw the painter René watching her from his niche in the gable, with eyes that glowed and yet were dim.

I think women foresee with certain prescience when they will be loved. She drew the lattice quickly to, and blew the lamp out: she kissed me in the darkness. Because her heart was glad or sorry? Both, perhaps.

Love makes one selfish. For the first time she left my lattice closed all through the oppressive hours until daybreak.

"Whenever a woman sees anything out of her window that makes her eager to look again, she always shuts the shutter. Why, I wonder?" said the balsam to me.

"That she may peep unsuspected through a chink," said the vine round the corner, who could overhear.

It was profane of the vine, and in regard to Lili untrue. She did not know very well, I dare say, why she withdrew herself on that sudden impulse, as the pimpernel shuts itself up at the touch of a raindrop.

But she did not stay to look through a crevice; she went straight to her little narrow bed, and told her beads and prayed, and slept till the cock crew in a stable near and the summer daybreak came.

She might have been in a chamber all mirror and velvet and azure and gold in any one of the ten thousand places of pleasure, and been leaning over gilded balconies under the lime leaves, tossing up little paper balloons in the air for gay wagers of love and wine and jewels. Pleasure had asked her more than once to come down from her attic and go with its crowds; for she was fair of feature and lithe of limb, though only a work-girl of Paris. And she would not, but slept here under the eaves, as the swallows did.

"We have not sun enough, little rose, you and I," she would say to me with a smile and a sigh. "But it is better to be a little pale, and live a little in the dark, and be a little cramped in a garret window, than to live grand in the sun for a moment, and the next to be tossed away in a gutter. And one can be so happy anyhow—almost anyhow!—when one is young. If I could only see a very little piece more of the sky, and get every Sunday out to the dear woods, and live one floor lower, so that the winters were not quite so cold and the summers not quite so hot, and find a little more time to go to mass in the cathedral, and be able to buy a pretty blue-and-white home of porcelain for you, I should ask nothing more of the blessed Mary—nothing more upon earth."

She had had the same simple bead-roll of innocent wishes ever since the first hour that she had raised me from the dust of the street; and it would, I doubt not, have remained her only one all the years of her life, till she should have glided down into a serene and cheerful old age of poverty and labour under that very same roof, without the blessed Mary ever deigning to hearken or answer. Would have done so if the painter René could have seen the stars, and so had not been driven to look instead at the glow-worm of her lamp as it was shining through my leaves.

But after that night on which she shut to the lattice so suddenly, I think the bead-roll of her pure desires lengthened—lengthened, though for some time the addition to it was written on her heart in a mystical language which she did not try to translate even to herself—I suppose fearing its meaning.

René made approaches to his neighbour's friendship soon after that night. He was but an art-student, the son of a poor mountaineer, and with scarce a thing he could call his own except an easel of deal, a few plaster casts and a bed of straw. She was but a working-girl, born of Breton peasants, and owning as her sole treasures two silver ear-rings and a white rose.

But for all that, no courtship could have been more reverential on the one side or fuller of modest grace on the other, if the scene of it had been a palace of princes or a château of the nobles.

He spoke very little.

The vine had said that at the club round the corner he was very eloquent, with all the impassioned and fierce eloquence common to men of the south. But with Lili he was almost mute. The vine, who knew human nature well—as vines always do, since their juices unlock the secret thoughts of men and bring to daylight their darkest passions—the wine said that such silence, in one by nature eloquent, showed the force of his love and its delicacy.

This may be so; I hardly know. My lover the wind, when he is amorous, is loud, but then it is true his loves are not often very constant.

René chiefly wooed her by gentle service. He brought her little lovely wild flowers, for which he ransacked the woods of St. Germain's and Meudon. He carried the billets of her fire-wood up the seven long, twisting, dirty flights of stairs. He fought for her with the wicked old porteress at the door down stairs. He played to her in the grey of the evening on a quaint simple flute, a relic of his boyhood, the sad, wild, touching airs of his own southern mountains—played at his open window while the lamps burned through the dusk, till the people listened at their doors and casements, and gathered in groups in the passage below, and said to one another, "How clever he is!—and yet he starves."

He did starve very often, or at least he had to teach himself to keep down hunger with a morsel of black chaff-bread and a stray roll of tobacco. And yet I could see that he had become happy.

Lili never asked him within her door. All the words they exchanged were from their open lattices, with the space of the roadway between them.

I heard every syllable they spoke, and they were on the one side most innocent, and on the other most reverential. Ay, though you may not believe it—you who know the people of Paris from the travesties of theatres and the slanders of salons.

And all this time secretly he worked on at her portrait. He worked out of my sight and hers, in the inner part of his garret, but the swallows saw and told me.

There are never any secrets between birds and flowers.

We used to live in Paradise together, and we love one another as exiles do; and we hold in our cups the raindrops to slake the thirst of the birds, and the birds in return bring to us from many lands and over many waters tidings of those lost ones who have been torn from us to strike the roots of our race in far-off soils and under distant suns.

Late in the summer of the year, one wonderful fête-day, Lili did for once get out to the woods, the old kindly green woods of Vincennes.

A neighbour on a lower floor, a woman who made poor scentless, senseless, miserable imitations of all my race in paper, sat with the old bed-ridden grandmother while Lili took her holiday—so rare in her life, though she was one of the motes in the bright champagne of the dancing air of Paris. I missed her solely on each of those few sparse days of her absence, but for her I rejoiced.

"*Je reste: tu t'en vas*," says the rose to the butterfly in the poem; and I said so in my thoughts to her.

She went to the broad level grass, to the golden fields of the sunshine, to the sound of the bees murmuring over the wild purple thyme, to the sight of the great snowy clouds slowly sailing over the sweet blue freedom of heaven—to all the things of my birthright and my deathless remembrance—all that no woman can love as a rose can love them.

But I was not jealous; nay, not though she had cramped me in a little earth-bound cell of clay. I envied wistfully indeed, as I envied the swallows their wings which cleft the air, asking no man's leave for their liberty. But I would not have maimed a swallow's pinion had I had the power, and I would not have abridged an hour of Lili's freedom. Flowers are like your poets: they give ungrudgingly, and, like all lavish givers, are seldom recompensed in kind.

We cast all our world of blossom, all our treasury of fragrance, at the feet of the one we love; and then, having spent ourselves in that too abundant sacrifice, you cry, "A yellow, faded thing!— to the dust-hole with it!" and root us up violently and fling us to rot with the refuse and offal; not remembering the days when our burden of beauty made sunlight in your darkest places, and brought the odours of a lost paradise to breathe over your bed of fever.

Well, there is one consolation. Just so likewise do you deal with your human wonder-flower of genius.

Lili went for her day in the green midsummer world—she and a little blithe, happy-hearted group of young work-people—and I stayed in the garret window, hot and thirsty, and drooping and pale, choked by the dust that drifted up from the pavement, and hearing little all day long save the quarrels of the sparrows and the whirr of the engine-wheels in a baking-house close at hand.

For it was some great day or other, when all Paris was out *en fête*, and everyone was away from his or her home, except such people as the old bedridden woman and the cripple who watched her. So, at least, the white roof-pigeons told me, who flew where they listed, and saw the whole splendid city beneath them—saw all its glistening of arms and its sheen of palace roofs, all its gilded domes and its white, wide squares, all its crowds, many-hued as a field of tulips, and all its flashing eagles, golden as the sun.

When I had been alone two hours, and whilst the old building was silent and empty, there came across the street from his own dwelling-place, the artist René, with a parcel beneath his arm.

He came up the stairs with a light and noiseless step, and pushed open the door of our attic. He paused on the threshold a moment with the sort of reverent hushed look on his face that I had seen on the faces of one or two swarthy, bearded, scarred soldiers as they paused before the shrine at the door of the little chapel which stood in my sight on the other side of our street.

Then he entered, placed the thing which he carried on a wooden chair fronting the light, uncovered it, and went quietly out again without the women in the inner closet hearing him.

What he had brought was the canvas I had seen grow under his hand, the painting of me and the lamp and Lili. I do not doubt how he had done it: it was surely the little attic window, homely and true in likeness, and yet he had glorified us all, and so framed in my leaves and my white flowers, the low oil flame and the fair head of my mistress, that there was that in the little picture which made me tremble and yet be glad.

On a slender slip of paper attached to it there was written, "*Il n'y a pas de nuit sans étoile.*"

Of him I saw no more. The picture kept me silent company all that day.

At evening Lili came. It was late. She brought with her a cool perfume of dewy mosses and fresh leaves, and strawberry plants—sweet as honey. She came in with a dark dreamy brilliance in her eyes, and long coils of foliage in her hands.

She brought to the canary chickweed and a leaf of lettuce. She kissed me and laid wet mosses on my parching roots, and fanned me with the breath of her fresh lips. She took to the old women within a huge cabbage leaf full of cherries, having, I doubt not, gone herself without in order to bring the ruddy fruit to them.

She had been happy, but she was very quiet.

To those who love the country as she did, and, thus loving it, have to dwell in cities, there is as much of pain, perhaps, as of pleasure in a fleeting glimpse of the lost heaven.

She was tired, and sat for a while, and did not see the painting, for it was dusk. She only saw it when she rose to light the lamp: then, with a little shrill cry, she fell on her knees before it in her wonder and her awe, and laughed and sobbed a little, and then was still again, looking at this likeness of herself.

The written words took her long to spell out, for she could scarcely read, but when she had mastered them, her head sank on her breast with a flush and a smile, like the glow of dawn over my own native Provence, I thought.

She knew whence it came, no doubt, though there were many artists and students of art in that street.

But then there was only one who had watched her night after night as men watched the stars of old to read their fates in the heavens.

Lili was only a young ouvrière, she was only a girl of the people: she had quick emotions and innocent impulses; she had led her life straightly because it was her nature, as it is of the lilies— her namesakes, my cousins—to grow straight to the light, pure and spotless. But she was of the populace: she was frank, fearless, and strong, despite all her dreams. She was glad, and she sought not to hide it.

With a gracious impulse of gratitude she turned to the lattice, and leaned past me, and looked for my neighbour.

He was there in the gloom: he strove not to be seen, but a stray ray from a lamp at the vintner's gleamed on his handsome dark face, lean, and pallid, and yearning, and sad, but full of force and of soul, like a head of Rembrandt's. Lili stretched her hands to him with a noble, candid gesture and a sweet, tremulous laugh:

"What you have given me!—it is you?—it *is* you?"

"Mademoiselle forgives?" he murmured, leaning as far out as the gable would permit.

The street was still deserted, and very quiet. The theatres were all open to the people that night free, and bursts of music from many quarters rolled in through the sultry darkness.

Lili coloured over all her fair pale face, even as I have seen my sisters' white breasts glow to a wondrous wavering warmth as the sun of the west kissed them. She drew her breath with a quick sigh. She did not answer him in words, but with a sudden movement of exquisite eloquence, she broke from me my fairest and my last-born blossom and threw it from her lattice into his.

Then, as he caught it, she closed the lattice with a swift, trembling hand, and fled to the little sleeping-closet where her crucifix and her mother's rosary hung together above her bed.

As for me, I was left bereaved and bleeding. The dew which waters the growth of your human love is usually the tears or blood of some martyred life.

I was sacrificed for Lili.

I prayed, as my torn stem quivered, and my fairest begotten sank to her death in the night and in the silence, that I might be the first and the last to suffer from the human love born that night.

I, a rose—Love's flower.

III.

Now before that summer was gone, these two were betrothed to one another, and my little, fair, dead daughter, the Rosebud, all faded and scentless though her half-opened leaves were, remained always on René's heart as a tender and treasured relic.

They were betrothed, I say,—not wedded, for they were so terribly poor.

Many a day he, I think, had not so much as a

crust to eat; and there passed many weeks when the works on his canvas stood unfinished because he had not wherewithal to buy the oils and the colours to finish them.

René was frightfully poor, indeed; but then, being an artist and a poet, and the lover of a fair and noble woman, and a dreamer of dreams, and a man God-gifted, he was no longer wretched.

For the life of a painter is beautiful when he is still young, and loves truly, and has a genius in him stronger than calamity, and hears a voice in which he believes say always in his ear, "Fear nothing. Men must believe as I do in thee, one day. And meanwhile—we can wait!"

And a painter in Paris, even though he starve on a few sous a day, can have so much that is lovely and full of picturesque charm in his daily pursuits: the long, wondrous galleries full of the arts he adores; the "*réalité de l'idéal*" around him in that perfect world; the slow, sweet, studious hours in the calm wherein all that is great in humanity alone survives; the trance—half adoration, half aspiration, at once desire and despair—before the face of the Mona Lisa; then, without, the streets so glad and so gay in the sweet, living sunshine; the quiver of green leaves among gilded balconies; the groups at every turn about the doors; the glow of colour in market-place and peopled square; the quaint gray piles in old historic ways; the stones, from every one of which some voice from the imperishable Past cries out; the green and silent woods, the little leafy villages, the winding waters gardengirt; the forest heights, with the city gleaming and golden in the plain;—all these are his.

With these,—and youth,—who shall dare say the painter is not rich—ay, though his board be empty and his cup be dry?

I had not loved Paris,—I, a little imprisoned rose, caged in a clay pot, and seeing nothing but the sky-line of the roofs. But I grew to love it, hearing from René and from Lili of all the poetry and gladness that Paris made possible in their young and burdened lives, and which could have been thus possible in no other city of the earth.

City of Pleasure you have called her, and with truth; but why not also City of the Poor? For what city, like herself, has remembered the poor in her pleasure, and given to them, no less than to the richest, the treasure of her laughing sunlight, of her melodious music, of her gracious hues, of her million flowers, of her shady leaves, of her divine ideals?

Oh, world! when you let Paris die, you let your last youth die with her! Your rich will mourn a paradise deserted, but your poor will have need to weep with tears of blood for the ruin of the sole Eden whose sunlight sought them in their shadow, whose music found them in their loneliness, whose glad green ways were open to their tired feet, whose radiance smiled the sorrow from their aching eyes, and in whose wildest errors and whose vainest dreams their woes and needs were unforgotten.

Well, this little, humble love-idyl, which grew into being in an attic of Paris, had a tender grace of its own; and I watched it with tenderness, and it seemed to me fresh as the dews of the morning in the midst of the hot stifling world.

They could not marry: he had nothing but famine for his wedding-gift, and all the little that she made was taken for the food and wine of the bedridden old grandam in that religious execution of a filial duty which is so habitual in the French family-life, that no one dreams of counting it as any virtue.

But they spent their leisure-time together: they passed their rare holiday hours in each other's society in the woods which they both loved, or in the public galleries of art; and when the autumn came on apace, and they could no longer sit at their open casements, he still watched the gleam of her pale lamp as a pilgrim the light of a shrine, and she, ere she went to rest, would push ajar the closed shutter and put her pretty fair head into the darkling night and waft him a gentle good-night, and then go and kneel down by her bed and pray for him and his future before the cross which had been her dead mother's.

On that bright summer, a hard winter followed. The poor suffered very much; and I, in the closed lattice, knew scarcely which was the worse,—the icy shivering chills of the snow-burdened air, or the close noxious suffocation of the stove.

I was very sickly and ill, and cared little for my life during that bitter cold weather, when the panes of the lattice were all blocked from week's end to week's end with the solid silvery foliage of the frost.

René and Lili both suffered greatly: he could only keep warmth in his veins by the stoves of the public libraries, and she lost her work in the box trade after the New Year fairs, and had to eke out as best she might the few francs she had been able to lay back in the old brown pipkin in the closet.

She had, moreover, to sell most of the little things in her garret: her own mattress went, though she kept the bed under her grandmother. But there were two things she would not sell, though for both was she offered money: they were her mother's reliques and myself.

She would not, I am sure, have sold the picture, either. But for that no one offered her a centime.

One day, as the last of the winter solstice was passing away, the old woman died.

Lili wept for her sincere and tender tears, though never in my time—nor in any other, I believe, had the poor, old, querulous, paralytic sufferer rewarded her with anything except lamentation and peevish discontent.

"*Now* you will come to me?" murmured her lover, when they had returned from laying the old dead peasant in the quarter of the poor.

Lili drooped her head softly upon his breast.

"If you wish it!" she whispered, with a whisper as soft as the first low breath of summer.

If he wished it!

A gleam of pale gold sunshine shone through the dulled panes upon my feeble branches; a little timid fly crept out and spread its wings; the bells of the church rang an angelus; a child laughed in the street below; there came a smile of greenness spreading over the boughs of leafless trees; my lover, the wind, returned from the south, fresh from desert and ocean, with the scent of the spice-groves and palm-aisles of the east in his breath, and softly unclosing my lattice, murmured to me, "Didst thou think I was faithless? See, I come with the spring!"

So, though I was captive and they two were poor, yet we three were all happy; for love and a new year of promise were with us.

I bore a little snowy blossom (sister to the one which slept lifeless on René's heart) that spring, whilst yet the swallows were not back from the African gardens, and the first violets were carried in millions through the streets,—the only innocent imperialists that the world has ever seen.

That little winter-begotten darling of mine was to be Lili's nuptial-flower. She took it so tenderly from me, that it hardly seemed like its death.

"My little dear rose, who blossoms for me, though I can only cage her in clay, and only let her see the sun's rays between the stacks of the chimneys!" she said softly over me as she kissed me; and when she said that, could I any more grieve for Provence?

"What do they wed upon, those two?" said the old vine to me.

And I answered him: "Hope and dreams."

"Will those bake bread and feed babes?" said

the vine, as he shook his wrinkled tendrils despondently in the March air.

We did not ask in the attic.

Summer was nigh at hand, and we loved one another.

René had come to us—we had not gone to him. For our garret was on the sunny, his on the dark, side of the street, and Lili feared the gloom for me and the bird; and she could not bring herself to leave that old red-leaved creeper who had wound himself so close about the rain-pipe and the roof, and who could not have been dislodged without being slain.

With the Mardi Gras her trade had returned to her. René, unable to prosecute his grand works, took many of the little boxes in his own hands, and wrought on them with all the nameless mystical charm and the exquisite grace of touch which belong to the man who is by nature a great artist. The little trade could not at its best price bring much, but it brought bread; and we were happy.

While he worked at the box-lids she had leisure for her household labours: when these were done she would draw out her mother's old Breton distaff, and would sit and spin. When twilight fell they would go forth together to dream under the dewy avenues and the glistening stars, or as often would wait within whilst he played on his mountain flute to the people at the doorways in the street below.

"Is it better to go out and see the stars and the leaves ourselves, or to stay in-doors and make all these forget the misfortune of not seeing them?" said Lili, on one of those evenings when the warmth and the sunset almost allured her to draw the flute from her husband's hands and give him his hat instead; and then she looked down into the narrow road, at the opposite houses, at the sewing-girls stitching by their little windows, at the pale students studying their sickly lore with scalpel and with skeleton, at the hot dusty little children at play on the asphalte sidewalk, at the sorrowful darkened casements behind which she knew beds of sickness or of paralyzed old age were hidden — looked at all this from behind my blossoms, and then gave up the open air and the evening stroll that were so dear a pastime to her, and whispered to René, "Play, or they will be disappointed."

And he played, instead of going to the debating-club in the room round the corner.

"He has ceased to be a patriot," grumbled the old vine. "It is always so with every man when once he has loved a woman!"

Myself, I could not see that there was less patriotism in breathing the poetry of sound into the ears of his neighbours than in rousing the passions of hell in the breasts of his brethren.

But perhaps this was my ignorance: I believe that of late years people have grown to hold that the only pure patriotism is, and ought to be, evinced in the most intense and the most brutalized form of one passion—"Envy, eldest born of Hell."

So these two did some good, and were happy, though more than once it chanced to them to have to go a whole day without tasting food of any sort.

I have said that René had genius—a genius bold, true, impassioned, masterful—such a genius as colours the smallest trifles that it touches. René could no more help putting an ideal grace into those little sweetmeat boxes—which sold at their very highest, in the booths of the fairs, at fifty centimes apiece—than we, the roses, can help being fragrant and fair.

Genius has a way of casting its pearls in the dust as we scatter our fragrance to every breeze that blows. Now and then the pearl is caught and treasured, as now and then some solitary creature pauses to smell the sweetness of the air in which we grow, and thanks the God who made us.

But as ninety-nine roses bloom unthanked for one that is thus remembered, so ninety-nine of the pearls of genius are trodden to pieces for one that is set on high and crowned with honour.

In the twilight of a dull day a little, feeble, brown old man climbed the staircase and entered our attic with shambling step.

We had no strangers to visit us: who visits the poor? We thought he was an enemy: the poor always do think so, being so little used to strangers.

René drew himself erect, and strove to hide the poverty of his garments, standing by his easel. Lili came to me, and played with my leaves in her tender, caressing fashion.

"You painted this, M. René Claude?" asked the little brown old man.

He held in his hand one of the bonbon boxes, the prettiest of them all, with a tambourine-girl dancing in a wreath of Provence roses. René had copied me with loving fidelity in the flowers, and with a sigh had murmured as he cast the box aside when finished, "That ought to fetch at least a franc!" But he had got no more than the usual two sous for it.

The little old man sat down on the chair which Lili placed for him.

"So they told me, where I bought this. It was at a booth at St. Cloud. Do you know that it is charming?"

René smiled a little sadly: Lili flushed with joy. It was the first praise which she had ever heard given to him.

"You have a great talent," pursued the little man.

René bowed his handsome haggard face—his mouth quivered a very little: for the first time Hope entered into him.

"Genius, indeed," said the stranger; and he sauntered a little about and looked at the canvasses, and wondered and praised, and said not very much, but said that little so well and so judiciously that it was easy to see he was no mean judge of art, and possibly no slender patron of it.

As Lili stood by me, I saw her colour come and go and her breast heave. I too trembled in all my leaves: were recognition and the world's homage coming to René at last?

"And I have been so afraid always that I had injured, burdened him, clogged his strength in that endless strife!" she murmured below her breath. "O, dear little rose! if only the world can but know his greatness!"

Meanwhile the old man looked through the sketches and studies with which the room was strewed.

"You do not finish your things?" he said abruptly.

René flushed darkly.

"Oil pictures cost money," he said, briefly, "and —I am very poor."

Though a peasant's son, he was very proud: the utterance must have hurt him much.

The stranger took snuff.

"You are a man of singular genius," he said simply. "You only want to be known to get the prices of Meissonier."

Meissonier!—the Rothschild of the studios, the artist whose six-inch canvas would bring the gold value of a Raphael or a Titian!

Lili, breathing fast and white as death with ecstasy, made the sign of the cross on her breast: the delicate brown hand of René shook where it leaned on his easel.

They were both silent—silent from the intensity of their hope.

"Do you know who I am?" the old man pursued, with a cordial smile.

"I have not that honour," murmured René.

The stranger, taking his snuff out of a gold box, named a name at which the painter started. It was that of one of the greatest art-dealers in the whole of Europe; one who at a word could make or mar an artist's reputation; one whose accuracy of judgment was considered infallible by all connoisseurs, and the passport to whose galleries was to any unknown painting a certain passport also to the fame of men.

"You are a man of singular genius," repeated the great purchaser, taking his snuff in the middle of the little bare chamber. "It is curious—one always finds genius either in a cellar or in an attic: it never, by any chance, is to be discovered midway on the stairs—never in the *mezzanino*. But to the point. You have great delicacy of touch, striking originality of idea, a wonderful purity yet bloom in your colour, and an exquisite finish of minutiæ, without any weakness—a combination rare, very rare. That girl yonder, feeding white pigeons on the leads of a roof, with an atom of blue sky, and a few vine leaves straying over the parapet—that is perfectly conceived. Finished it must be. So must that little study of the beggar-boy looking through the gilded gates into the rose-gardens—it is charming, charming. Your price for those?"

René's worn young face coloured to the brows.

"Monsieur is too good," he muttered brokenly. "A nameless artist has no price, except—"

"Honour," murmured Lili, as she moved forward with throbbing heart and dim eyes. "Ah, monsieur, give him a name in Paris! We want nothing else —nothing else!"

"Poor fools!" said the dealer to the snuff-box.
I heard him—they did not.

"Madame," he answered aloud, "Paris herself will give him that the first day his first canvas hangs in my galleries. Meanwhile, I must in honesty be permitted to add something more. For each of those little canvases, the girl on the roof and the boy at the gate, I will give you now two thousand francs, and two thousand more when they shall be completed. Provided—"

He paused and glanced musingly at René.

Lili had turned away, and was sobbing for very joy at this undreamed-of deliverance.

René stood quite still, with his hands crossed on the easel and his head bent on his chest. The room, I think, swam round him.

The old man sauntered again a little about the place, looking here and looking there, murmuring certain artistic disquisitions technical and scientific, leaving them time to recover from the intensity of their emotion.

What a noble thing old age was, I thought, living only to give hope to the young in their sorrow, and to release captive talents from the prison of obscurity!

We should leave the little room in the roof, and dwell in some bright quarter where it was all leaves and flowers; and René would be great, and go to dine with princes, and drive a team of belled horses, like a famous painter who had dashed once with his splendid equipage through our narrow passage; and we should see the sky always—as much of it as ever we chose, and Lili would have a garden of her own, all grass, and foliage, and falling waters, in which I should live in the open air all the day long, and make believe that I was in Provence.

My dreams and my fancies were broken by the sound of the old man's voice taking up the thread of his discourse once more in front of René.

"I will give you four thousand francs each for those two little canvases," he repeated. "It is a mere pinch of dust to what you will make in six months' time,—if—if—you hear me?—your name is brought before the public of Paris in my galleries and under my auspices. I suppose you have heard something of what I can do, eh? Well, all I can do I will do for you; for you have a great talent, and without introduction, my friend, you may as well roll up your pictures and burn them in your stove to save charcoal? You know that?"

René indeed knew—none better. Lili turned on the old man her sweet, frank Breton eyes, smiling their radiant gratitude through tenderest tears.

The saints will reward you, monsieur, in a better world than this," she murmured softly.

The old man took snuff a little nervously.

"There is one condition I must make," he said with a trifling hesitation—"one only."

"Ask of my gratitude what you will," answered René quickly, while he drew a deep breath of relief and freedom—the breath of one who casts to the ground the weight of a deadly burden.

"It is that you will bind yourself only to paint for me."

"Certainly."

René gave the assent with eagerness. Poor fellow! it was a novelty so exquisite to have any one save the rats to paint for. It never dawned upon his thoughts that when he stretched his hands out with such passionate desire to touch the hem of the garment of Fortune and catch the gleam of the laurels of Fame, he might be in truth only holding them out to fresh fetters.

"Very well," said the old man quietly, and he sat down again and looked full in René's face, and unfolded his views for the artist's future.

He used many words, and was slow and suave in their utterance, and paused often and long to take out his heavy gold box; but he spoke well. Little by little his meaning gleamed out from the folds of verbiage in which he skilfully enwrapped it.

It was this.

The little valueless drawings on the people's sweetmeat boxes of gilded cardboard had a grace, a colour, and a beauty in them which had caught, at a fair-booth in the village of St. Cloud, the ever-watchful eyes of the great dealer. He had bought half-a-dozen of the boxes for a couple of francs. He had said, "Here is what I want." Wanted for what? Briefly, to produce Petitôt enamels and Fragonard cabinets, and perhaps now and then a Greuze portrait—genuine eighteenth-century work. There was a rage for it. René would understand?

René's dark southern eyes lost a little of their new lustre of happiness and grew troubled with a sort of cloud of perplexity. He did not seem to understand.

The old man took more snuff, and used phrases clearer still.

There were great collectors—dilettanti of houses imperial, and royal, and princely, and noble, of all the grades of greatness—who would give any sum for bonbonnières and tabatières of eighteenth-century work by anyone of the few famous masters of that time. A genuine, incontestable sweetmeat box from the ateliers of the Louis XIV. or Louis XV.

period would fetch almost a fabulous sum. Then again he paused, doubtfully.

René bowed, and his wondering glance said without words, "I know this. But I have no eighteenth-century work to sell you: if I had, should we starve in an attic?"

His patron coughed a little, looked at Lili, then proceeded to explain still farther.

In René's talent he had discerned the hues, the grace, the delicacy yet brilliancy, the voluptuousness and the *désinvolture* of the best eighteenth-century work. René doubtless did other and higher things which pleased himself far more than these airy trifles. Well, let him pursue the greater line of art if he chose; but he, the old man who spoke, could assure him that nothing would be so lucrative to him as those bacchantes in wreaths of roses and young tambourine-players *gorge au vent* dancing in a bed of violets, and beautiful marquises, powdered and jewelled, looking over their fans, which he had painted for those poor little two-sous boxes of the populace, and the like of which, exquisitely finished on enamel or ivory, set in gold and tortoise-shell rimmed with pearls and turquoises or opals and diamonds, would deceive the finest connoisseur in Europe into receiving them as—whatever they might be signed and dated.

If René would do some half dozen of these at dictation and a Greuze or Boucher head in a year, not more—more would be perilous—paint and sign them, and produce them with any touches that might be commanded; never ask what became of them when finished, nor recognize them if hereafter he might see them in any illustrious collection,—if René would bind himself to do this, he, the old man who spoke, would buy his other paintings, place them well in his famous galleries, and, using all his influence, would make him in a twelvemonth's time the most celebrated of all the young painters in Paris.

It was a bargain? Ah, how well it was, he said, to put the best of one's powers into the most trifling things one did! If that poor little two-sous box had been less lavishly and gracefully decorated, it would never have arrested his eyes in the bon-bon-booth at St. Cloud. The old man paused to take snuff and receive an answer.

René stood motionless.

Lili had sunk into a seat, and was gazing at the tempter with wide-open, puzzled, startled eyes. Both were silent.

"It is a bargain?" said the old man again. "Understand me, M. René Claude. You have no risk, absolutely none, and you have the certainty of fair fame and fine fortune in the space of a few years. You will be a great man before you have a gray hair: that comes to very few. I shall not trouble you for more than six dix-huitième siècle enamels in the year—perhaps for only four. You can spend ten months out of the twelve on your own canvases, making your own name and your own wealth as swiftly as your ambition and impatience can desire. Madame here," said the acute dealer with a pleasant smile—"Madame here can have a garden sloping on the Seine and a glasshouse of choicest flowers—which I see are her graceful weakness—ere another rose-season has time to come round, if you choose."

His voice lingered softly on the three last words.

The dew stood on René's forehead, his hands clenched on the easel:

"You wish me—to paint—forgeries of the Petitôt enamels?"

The old man smiled unmoved:

"Chut, chut! Will you paint me little bonbonnières on enamel or porcelain instead of on cardboard? That is all the question. I have said where they go, how they are set: what they are called shall be my affair. You know nothing. The only works of yours which you will be concerned to acknowledge will be your own canvas pictures. What harm can it do any creature? You will gratify a connoisseur or two innocently, and you will meanwhile be at leisure to follow the bent of your own genius, which otherwise—"

He paused: I heard the loud throbs of René's heart under that cruel temptation.

Lili gazed at his tempter with the same startled terror and bewilderment still dilating her candid eyes with a woeful pain.

"Otherwise," pursued the old man with merciless tranquillity, "you will never see me any more, my friends. If you try to repeat any story to my hindrance, no one will credit you. I am rich, you are poor. You have a great talent: I shall regret to see it lost, but I shall let it die—so."

And he trod very gently on a little gnat that crawled near his foot, and killed it.

A terrible agony gathered in the artist's face.

"O God!" he cried in his torture, and his eyes went to the canvases against the wall, and then to the face of his wife, with an unutterable yearning desire.

For them, for *them*,—his genius and his love,—this sin which tempted him looked virtue.

"Do you hesitate?" said the merciless old man. "Pshaw! whom do you hurt? You give me work as good as that which you imitate, and I call it only by a dead man's name: who is injured? What harm can there be in humouring the fanaticism of fashion? Choose—I am in haste."

René hid his face with his hands, so that he should not behold those dear creations of his genius which so cruelly, so innocently, assailed him with a temptation beyond his strength.

"Choose for me—you!" he muttered in his agony to Lili.

Lili, white as death, drew closer to him.

"My René, your heart has chosen," she murmured through her dry and quivering lips. "You cannot buy honour by a fraud."

René lifted his head and looked straight in the eyes of the man who held the scales of his fate, and could weigh out for his whole life's portion either fame and fortune or obscurity and famine.

"Sir," he said slowly, with a bitter tranquil smile about his mouth, "my garret is empty, but it is clean. May I trouble you to leave it as you found it?"

So they were strong to the end, these two famished children of frivolous Paris.

But when the door had closed and shut their tempter out, the revulsion came: they wept those tears of blood which come from the hearts' depths of those who have seen Hope mock them with a smile a moment, to leave them face to face with Death.

"Poor fools!" sighed the old vine from his corner in the gray, dull twilight of the late autumn day.

Was the vine right?

The air which he had breathed for fifty years through all his dust-choked leaves and tendrils had been the air off millions of human lungs, corrupted in its passage through millions of human lips, and the thoughts which he thought were those of human wisdom.

The sad day died; the night fell; the lattice was closed; the flute lay untouched.

A great misery seemed to enfold us. True, we were no worse off than we had been when the same day dawned. But that is the especial cruelty of every tempter always: he touches the innocent closed eyes of his victims with a collyrium which makes the happy blindness of content no longer possible. If the tempted be strong to resist him, the tempter has still his vengeance, for they are never again at peace as they were before that fatal hour in which he showed them all that they were not, all that they might be.

Our stove was not more chill, our garret not more empty; our darkness not more dark amidst the gay, glad, dazzling city; our dusky roof and looming crown that shut the sky out from us not more gloomy and impenetrable than they had been on all those other earlier nights when yet we had been happy. Yet how intensified millionfold seemed cold and loneliness and poverty and darkness, all!—for we had for the first time known what it was to think of riches, of fame, of homage, of light, as *possible*, and then to lose them all for ever!

I had been resigned for love's sake to dwell amongst the roofs, seeing not the faces of the stars, nor feeling ever the full glory of the sun; but now —I had dreamed of the fair freedom of gardenways and the endless light of summer suns on palace terraces, and I drooped and shivered and sickened, and was twice captive and twice exiled; and knew that I was a little nameless, worthless, hapless thing, whose fairest chaplet of blossom no hand would ever gather for a crown.

As with my life, so was it likewise with theirs.

They had been so poor, but they had been so happy: the poverty remained, the joy had flown.

That winter was again very hard, very cold: they suffered greatly.

They could scarcely keep together body and soul, as your strange phrase runs: they went without food sometimes for days and days, and fuel they had scarcely ever.

The bird in his cage was sold: they would not keep the little golden singing thing to starve into silence like themselves.

As for me, I nearly perished of the cold: only the love I bore to Lili kept a little life in my leafless branches.

All that cruel winter-time they were strong still, those children of Paris.

For they sought no alms, and in their uttermost extremity neither of them ever whispered to the other, "Go seek the tempter: repent, be wise. Give not up our lives for a mere phantasy of honour."

"When the snow is on the ground, and the canvases have to burn in the stove, then you will change your minds and come to me on your knees," the old wicked, foul spirit had said, mocking them, as he had opened the door of the attic and passed away creaking down the dark stairs.

And I suppose he had reckoned on this; but if he had done so he had reckoned without his host, as your phrase runs: neither René nor Lili ever went to him, either on their knees or in any other wise.

When the spring came we three were still all living—at least their hearts still beat and their lips still drew breath, as my boughs were still green and my roots still clung to the soil. But no more to them or to me did the coming of spring bring, as of old, the real living of life, which is joy.

And my lover the wind wooed me no more, and the birds no more brought me the rose-whispers of my kindred in Provence. For even the little pigeon-hole in the roof had become too costly a home for us, and we dwelt in a den under the stones of the streets, where no light came and scarce a breath of air ever strayed to us.

There the uncompleted canvases on which the painter whom Lili loved had tried to write his title to the immortality of fame, were at last finished—finished,—for the rats ate them.

All this while we lived—the man whose genius and misery were hell on earth; the woman whose very purity and perfectness of love were her direst torture; and I, the little white flower born of the sun and the dew, of fragrance and freedom, to whom every moment of this blindness, this suffocation, this starvation, this stench of putrid odours, this horrible roar of the street above, was a moment worse than any pang of death.

Away there in Provence so many a fair rose-sister of mine bowed her glad, proud, innocent head with anguish and shuddering terrors to the sharp summons of the severing knife that cut in twain her life, whilst I—I, on and on—was forced to keep so much of life as lies in the capacity to suffer and to love in vain.

So much was left to them: no more.

"Let us compel Death to remember us, since even Death forgets us!" René murmured once in his despair to her.

But Lili had pressed her famished lips to his: "Nay, dear, wait: God will remember us even yet, I think."

It was her faith. And of her faith she was justified at last.

There came a ghastlier season yet, a time of horror insupportable—of ceaseless sound beside which the roar of the mere traffic of the streets would have seemed silence—a stench beside which the sulphur smoke and the gas fumes of a previous time would have been as some sweet fresh woodland air—a famine beside which the daily hunger of the poor was remembered as the abundance of a feast—a cold beside which the chillness of the scant fuel and empty braziers of other winters were recalled as the warmth of summer—a darkness only lit by the red flame of burning houses—a solitude only broken by the companionship of woe and sickness and despair—a suffocation only changed by a rush of air strong with the scent of blood, of putridity, of the million living plague-stricken, of the million dead lying unburied.

For there was War.

Of year or day or hour I knew nothing. It was always the same blackness as of night; the same horror of sound, of scent, of cold; the same misery; the same torture. I suppose that the sun was quenched, that the birds were dumb, that the winds were stilled for ever—that all the world was dead: I do not know. They called it the Siege of Paris. I suppose that they meant the Revolt of Hell.

Yet Lili lived, and I: in that dread darkness we had lost René—we saw his face no more. Yet he could not be in his grave, I knew, for Lili, clasping my barren branches to her breast, would murmur, "Whilst he still lives I will live—yes, yes, yes!"

And she did live—so long, so long!—on a few draughts of water and a few husks of grain.

I knew that it was long, for full a hundred times she muttered aloud, "Another day? O God!—how long? how long?"

At last in the darkness a human hand was stretched to her, close beside me.

A foul and fierce light, the light of flame, was somewhere on the air above us, and at that moment glowed through the horrid gloom we dwelt in in the bowels of the earth. I saw the hand and what it held to her: it was a stranger's, and it held the little colourless dead rosebud, my sweetest blossom, that had lain ever upon René's heart.

She took it—she who had given it as her first love-gift. She was mute. In the glare of the flame that quivered through the darkness I saw her standing quite erect and very still.

The voice of a stranger thrilled through the din from the world above.

"He fought as only patriots can," it said softly and as through tears. "I was beside him. He fell with Regnault in the sortie yesterday. He could not speak: he had only strength to give me this for you. Be comforted: he has died for Paris."

On Lili's face there came once more the radiance of a perfect peace, a glory pure and endless as the glory of the sun.

"Great in death!" she murmured. "My love, my love, I come!"

I lost her in the darkness.

I heard a voice above me say that life had left her lips as the dead rose touched them.

What more is there for me to tell?

I live, since to breathe, and to feel pain, and to desire vainly, and to suffer always, are surest proofs of life.

I live, since that stranger's hand which brought

my little dead blossom as the message of farewell, had pity on me and brought me away from that living grave. But the pity was vain: I died the only death that had any power to hurt me when the human heart I loved grew still for ever.

The light of the full day now shines on me; the shadows are cool, the dews are welcome: they speak around me of the coming of spring, and in the silence of the dawns I hear from the woods without the piping of the nesting birds; but for me the summer can never more return—for me the sun can never again be shining—for me the greenest garden world is barren as a desert.

For I am only a little rose, but I am in exile and France is desolate.

A LEAF IN THE STORM.

I.

The Berceau de Dieu was a little village in the valley of the Seine.

As a lark drops its nest amongst the grasses, so a few peasant people had dropped their little farms and cottages amidst the great green woods on the winding river. It was a pretty place, with one steep, stony street, shady with poplars and with elms; quaint houses, about whose thatch a cloud of white and gray pigeons fluttered all day long; a little aged chapel with a conical red roof; and great barns covered with ivy and thick creepers, red and purple, and lichens that were yellow in the sun.

All around it there were the broad, flowering meadows, with the sleek cattle of Normandy fattening in them, and the sweet dim forests where the young men and maidens went on every holyday and feast-day in the summer-time to seek for wood-anemones, and lilies of the pools, and the wild campanula, and the fresh dog-rose, and all the boughs and grasses that made their house-doors like garden bowers, and seemed to take the cushat's note and the linnet's song into their little temple of God.

The Berceau de Dieu was very old indeed.

Men said that the hamlet had been there in the day of the Virgin of Orléans; and a stone cross of the twelfth century still stood by the great pond of water at the bottom of the street, under the chestnut-tree, where the villagers gathered to gossip at sunset when their work was done.

It had no city near it, and no town nearer than four leagues. It was in the green core of a pastoral district, thickly wooded and intersected with orchards. Its produce of wheat, and oats, and cheese, and fruit, and eggs, was more than sufficient for its simple prosperity. Its people were hardy, kindly, labourious, happy; living round the little gray chapel in amity and goodfellowship.

Nothing troubled it. War and rumours of war, revolutions and counter-revolutions, empires and insurrections, military and political questions,—these all were for it things unknown and unheard of— mighty winds that arose and blew and swept the lands around it, but never came near enough to harm it, lying there, as it did, in its loneliness like any lark's nest.

Even in the great days of the Revolution it had been quiet. It had had a lord whom it loved in the old castle on the hill at whose feet it nestled: it had never tried to harm him, and it had wept bitterly when he had fallen at Jemappes, and left no heir, and the château had crumbled into ivy-hung ruins.

The thunder-heats of that dread time had scarcely scorched it. It had seen a few of its best youth march away to the chant of the Marseillaise to fight on the plains of Champagne; and it had been visited by some patriots in *bonnets rouges* and soldiers in blue uniforms, who had given it tricoloured cockades and bade it wear them in the holy name of the Republic one and indivisible. But it had not known what these meant, and its harvests had been reaped without the sound of a shot in its fields or any gleam of steel by its innocent hearths; so that the terrors and the tidings of those noble and ghastly years had left no impress on its generations.

Reine Allix, indeed, the oldest woman amongst them all, numbering more than ninety years, remembered when she was a child hearing her father and his neighbours talk, in low awestricken tones, one bitter wintry night, of how a king had been slain to save the people; and she remembered likewise—remembered it well, because it had been her betrothal-night and the sixteenth birthday of her life—how a horseman had flashed through the startled street like a comet, and had called aloud, in a voice of fire, "Gloire! gloire! gloire!—Marengo! Marengo! Marengo!" And how the village had dimly understood that something marvellous for France had happened afar off, and how her brothers, and her cousins, and her betrothed, and she with them, had all gone up to the high slope over the river, and had piled up a great pyramid of pine-wood and straw and dried mosses, and had set flame to it, till it had glowed in its scarlet triumph all through that wondrous night of the sultry summer of victory.

These and the like memories she would sometimes relate to the children at evening, when they gathered round her begging for a story.

Otherwise, no memories of the Revolution or the Empire disturbed the tranquillity of the Berceau; and even she, after she had told them, would add:

"I am not sure now what Marengo was. A battle, no doubt, but I am not sure where nor why. But we heard later that little Claudis, my aunt's youngest born, a volunteer, not nineteen, died at it. If we had known, we should not have gone up and lit the bonfire."

This woman, who had been born in that time

of famine and flame, was the happiest creature in the whole hamlet of the Berceau.

"I am old: yes, I am very old," she would say, looking up from her spinning-wheel in her house-door, and shading her eyes from the sun, "very old—ninety-two last summer. But when one has a roof over one's head, and a pot of soup always, and a grandson like mine, and when one has lived all one's life in the Berceau de Dieu, then it is well to be so old. Ah, yes, my little ones—yes, though you doubt it, you little birds that have just tried your wings—it is well to be so old. One has time to think, and thank the good God, which one never seemed to have a minute to do in that work, work, work, when one was young."

Reine Allix was a tall and strong woman, very withered, and very bent, and very brown, yet with sweet, dark, flashing eyes that had still light in them, and a face that was still noble, though nearly a century had bronzed it with its harvest suns and blown on it with its winter winds.

She wore always the same garb of homely dark-blue serge, always the same tall white headgear, always the same pure silver ear-rings, that had been at once an heirloom and a nuptial gift. She was always shod in her wooden sabots, and she always walked abroad with her staff of ash.

She had been born in the Berceau de Dieu; had lived there and wedded there; had toiled there all her life, and never left it for a greater distance than a league or a longer time than a day.

She loved it with an intense love: the world beyond it was nothing to her: she scarcely believed in it as existing. She could neither read nor write. She told the truth, reared her offspring in honesty, and praised God always—had praised Him when starving in a bitter winter after her husband's death, when there had been no field-work, and she had had five children to feed and clothe; and still praised Him now that her sons were all dead before her, and all she had living of her blood was her grandson Bernadou.

Her life had been a hard one.

Her parents had been hideously poor. Her marriage had scarcely bettered her condition. She had laboured in the fields always, hoeing and weeding, and reaping, and carrying wood, and driving mules, and continually rising with the first streak of the daybreak. She had known fever and famine, and all manner of earthly ills. But now in her old age she had peace.

Two of her dead sons, who had sought their fortunes in the other hemisphere, had left her a little money, and she had a little cottage and a plot of ground, and a pig, and a small orchard. She was well-to-do, and could leave it all to Bernadou; and for ten years she had been happy, perfectly happy, in the coolness, and the sweetness and the old familiar ways and habits of the Berceau.

Bernadou was very good to her.

The lad, as she called him, was five-and-twenty years old, tall and straight and clean-limbed, with the blue eyes of the North, and a gentle frank face. He worked early and late in the plot of ground that gave him his livelihood. He lived with his grandmother, and tended her with a gracious courtesy and veneration that never altered. He was not very wise; he also could neither read nor write; he believed in his priest and his homestead, and loved the ground that he had trodden ever since his first steps from the cradle had been guided by Reine Allix.

He had never been drawn for the conscription, because he was the only support of a woman of ninety: he, likewise, had never been half-a-dozen kilometres from his birth-place.

When he was bidden to vote, and he asked what his vote of assent would pledge him to, they told him,—

"It will bind you to honour your grandmother so long as she shall live, and to get up with the lark, and to go to mass every Sunday, and to be a loyal son to your country. Nothing more."

And thereat he had smiled and straightened his stalwart frame, and gone right willingly to the voting-urn.

He was very stupid in these things; and Reine Allix, though clear-headed and shrewd, was hardly more learned in them than he.

"Look you," she had said to him oftentimes, "in my babyhood there was the old white flag upon the château. Well, they pulled that down and put up a red one. That toppled and fell, and there was one of three colours. Then somebody with a knot of white lilies in his hand came one day and set up the old white one afresh; and before the day was done that was down again, and the tricolour again up where it is still. Now some I know fretted themselves greatly because of all these changes of the flags, but as for me, I could not see that any one of them mattered: bread was just as dear, and sleep was just as sweet, whichever of the three was uppermost."

Bernadou, who had never known but the flag of three colours, believed her, as, indeed, he believed every word that those kindly and resolute old lips ever uttered to him.

He had never been in a city, and only once,

on the day of his first communion, in the town four leagues away. He knew nothing more than this simple, cleanly, honest life that he led. With what men did outside his little world of meadowland and woodland he had no care nor any concern.

Once a man had come through the village of the Berceau, a travelling hawker of cheap prints,—a man with a wild eye and a restless brain—who told Bernadou that he was a downtrodden slave, a clod, a beast like a mule, who fetched and carried that the rich might fatten,—a dolt, an idiot, who cared nothing for the rights of man and the wrongs of the poor.

Bernadou had listened with a perplexed face: then, with a smile, that had cleared it like sunlight, he had answered in his country dialect.

"I do not know of what you speak. Rights? Wrongs? I cannot tell. But I have never owed a sou; I have never told a lie; I am strong enough to hold my own with any man that flouts me; and I am content where I am. That is enough for me."

The peddler had called him a poor-spirited beast of burden, but had said so out of reach of his arm, and by night had slunk away from the Berceau de Dieu, and had been no more seen there to vex the quiet contentment of its peaceful and peace-loving ways.

At night, indeed, sometimes, the little wine-shop of the village would be frequented by some half-dozen of the peasant proprietors of the place, who talked Communism after their manner, not a very clear one, in excited tones and with the feverish glances of conspirators. But it meant little, and came to less.

The weather and the price of wheat were dearer matters to them; and in the end they usually drank their red wine in amity, and went up the village street arm in arm, singing patriotic songs until their angry wives flung open their lattices and thrust their white headgear out into the moonlight, and called to them shrewishly to get to bed and not make fools of themselves in that fashion; which usually silenced and sobered them all instantly; so that the revolutions of the Berceau de Dieu, if not quenched in a wine-pot, were always smothered in a nightcap, and never, by any chance, disturbed its repose.

But of these noisy patriots, Bernadou was never one. He had the instinctive conservatism of the French peasant, which is in such direct and tough antagonism with the feverish Socialism of the French artisan.

His love was for the soil—a deep-rooted love as the oaks that grew in it. Of Paris he had a dim, vague dread, as of a superb beast continually draining and devouring. Of all forms of government he was alike ignorant. So long as he tilled his little angle of land in peace, so long as the sun ripened his fruits and corn, so long as famine was away from his door and his neighbours dwelt in good-fellowship with him, so long he was happy, and cared not whether he was thus happy under a monarchy, an empire, or a republic.

This wisdom, which the peddler called apathy and cursed, the young man had imbibed from Nature and the teachings of Reine Allix.

"Look at home and mind thy work," she had said always to him. "It is labour enough for a man to keep his own life clean and his own hands honest. Be not thou at any time as they are who are for ever telling the good God how He might have made the world on a better plan, while the rats gnaw at their haystacks and the children cry over an empty platter."

And he had taken heed to her words; so that in all the countryside there was not any lad truer, gentler, braver or more patient at labour than was Bernadou; and though some thought him mild even to foolishness, and meek even to stupidity, he was no fool; and he had a certain rough skill at music, and a rare gift at the culture of plants, that made his little home bright within in the winter-time with melody, and in the summer gay without as a king's parterre.

At any rate, Reine Allix and he had been happy together for a quarter of a century under the old gray thatch of the wayside cottage, where it stood at the foot of the village-street, with its great sycamores spread above it. Nor were they less happy when in mid-April, in the six-and-twentieth year of his age, Bernadou had come in with a bunch of primroses in his hand, and had bent down to her and saluted her with a respectful tenderness, and said, softly and a little shyly, "Gran'mère, would it suit you if I were ever—to marry?"

Reine Allix was silent a minute and more, cherishing the primroses and placing them in a little brown cupful of water. Then she looked at him steadily with her clear dark eyes:

"Who is it, my child?"

He was always a child to her, this last-born of the numerous brood that had once dwelt with her under the spreading branches of the sycamores, and had now all perished off the face of the earth, leaving himself and her alone.

Bernadou's eyes met hers frankly:

"It is Margot Dax: does that please you, gran'-mère, or no?"

"It pleases me well," she said simply. But there was a little quiver about her firm-set mouth, and her aged head was bent over the primroses. She had foreseen it; she was glad of it; and yet, for the instant it was a pang to her.

"I am very thankful," said Bernadou, with a flash of joy on his face.

He was independent of his grandmother: he could make enough to marry upon by his daily toil, and he had a little store of gold and silver in his bank in the thatch, put by for a rainy day; but he would have no more thought of going against her will than he would have thought of lifting his hand against her. In the primitive homesteads of the Berceau de Dieu, filial reverence was still accounted the first of virtues, yet the simplest and the most imperative.

"I will go see Margot this evening," said Reine Allix, after a little pause. "She is a good girl, and a brave, and of pure heart and fair name. You have chosen well, my grandson."

Bernadou stooped his tall, fair, curly head, and she laid her hands on him and blessed him.

That evening, as the sun set, Reine Allix kept

her word, and went to the young maiden who had allured the eyes and heart of Bernadou.

Margot was an orphan: she had not a penny to her dower; she had been brought up on charity, and she dwelt now in the family of the largest landowner of the place, a miller, with a numerous offspring, and several head of cattle, and many stretches of pasture and of orchard.

Margot worked for a hard master, living, indeed, as one of the family, but sharply driven all day long at all manner of house-work and field-work. Reine Allix had kept her glance on her, through some instinctive sense of the way that Bernadou's thoughts were turning, and she had seen much to praise, nothing to chide, in the young girl's modest, industrious, cheerful, uncomplaining life.

Margot was very pretty too, with the brown oval face, and the great black soft eyes, and the beautiful form of the southern blood that had run in the veins of her father, who had been a sailor of Marseilles, whilst her mother had been a native of the Provençal country. Altogether, Reine Allix knew that her beloved one could not have done better or more wisely, if choose at all he must.

"Some people indeed," she said to herself as she climbed the street whose sharp-set flints had been trodden by her wooden shoes for ninety years—

"Some people would mourn and scold because there is no store of linen, no piece of silver plate, no little round sum in money with the poor child. But what does it matter? We have enough for three. It is wicked indeed for parents to live so that they leave their daughter portionless, but it is no fault of the child's. Let them say what they like, it is a reason the more that she should want a roof over her head and a husband to care for her good."

So she climbed the steep way and the slanting road round the hill, and went in by the door of the mill-house, and found Margot busy in washing some spring lettuces and other green things in a bowl of bright water.

Reine Allix, in the fashion of her country and her breeding, was about to confer with the master and mistress ere saying a word to the girl, but there was that in Margot's face and in her timid greeting that lured speech out of her.

She looked long and keenly into the child's downcast countenance, then touched her with a tender smile:

"Petite Margot, the birds told me a little secret to-day. Canst guess what it is? Say?"

Margot coloured and then grew pale. True, Bernadou had never really spoken to her, but still, when one is seventeen, and has danced a few times with the same person, and has plucked the leaves of a daisy away to learn one's fortune, spoken words are not very much wanted.

At sight of her the eyes of the old woman moistened and grew dimmer than age had made them. She smiled still, but the smile had the sweetness of a blessing in it, and no longer the kindly banter of humour.

"You love him, my little one?" she said, in a soft hushed voice.

"Ah, Mère Alix!" Margot could not say more. She covered her face with her hands, and turned to the wall, and wept with a passion of joy.

Down in the Berceau there were gossips who would have said, with wise shakes of their heads, "Tut, tut! how easy it is to make believe in a little love when one is a serving-maid, and has not a sou, nor a roof, nor a friend in the world, and a comely youth, well-to-do, is willing to marry us!"

But Reine Allix knew better. She had not lived ninety years in the world not to be able to discern between true feeling and counterfeit. She was touched, and drew the trembling frame of Margot into her arms, and kissed her twice on the closed, blue-veined lids of her black eyes.

"Make him happy, only make him happy," she

murmured; "for I am very old, Margot, and he is alone, all alone."

And the child crept to her, sobbing for very rapture that she, friendless, homeless, and penniless, should be thus elected for so fair a fate, and whispered through her tears, "I will."

Reine Allix spoke in all form to the miller and his wife, and with as much earnestness in her demand as though she had been seeking the hand of rich Yacobé, the tavern-keeper's only daughter. The people assented: they had no pretext to oppose, and Reine Allix wrapt her cloak about her and descended the hill and the street just as the twilight closed in and the little lights began to glimmer through the lattices and the shutters and the green mantle of the boughs, whilst the red fires of the smithy forge glowed brightly in the gloom, and a white horse waited to be shod, with a boy in a blue blouse seated on its back and switching away with a branch of budding hazel the first grey gnats of the early year.

"It is well done, it is well done," she said to herself, looking at the low rosy clouds and the pale gold of the waning sky. "A year or two, and I shall be in my grave. I shall leave him easier if I know he has some creature to care for him, and I shall be quiet in my coffin, knowing that his children's children will live on and on and on in the Berceau, and sometimes perhaps think a little of me when the nights are long and they sit round the fire."

She went in, out of the dewy air, into the little low, square room of her cottage, and went up to Bernadou and laid her hands on his shoulders.

"Be it well with thee, my grandson, and with thy sons' sons after thee," she said solemnly. "Margot will be thy wife. May thy days and hers be long in thy birth-place!"

A MONTH later they were married.

It was then May.

The green nest of the Berceau seemed to overflow with the singing of birds and the blossoming of flowers. The corn-lands promised a rare harvest, and the apple orchards were weighed down with their red and white blossoms. The little brown streams in the woods brimmed over in the grass, and the air was full of a sweet mellow sunlight, a cool fragrant breeze, a continual music of humming bees and soaring larks and mule-bells ringing on the roads, and childish laughter echoing from the fields.

In this glad spring-time Bernadou and Margot

were wedded, going with their friends one sunny morning up the winding hill-path to the little grey chapel whose walls were hidden in ivy, and whose sorrowful Christ looked down through the open porch across the blue and hazy width of the river.

Georges, the baker, whose fiddle made merry melody at all the village dances, played before them tunefully; little children, with their hands full of wood-flowers, ran before them; their old blind poodle smelt its way faithfully by their footsteps; their priest led the way upward with the cross held erect against the light; Reine Allix walked beside them, nearly as firmly as she had trodden the same road seventy years before in her own bridal hour; in the hollow below lay the Berceau de Dieu, with its red gables and its thatched roofs hidden beneath leaves, and its peaceful pastures smiling under the serene blue skies of France.

They were happy—ah Heaven, so happy!—and all their little world rejoiced with them.

They came home, and their neighbours entered with them, and ate and drank, and gave them good wishes and gay songs; and the old priest blessed them with a father's tenderness upon their threshold; and the fiddle of Georges sent gladdest dance-music flying through the open casements, across the road, up the hill, far away to the clouds and the river.

At night, when the guests had departed, and all was quite still within and without, Reine Allix sat alone at her window in the roof, thinking of their future and of her past, and watching the stars come out, one by another, above the woods. From her lattice in the eaves she saw straight up the village street; saw the dwellings of her lifelong neighbours, the slopes of the rich fields, the gleam of the broad grey water, the whiteness of the crucifix against the darkened sky.

She saw it all—all so familiar, with that intimate association only possible to the peasant who has dwelt on one spot from birth to age.

In that faint light, in those deep shadows, she could trace all the scene as though the brightness of the noon shone on it; it was all, in its homeliness and simplicity, intensely dear to her.

In the playtime of her childhood, in the courtship of her youth, in the joys and woes of her wifehood and widowhood, the bitter pains and sweet ecstasies of her maternity, the hunger and privation of struggling, desolate years, the contentment and serenity of old age,—in all these her eyes had rested only on this small quaint leafy street, with its dwellings close and low, like beehives in a garden, and its pasture-lands and corn-lands, wood-girt and water-fed, stretching as far as the sight could reach.

Every inch of its soil, every turn of its paths, was hallowed to her with innumerable memories: all her beloved dead were garnered there where the white Christ watched them: when her time should come, she thought, she would rest with them nothing loth.

As she looked the tears of thanksgiving rolled down her withered cheeks, and she bent her feeble limbs and knelt down in the moonlight, praising God that He had given her to live and die in this cherished home, and beseeching Him for her children that they likewise might dwell in honesty, and with length of days abide beneath that roof.

"God is good," she murmured as she stretched herself to sleep beneath the eaves—"God is good. Maybe, when He takes me to Himself, if I be worthy, He will tell His holy saints to give me a little corner in His kingdom, that He shall fashion for me in the likeness of the Berceau."

For it seemed to her that, than the Berceau, heaven itself could hold no sweeter or fairer nook of Paradise.

The year rolled on, and the cottage under the sycamores was but the happier for its new inmate.

Bernadou was serious of temper, though so gentle, and the arch gay humour of his young wife was like perpetual sunlight in the house. Margot, too, was so docile, so eager, so bright, and so imbued with devotional reverence for her husband and his home, that Reine Allix day by day blessed the fate that had brought to her this fatherless and penniless child.

Bernadou himself spoke little: words were not in his way, but his blue frank eyes shone with an unclouded radiance that never changed, and his voice, when he did speak, had a mellow softness in it that made his slightest speech to the two women with him tender as a caress.

"Thou art a happy woman, my sister," said the priest, who was wellnigh as old as herself.

Reine Allix bowed her head and made the sign of the cross: "I am, praise be to God!"

And being happy, she went to the hovel of poor Madelon Dreux, the cobbler's widow, and nursed her and her children through a malignant fever, sitting early and late, and leaving her own peaceful hearth for the desolate hut with the delirious ravings and heart-rending moans of the fever-stricken.

"How ought one to dare to be happy if one is not of use?" she would say to those who sought to dissuade her from running such peril.

Madelon Dreux and her family recovered, owing to her their lives, and she was happier than before, thinking of them when she sat on the settle before the wood-fire roasting chestnuts and spinning flax on the wheel, and ever and again watching the flame reflected on the fair head of Bernadou or in the dark, smiling eyes of Margot.

Another spring passed and another year went by, and the little home under the sycamores was still no less honest in its labours or bright in its rest.

It was one amongst a million of such homes in France, where a sunny temper made mirth with a meal of herbs, and filial love touched to poetry the prose of daily household tasks.

A child was born to Margot in the spring-time with the violets and daisies, and Reine Allix was proud of the fourth generation, and as she caressed the boy's healthy fair limbs, thought that God was indeed good to her, and that her race would live long in the place of her birth.

The child resembled Bernadou, and had his clear and candid eyes. It soon learned to know the voice of "Gran'mère," and would turn from its young mother's bosom to stretch its arms to Reine Allix. It grew fair and strong, and all the ensuing winter passed its hours curled like a dormouse or playing like a puppy at her feet in the chimney corner.

Another spring and summer came, and the boy was more than a year old, with curls of gold, and cheeks like apples, and a mouth that always smiled.

He could talk a little, and tumbled like a young rabbit amongst the flowering grasses.

Reine Allix watched him, and her eyes filled.

"God is too good," she thought. She feared that she should scarce be so willing to go to her last sleep under the trees on the hillside as she had used to be. She could not help a desire to see this child, this second Bernadou, grow up to youth and manhood; and of this she knew it was wild to dream.

It was ripe midsummer.

The fields were all russet and amber with an abundance of corn. The little gardens had seldom yielded so rich a produce. The cattle and the flocks were in excellent health.

There had never been a season of greater promise and prosperity for the little traffic that the village and its farms drove in sending milk and sheep and vegetable wealth to that great city which was to it as a dim, wonderful, mystic name without meaning.

One evening in this gracious and golden time the people sat out as usual when the day was done, talking from door to door, the old women knitting or spinning, the younger ones mending their husbands' or brothers' blouses or the little blue shirts of their infants, the children playing with the dogs on the sward that edged the stones of the street, and above all the great calm heavens and the glow of the sun that had set.

Reine Allix, like the others, sat before the door, for once doing nothing, but with folded hands and bended head dreamily taking pleasure in the coolness that had come with evening, and the smell of the limes that were in blossom, and the blithe chatter of Margot with the neighbours.

Bernadou was close beside them, watering and weeding those flowers that were at once his pride and his recreation, making the face of his dwelling bright and the air around it full of fragrance.

The little street was quiet in the evening light, only the laughter of the children and the gay gossip of their mothers breaking the pleasant stillness: it had been thus at evening with the Berceau centuries before their time—they thought that it would thus likewise be when centuries should have seen the youngest-born there travel to his grave.

Suddenly there came along the road between the trees an old man and a mule: it was Mathias Rével the miller, who had been that day to a little town four leagues off, which was the trade-mart and the corn-exchange of the district. He paused before the cottage of Reine Allix: he was dusty, travel-stained and sad. Margot ceased laughing among her flowers as she saw her old master. None of them knew why, yet the sight of him made the air seem cold and the night seem near.

"There is terrible news," he said, drawing a sheet of printed words from his coat-pocket—"terrible news! We are to go to war."

"War!" The whole village clustered round him. They had heard of war, far-off wars in Africa and Mexico, and some of their sons had been taken off like young wheat mown before its time; but it still remained to them a thing remote, impersonal, inconceivable, with which they had nothing to do, nor ever would have anything.

"Read!" said the old man, stretching out his sheet. The only one there who could do so, Picot the tailor, took it and spelled the news out to their wondering ears.

It was the declaration of France against Prussia.

There arose a great wail from the mothers whose sons were conscripts.

The rest asked in trembling, "Will it touch us?"

"Us!" echoed Picot the tailor, in contempt. "How should it touch us? Our braves will be in Berlin with another fortnight. The paper says so."

The people were silent: they were not sure what he meant by Berlin, and they were afraid to ask.

"My boy! my boy!" wailed one woman, smiting her breast. Her son was in the army.

"Marengo!" murmured Reine Allix, thinking of that far-off time in her dim youth when the horseman had flown through the dusky street and the bonfire blazed on the highest hill above the river.

"Bread will be dear," muttered Mathias the miller, going onward with his foot-weary mule.

Bernadou stood silent, with his roses dry and thirsty round him.

"Why art thou sad?" whispered Margot, with wistful eyes. "Thou art exempt from war-service, my love?"

Bernadou shook his head.

"The poor will suffer somehow," was all he answered.

Yet to him, as to all in the Berceau, the news was not very terrible, because it was so vague and distant—an evil so far off and shapeless.

Picot the tailor, who alone could read, ran from house to house, from group to group, breathless, gay and triumphant, telling them all that in two weeks more their brethren would sup in the king's palace at Berlin; and the people believed and laughed and chattered, and, standing outside their doors in the cool nights, thought that some good had come to them and theirs.

Only Reine Allix looked up the hill above the river, and murmured, "When we lit the bonfire there, Claudis lay dead."

And Bernadou, standing musing amongst his roses, said with a smile that was very grave,

"Margot, see here! When Picot shouted, 'à Berlin!' he trod on my Gloire de Dijon rose and killed it."

The sultry heats and cloudless nights of the wondrous and awful summer of the year eighteen hundred and seventy passed by, and to the Berceau de Dieu it was a summer of fair promise and noble harvest, and never had the land brought forth in richer profusion for man and beast.

Some of the youngest and ablest-bodied labourers were indeed drawn away to join those swift trains that hurried thousands and tens of thousands to the frontier by the Rhine. But most of the male population were married, and were the fathers of young children, and the village was only moved to a thrill of love and of honest pride to think how its young Louis and Jean and André and Valentin were gone full of high hope and high spirit, to come back, maybe—who could say not?—with epaulettes and ribbons of honour.

Why they were gone they knew not very clearly, but their superiors affirmed that they were gone to make greater the greatness of France; and the folk of the Berceau believed it, having in a corner of their quiet hearts a certain vague, dormant, yet deep-rooted love, on which was written the name of their country.

News came slowly and seldom to the Berceau.

Unless some one of the men rode his mule to the little town, which was but very rarely, or unless some peddler came through the village with a newssheet or so in his pack, or rumours and tidings on his lips, nothing that was done beyond its fields and woods came to it. And the truth of what it heard it had no means of measuring or sifting.

It believed what it was told, without questioning; and as it reaped the harvests in the rich hot sun of August, its peasants laboured cheerily in the simple and firm belief that mighty things were being done for them and theirs in the far eastern provinces by their great army, and that Louis and Jean and André and Valentin and the rest—though, indeed, no tidings had been heard of them—were safe and well and glorious somewhere, away where the sun rose, in the sacked palaces of the German king.

Reine Allix alone of them was serious and sorrowful—she whose memories stretched back over the wide space of near a century.

"Why art thou anxious, gran'mère?" they said

to her. "There is no cause. Our army is victorious everywhere; and they say our lads will send us all the Prussians' corn and cattle, so that the very beggars will have their stomachs full."

But Reine Allix shook her head, sitting knitting in the sun:

"My children, I remember the days of my youth. Our army was victorious then; at least they said so. Well, all I know is that little Claudis and the boys with him never came back; and as for bread, you could not get it for love or money, and the people lay dead of famine out on the public roads."

"But that is so long ago, gran'mère!" they urged.

Reine Allix nodded.

"Yes. It is long ago, my dears. But I do not think that things change very much."

They were silent out of respect for her, but amongst themselves they said, "She is very old. Nothing is as it was in her time."

One evening, when the sun was setting red over the reapen fields, two riders on trembling and sinking horses went through the village, using whip and spur, and scarcely drew rein as they shouted to the cottagers to know whether they had seen go by a man running for his life.

The people replied that they had seen nothing of the kind, and the horsemen pressed on, jamming their spurs into their poor beasts' steaming flanks.

"If you see him, catch and hang him," they shouted as they scoured away: "he is a Prussian spy!"

"A Prussian!" the villagers echoed with a stupid stare—"a Prussian in France!"

One of the riders looked over his shoulders for a moment:

"You fools! do you not know? We are beaten—beaten everywhere—and the Prussian pigs march on Paris."

The spy was not seen in the Berceau, but the news brought by his pursuers scared sleep from the eyes of every grown man that night in the little village.

"It is the accursed Empire!" screamed the patriots of the wine-shop.

But the rest of the people were too terrified and downstricken to take heed of empires or patriots: they only thought of Louis and Jean and André and Valentin; and they collected round Reine Allix, who said to them, "My children, for love of money all our fairest fruits and flowers—yea, even to the best blossoms of our maiden-hood—were sent to be bought and sold in Paris. We sinned therein, and this is the will of God."

This was all for a time that they heard.

It was a place lowly and obscure enough to be left in peace. The law pounced down on it once or twice and carried off a few more of its men for army-service, and arms were sent to it from its neighbouring town, and an old soldier of the First Empire tried to instruct its remaining sons in their use. But he had no apt pupil except Bernadou, who soon learned to handle a musket with skill and with precision, and who carried his straight form gallantly and well, though his words were seldom heard and his eyes were always sad.

"You will not be called till the last, Bernadou," said the old soldier: "you are married, and maintain your grandame and wife and child. But a strong, muscular, well-built youth like you should not wait to be called—you should volunteer to serve France."

"I will serve France when my time comes," said Bernadou, simply, in answer. But he would not leave his fields barren, and his orchard uncared for, and his wife to sicken and starve, and his grandmother to perish alone in her ninety-third year.

They jeered and flouted and upbraided him, those patriots who screamed against the fallen Empire in the wine-shop, but he looked them straight in the eyes, and held his peace, and did his daily work.

"If he be called, he will not be found wanting," said Reine Allix, who knew him better than did even the young wife whom he loved.

Bernadou clung to his home with a dogged devotion.

He would not go from it to fight unless compelled, but for it he would have fought like a lion. His feeling for his country was a feeling for only an indefinite, shadowy existence that was not clear to him: he could not love a land that he had never seen, a capital that was only to him as an empty name; nor could he comprehend the danger that his nation ran, nor could he desire to go forth and spend his life-blood in defence of things unknown to him. He was only a peasant, and he could not read nor greatly understand.

But affection for his birth-place was a passion with him—mute indeed, but deep-seated as an oak. For his birth-place he would have struggled as a man can only struggle when supreme love as well as duty nerves his arm. Neither he nor Reine Allix could see that a man's duty might lie from home;

but in that home both were alike ready to dare anything and to suffer everything.

It was a narrow form of patriotism, yet it had nobleness, endurance, and patience in it: in song it has been oftentimes deified as heroism, but in modern philosophy it is derided, and in modern warfare it is punished as the blackest crime.

So Bernadou tarried in his cottage till he should be called, keeping watch by night over the safety of his village, and by day doing all he could to aid the deserted wives and mothers of the place by the tilling of their ground for them and the tending of such poor cattle as were left in their desolate fields.

He and Margot and Reine Allix, between them, fed many mouths that would otherwise have been closed in death by famine, and denied themselves all except the barest and most meagre subsistence, that they might give away the little they possessed.

And all this while the war went on, but seemed far from them, so seldom did any tidings of it pierce the seclusion in which they dwelt. By and by, as the autumn went on, they learned a little more.

Fugitives coming to the smithy for a horse's shoe; women fleeing to their old village homes from their base, gay life in the city; mandates from the government of defence sent to every hamlet in the country; stray news-sheets brought in by carriers, or hawkers, and hucksters,—all these by degrees told them of the peril of their country—vaguely, indeed, and seldom truthfully, but so that by mutilated rumours they came at last to know the awful facts of the fate of Sedan, the fall of the Empire, the siege of Paris.

It did not alter their daily lives: it was still too far off, and too impalpable. But a foreboding, a dread, an unspeakable woe settled down on them.

Already their lands and cattle had been harassed to yield provision for the army and large towns; already their best horses had been taken for the siege-trains and the forage-waggons; already their ploughshares were perforce idle, and their children cried because of the scarcity of nourishment; already the iron of war had entered into their souls.

The little street at evening was mournful and very silent: the few who talked spoke in whispers, lest a spy should hear them, and the young ones had no strength to play: they wanted food.

"It is as it was in my youth," said Reine Allix, eating her piece of black bread and putting aside the better food prepared for her, that she might save it, unseen, for "the child."

It was horrible to her and to all of them to

live in that continual terror of an unknown foe—that perpetual expectation of some ghastly, shapeless misery.

They were quiet—so quiet!—but by all they heard they knew that any night, as they went to their beds, the thunder of cannon might awaken them; any morning, as they looked on their beloved fields, they knew that ere sunset the flames of war might have devoured them.

They knew so little, too: all they were told was so indefinite and garbled that sometimes they thought the whole was some horrid dream—thought so, at least, until they looked at their empty stables, their untilled land, their children who cried from hunger, their mothers who wept for the conscripts.

But as yet it was not so very much worse than it had been in times of bad harvest and of dire distress; and the storm which raged over the land had as yet spared this little green nest among the woods on the Seine.

November came.

"It is a cold night, Bernadou: put on more wood," said Reine Allix. Fuel at the least was plentiful in that district, and Bernadou obeyed.

He sat at the table, working at a new churn for his wife: he had some skill at turnery and at invention in such matters. The child slept soundly in its cradle by the hearth, smiling while it dreamed. Margot spun at her wheel. Reine Allix sat by the fire, seldom lifting her head from her long knitting-needles, except to cast a look on her grandson or at the sleeping child. The little wooden shutter of the house was closed. Some winter roses bloomed in a pot beneath the little crucifix. Bernadou's flute lay on a shelf: he had not had heart enough to play it since the news of the war had come.

Suddenly a great sobbing cry rose without—the cry of many voices, all raised in woe together.

Bernadou rose, took his musket in his hand, undid his door, and looked out. All the people were turned out into the street, and the women, loudly lamenting, beat their breasts and strained their children to their bosoms.

There was a sullen red light in the sky to the eastward, and on the wind a low, hollow roar stole to them.

"What is it?" he asked.

"The Prussians are on us!" answered twenty voices in one accord. "That red glare is the town burning."

Then they were all still—a stillness that was more horrible than their lamentations.

Reine Allix came and stood by her grandson.

"If we must die, let us die *here*," she said, in a voice that was low, and soft, and grave.

He took her hand and kissed it. She was content with his answer.

Margot stole forth too, and crouched behind them, holding her child to her breast. "What can they do to us?" she asked, trembling, with the rich colours of her face blanched white.

Bernadou smiled on her: "I do not know, my dear. I think even they can hardly bring death upon women and children."

"They can, and they will," said a voice from the crowd.

None answered. The street was very quiet in the darkness. Far away in the east the red glare glowed. On the wind there was still that faint, distant ravening roar, like the roar of famished wolves: it was the roar of fire and of war.

In the silence Reine Allix spoke: "God is good. Shall we not trust in Him?"

With one great choking sob the people answered: their hearts were breaking. All night long they watched in the street—they who had done no more to bring this curse upon them than the flower-roots that slept beneath the snow. They dared not go to their beds: they knew not when the enemy might be upon them. They dared not flee: even in their own woods the foe might lurk for them. One man indeed did cry aloud, "Shall we stay here in our houses to be smoked out like bees from their hives? Let us fly!"

But the calm, firm voice of Reine Allix rebuked him: "Let who will, run like a hare from the hounds. For me and mine, we abide by our homestead."

And they were ashamed to be outdone by a woman, and a woman ninety years old, and no man spoke any more of flight. All the night long they watched in the cold and the wind, the children shivering beneath their mothers' skirts, the men sullenly watching the light of the flames in the dark, starless sky. All night long they were left alone, though far off they heard the dropping shots of scattered firing, and in the leafless woods around them the swift flight of woodland beasts startled from their sleep, and the hurrying feet of sheep terrified from their folds in the outlying fields.

The daybreak came, gray, cheerless, very cold. A dense fog, white and raw, hung over the river: in the east, where the sun, they knew, was rising, they could only see the livid light of the still towering flames and pillars of black smoke against the leaden clouds.

"We will let them come and go in peace if

they will," murmured old Mathurin. "What can we do? We have no arms—no powder, hardly—no soldiers—no defence."

Bernadou said nothing, but he straightened his tall limbs, and in his grave, blue eyes a light gleamed.

Reine Allix looked at him as she sat in the doorway of her house. "Thy hands are honest, thy heart pure, thy conscience clear. Be not afraid to die if need there be," she said to him.

He looked down and smiled on her. Margot clung to him in a passion of weeping. He clasped her close and kissed her softly, but the woman who read his heart was the woman who had held him at his birth.

By degrees the women crept timidly back into their houses, hiding their eyes, so that they should not see that horrid light against the sky, whilst the starving children clung to their breasts or to their skirts, wailing aloud in terror. The few men there were left, for the most part of them very old or else mere striplings, gathered together in a hurried council. Old Mathurin the miller and the patriots of the wine-shop were agreed that there could be no resistance, whatever might befall them—that it would be best to hide such weapons as they had and any provisions that still remained to them, and yield up themselves and their homes with humble grace to the dire foe. "If we do otherwise," they said, "the soldiers will surely slay us, and what can a miserable little hamlet like this achieve against cannon and steel and fire?"

Bernadou alone raised his voice in opposition. His eye kindled, his cheek flushed, his words for once sprang from his lips like fire. "What!" he said to them, "shall we yield up our homes and our wives and our infants without a single blow? Shall we be so vile as to truckle to the enemies of France, and show that we can fear them? It were a shame, a foul shame: we were not worthy of the name of men. Let us prove to them that there are people in France who are not afraid to die. Let us hold our own so long as we can. Our muskets are good, our walls strong, our woods in this weather morasses that will suck in and swallow them if only we have tact to drive them there. Let us do what we can. The camp of the francs-tireurs is but three leagues from us. They will be certain to come to our aid. At any rate, let us die bravely. We can do little—that may be. But if every man in France does that little that he can, that little will be great enough to drive the invaders off the soil."

Mathurin and the others screamed at him and hooted. "You are a fool!" they shouted. "You will be the undoing of us all. Do you not know that one shot fired—nay, only one musket found—and the enemy puts a torch to the whole place?"

"I know," said Bernadou, with a dark radiance in his azure eyes. "But then it is a choice between disgrace and the flames: let us only take heed to be clear of the first—the last must rage as God wills."

But they screamed and mouthed and hissed at him: "Oh yes! fine talk, fine talk! See your own roof in flames if you will: you shall not ruin ours. Do what you will with your own neck. Keep it erect or hang by it, as you choose. But you have no right to give your neighbours over to death, whether they will or no."

He strove, he pleaded, he conjured, he struggled with them half the night, with the salt tears running down his cheeks, and all his gentle blood burning with righteous wrath and loathing shame, stirred for the first time in all his life to a rude, simple, passionate eloquence. But they were not persuaded. Their few gold-pieces hidden in the rafters, their few feeble sheep starving in the folds, their own miserable lives, all hungry, woe-begone and spent in daily terrors,—these were still dear to them, and they would not imperil them. They called him a madman; they denounced him as one who would be their murderer; they threw themselves on him and demanded his musket to bury it with the rest under the altar in the old chapel on the hill.

Bernadou's eyes flashed fire; his breast heaved; his nerves quivered; he shook them off and strode a step forward. "As you live," he muttered, "I have a mind to fire on you, rather than let you live to shame yourselves and me!"

Reine Allix, who stood by him silent all the while, laid her hand on his shoulder.

"My boy," she said in his ear, "you are right, and they wrong. Yet let not dissension between brethren open the door, for the enemy to enter thereby into your homes. Do what you will with your own life, Bernadou—it is yours—but leave them to do as they will with theirs. You cannot make sheep into lions, and let not the first blood shed here be a brother's."

Bernadou's head dropped on his breast.

"Do as you will," he muttered to his neighbours. They took his musket from him, and in the darkness of the night stole silently up the wooded chapel-hill and buried it, with all their other arms, under the altar where the white Christ hung.

"We are safe now," said Mathurin the miller to

the patriots of the tavern. "Had that madman had his way, he had destroyed us all."

Reine Allix softly led her grandson across his own threshold, and drew his head down to hers and kissed him between the eyes.

"You did what you could, Bernadou," she said to him, "let the rest come as it will."

Then she turned from him, and flung her cloak over her head and sank down, weeping bitterly, for she had lived through ninety-three years only to see this agony at the last.

Bernadou, now that all means of defence was gone from him, and the only thing left to him to deal with was his own life, had become quiet and silent and passionless, as was his habit. He would have fought like a mastiff for his home, but this they had forbidden him to do, and he was passive and without hope. He shut to his door, and sat down with his hand in that of Reine Allix and his arm around his wife.

"There is nothing to do but to wait," he said sadly.

The day seemed very long in coming.

The firing ceased for a while: then its roll commenced afresh, and grew nearer to the village. Then again all was still.

At noon a shepherd staggered into the place,

pale, bleeding, bruised, covered with mire. The Prussians, he told them, had forced him to be their guide, had knotted him tight to a trooper's saddle, and had dragged him with them until he was half dead with fatigue and pain. At night he had broken from them and had fled: they were close at hand, he said, and had burned the town from end to end because a man had fired at them from a housetop. That was all he knew.

Bernadou, who had gone out to hear his news, returned into the house and sat down and hid his face within his hands.

"If I resist you are all lost," he muttered. "And yet to yield like a cur!"

It was a piteous question, whether to follow the instinct in him and see his birth-place in flames and his family slaughtered for his act, or to crush out the manhood in him and live, loathing himself as a coward for evermore?

Reine Allix looked at him, and laid her hand on his bowed head, and her voice was strong and tender as music:

"Fret not thyself, my beloved. When the moment comes, then do as thine own heart and the whisper of God in it bid thee."

A great sob answered her: it was the first time

since his earliest infancy that she had ever heard from Bernadou.

It grew dark. The autumn day died. The sullen clouds dropped scattered rain. The red leaves were blown in millions by the wind. The little houses on either side the road were dark, for the dwellers in them dared not show any light that might be a star to allure to them the footsteps of their foes. Bernadou sat with his arms on the table, and his head resting on them. Margot nursed her son: Reine Allix prayed.

Suddenly in the street without there was the sound of many feet of horses and of men, the shouting of angry voices, the splashing of quick steps in the watery ways, the screams of women, the flash of steel through the gloom.

Bernadou sprang to his feet, his face pale, his blue eyes dark as night.

"They are come!" he said under his breath. It was not fear that he felt, nor horror: it was rather a passion of love for his birth-place and his nation—a passion of longing to struggle and to die for both. And he had no weapon!

He drew his house door open with a steady hand, and stood on his own threshold and faced these, his enemies. The street was full of them—some mounted, some on foot: crowds of them swarmed in the woods and on the roads. They had settled on the village as vultures on a dead lamb's body.

It was a little, lowly place: it might well have been left in peace.

It had had no more share in the war than a child still unborn, but it came in the victors' way, and their mailed heel crushed it as they passed. They had heard that arms were hidden and francs-tireurs sheltered there, and they had swooped down on it and held it hard and fast. Some were told off to search the chapel; some to ransack the dwellings; some to seize such food and bring such cattle as there might be left; some to seek out the devious paths that crossed and recrossed the fields; and yet there still remained in the little street hundreds of armed men, force enough to awe a citadel or storm a breach.

The people did not attempt to resist.

They stood passive, dry-eyed in misery, looking on whilst the little treasures of their household lives were swept away for ever, and ignorant what fate by fire or iron might be their portion ere the night was done.

They saw the corn that was their winter store to save their offspring from famine poured out like ditch-water. They saw oats and wheat flung down to be trodden into a slough of mud and filth. They saw the walnut presses in their kitchens broken open, and their old heirlooms of silver, centuries old, borne away as booty. They saw the oak cupboards in their wives' bed-chambers ransacked, and the homespun linen and the quaint bits of plate that had formed their nuptial dowers cast aside in derision or trampled into a battered heap. They saw the pet lamb of their infants, the silver ear-rings of their brides, the brave tankards they had drunk their marriage wine in, the tame bird that flew to their whistle, all seized for food or seized for spoil.

They saw all this, and had to stand by with mute tongues and passive hands, lest any glance of wrath or gesture of revenge should bring the leaden bullet in their children's throats or the yellow flame amidst their homesteads. Greater agony the world cannot hold.

Under the porch of the cottage, by the sycamores, one group stood and looked, silent and very still—Bernadou, erect, pale, calm, with a fierce scorn burning in his eyes; Margot, quiet, because he wished her so, holding to her the rosy and golden beauty of her son; Reine Allix, with a patient horror on her face, her figure drawn to its full height, and her hands holding to her breast the crucifix.

They stood thus, waiting they knew not what, only resolute to show no cowardice and meet no shame.

Behind them was the dull, waning glow of the wood-fire on the hearth which had been the centre of all their hopes and joys; before them the dim, dark country, and the woestricken faces of their neighbours, and the moving soldiery with their torches, and the quivering forms of the half-dying horses.

Suddenly a voice arose from the armed mass:

"Bring me the peasant hither."

Bernadou was seized by several hands and forced and dragged from his door out to the place where the leader of the Uhlans sat on a white charger that shook and snorted blood in its exhaustion.

Bernadou cast off the alien grasp that held him, and stood erect before his foes. He was no longer pale, and his eyes were clear and steadfast.

"You look less a fool than the rest," said the Prussian commander. "You know this country well?"

"Well!"

The country in whose fields and woodlands he

had wandered from his infancy, and whose every meadow-path and wayside tree and flower-sown brook he knew by heart as a lover knows the lines of his mistress's face!

"You have arms here?" pursued the German.

"We had."

"What have you done with them?"

"If I had had my way, you would not need ask. You would have felt them."

The Prussian looked at him keenly, doing homage to the boldness of the answer. "Will you confess where they are?"

"No."

"You know the penalty for concealment of arms is death?"

"You have made it so."

"We have, and Prussian will is French law. You are a bold man: you merit death. But still, you know the country well?"

Bernadou smiled, as a mother might smile were any foolish enough to ask her if she remembered the look her dead child's face had worn.

"If you know it well," pursued the Prussian, "I will give you a chance. Lay hold of my stirrup-leather and be lashed to it, and show me straight as the crow flies to where the weapons are hidden. If you do, I will leave you your life. If you do not—"

"If I do not?"

"You will be shot."

Bernadou was silent: his eyes glanced through the mass of soldiers to the little cottage under the trees opposite: the two there were straining to behold him, but the soldiers pushed them back, so that in the flare of the torches they could not see, nor in the tumult hear. He thanked God for it.

"Your choice?" asked the Uhlan, impatiently, after a moment's pause.

Bernadou's lips were white, but they did not tremble as he answered, "I am no traitor." And his eyes as he spoke went softly to the little porch where the light glowed from that hearth beside which he would never again sit with the creatures he loved around him.

The German looked at him: "Is that a boast or a fact?"

"I am no traitor," Bernadou answered simply once more.

The Prussian gave a sign to his troopers. There was the sharp report of a double shot, and Bernadou fell dead. One bullet had pierced his brain, the other was bedded in his lungs. The soldiers kicked aside the warm and quivering body. It was only a peasant killed!

With a shriek that rose above the roar of the wind, and cut like steel to every human heart that beat there, Reine Allix forced her way through the throng, and fell on her knees beside him, and caught him in her arms, and laid his head upon her breast, where he had used to sleep his softest sleep in infancy and childhood.

"It is God's will! it is God's will!" she muttered; and then she laughed—a laugh so terrible that the blood of the boldest there ran cold.

Margot followed her and looked, and stood dry-eyed and silent; then flung herself and the child she carried in her arms beneath the hoof of the white charger.

"End your work!" she shrieked to them. "You have killed him—kill us. Have you not mercy enough for that?"

The horse, terrified and snorting blood, plunged and trampled the ground: his fore foot struck the child's golden head and stamped its face out of all human likeness. Some peasants pulled Margot from the lashing hoofs; she was quite dead, though neither wound nor bruise was on her.

Reine Allix neither looked nor paused. With

all her strength she had begun to drag the body of Bernadou across the threshold of his house.

"He shall lie at home, he shall lie at home," she muttered. She would not believe that already he was dead.

With all the force of her earliest womanhood she lifted him, and half drew half bore him into the home that he had loved, and laid him down upon the hearth, and knelt by him, caressing him as though he were once more a child, and saying softly. "Hush!" for her mind was gone, and she fancied that he only slept.

Without, the tumult of the soldiery increased: they found the arms hidden under the altar on the hill; they seized five peasants to slay them for the dire offence. The men struggled, and would not go as the sheep to the shambles. They were shot down in the street before the eyes of their children. Then the order was given to fire the place in punishment, and leave it to its fate.

The torches were flung with a laugh on the dry thatched roofs—brands snatched from the house-fires on the hearths were tossed amongst the dwelling-houses and the barns. The straw and timber flared alight like tow.

An old man, her nearest neighbour, rushed to the cottage of Reine Allix and seized her by the arm.

"They fire the Berceau," he screamed. "Quick! quick! or you will be burned alive!"

Reine Allix looked up with a smile: "Be quiet! Do you not see? He sleeps."

The old man shook her, implored her, strove to drag her away—in desperation pointed to the roof above, which was already in flames.

Reine Allix looked: at that sight her mind cleared and regained consciousness; she remembered all, she understood all: she knew that he was dead.

"Go in peace and save yourself," she said in the old, sweet, strong tones of an earlier day. "As for me, I am very old. I and my dead will stay together at home."

The man fled, and left her to her choice.

The great curled flames and the livid vapours closed around her: she never moved. The death was fierce but swift, and even in death she and the one whom she had loved and reared were not divided.

The end soon came.

From hill to hill the Berceau de Dieu broke into flames. The village was a lake of fire, into which the statue of the Christ, burning and reeling, fell. Some few peasants, with their wives and children, fled to the woods, and there escaped one torture to perish more slowly of cold and famine. All other things perished. The rapid stream of the flame licked up all there was in its path. The bare trees raised their leafless branches on fire at a thousand points. The stores of corn and fruit were lapped by millions of crimson tongues. The pigeons flew screaming from their roosts and sank into the smoke. The dogs were suffocated on the thresholds they had guarded all their lives. The calf was stifled in the byre. The sheep ran bleating with the wool burning on their living bodies. The little caged birds fluttered helpless, and then dropped, scorched to cinders. The aged and the sick were stifled in their beds. All things perished.

The Berceau de Dieu was as one vast furnace, in which every living creature was caught and consumed and changed to ashes.

The tide of war has rolled on and left it a blackened waste, a smoking ruin, wherein not so much as a mouse may creep or a bird may nestle. It is gone, and its place can know it never more.

Never more.

But who is there to care?

It was but as a leaf which the great storm withered as it passed.

THE END.

PRINTING OFFICE OF THE PUBLISHER.

*Sold by all Booksellers and at all Railway Bookstalls
on the Continent.*

No private orders are executed by the publisher.

TAUCHNITZ EDITION.

October 1, 1910.

(This list appears on the first of each month, and contains all publications up to date.)

Contents:

Collection of British and American Authors. Complete List *Page* 2
Series for the Young . *Page* 29 | Students' Series . . . „ 30. 31
German Authors . . . „ 29. 30 | Manuals & Dictionaries „ 31. 32

Important Notice.

The Tauchnitz Edition in two new and artistic bindings.

The publishers beg to call attention to the fact that from now on copies of the Tauchnitz Edition can also be obtained in two entirely new and original bindings, the one in red cloth (Original-Leinenband), the other in an elegant olive-brown soft material (Original-Geschenkband). The price of each volume is ℳ 1,60 or francs 2,00 sewed, ℳ 2,20 or francs 2,75 in cloth (Original-Leinenband), and ℳ 3,00 or francs 3,75 bound in soft material (Original-Geschenkband).

A larger and more fully detailed Catalogue

of the Tauchnitz publications—containing much important and useful information in regard to authors and their works, and specially arranged for ready reference—is to be had on application of all booksellers gratis.

Particulars of the Latest Tauchnitz Volumes

will be found: firstly, within and outside the *Covers* of each volume in the Collection; secondly, on the *Bookmark* supplied with each work; and thirdly, in a *Monthly Descriptive List* supplied gratis by all booksellers.

Complete List
of the
Collection of British and American Authors.

Published with Continental Copyright by special agreement with the authors. Vide p. 1.

4218 Volumes. 411 British, 60 American Authors.
3821 Volumes by British, 397 Volumes by American Authors.

Price of each Volume M. 1,60 or Fr. 2,00 sewed,
M. 2,20 or Fr. 2,75 cloth (Original-Leinenband),
M. 3,00 or Fr. 3,75 in elegant soft binding (Original-Geschenkband).

Adams, Rev. W., † 1848.
Sacred Allegories 1 v.

Aguilar, Grace, † 1847.
Home Influence 2 v. — The Mother's Recompense 2 v.

Aïdé, [Charles] Hamilton, † 1906.
Rita 1 v. — Carr of Carrlyon 2 v. — The Marstons 2 v. — In that State of Life 1 v. — Morals and Mysteries 1 v. — Penruddocke 2 v. — "A nine Days' Wonder" 1 v. — Poet and Peer 2 v. — Introduced to Society 1 v.

Ainsworth, W. Harrison, † 1882.
Windsor Castle 1 v. — Saint James's 1 v. — Jack Sheppard (with Portrait) 1 v. — The Lancashire Witches 2 v. — The Star-Chamber 2 v. — The Flitch of Bacon 1 v. — The Spendthrift 1 v. — Mervyn Clitheroe 2 v. — Ovingdean Grange 1 v. — The Constable of the Tower 1 v. — The Lord Mayor of London 2 v. — Cardinal Pole 2 v. — John Law 2 v. — The Spanish Match 2 v. — The Constable de Bourbon 2 v. — Old Court 2 v. — Myddleton Pomfret 2 v. — The South-Sea Bubble 2 v. — Hilary St. Ives 2 v. — Talbot Harland 1 v. — Tower Hill 1 v. — Boscobel 2 v. — The Good Old Times 2 v. — Merry England 2 v. — The Goldsmith's Wife 2 v. — Preston Fight 2 v. — Chetwynd Calverley 2 v. — The Leaguer of Lathom 2 v. — The Fall of Somerset 2 v. — Beatrice Tyldesley 2 v. — Beau Nash 2 v. — Stanley Brereton 2 v.

Albanesi, Madame.
Drusilla's Point of View 1 v.

Alcott, Louisa M. (Am.), † 1888.
Little Women 2 v. — Little Men 1 v. — An Old-Fashioned Girl 1 v. — Jo's Boys 1 v.

Aldrich, Thomas Bailey (Am.)
Marjorie Daw and other Tales 1 v. — The Stillwater Tragedy 1 v.

Alexander, Mrs. (Hector), † 1902.
A Second Life 3 v. — By Woman's Wit 1 v. — Mona's Choice 2 v. — A Life Interest 2 v. — A Crooked Path 2 v. — Blind Fate 2 v. — A Woman's Heart 2 v. — For His Sake 2 v. — The Snare of the Fowler 2 v. — Found Wanting 2 v. — A Ward in Chancery 1 v. — A Choice of Evils 2 v. — A Fight with Fate 2 v. — A Winning Hazard 1 v. — A Golden Autumn 1 v. — Mrs. Crichton's Creditor 1 v. — Barbara, Lady's Maid and Peeress 1 v. — The Cost of Her Pride 2 v. — Brown, V.C. 1 v. — Through Fire to Fortune 1 v. — A Missing Hero 1 v. — The Yellow Fiend 1 v. — Stronger than Love 2 v. — Kitty Costello 1 v.

Alice, Grand-Duchess of Hesse, † 1878.
Letters to Her Majesty the Queen (with Portrait). With a Memoir by H. R. H. Princess Christian 2 v.

Alldridge, Lizzie.
By Love and Law 2 v. — The World she awoke in 2 v.

Allen, Grant, † 1899.
The Woman who did 1 v.

"All for Greed," Author of (Baroness de Bury).
All for Greed 1 v. — Love the Avenger 2 v.

Anstey, F. (Guthrie).
The Giant's Robe 2 v. — A Fallen Idol 1 v. — The Pariah 3 v. — The Talking Horse and other Tales 1 v. — Voces Populi (First and Second Series) 1 v. — The Brass Bottle 1 v. — A Bayard from Bengal 1 v. — Salted Almonds 1 v.

Argles, Mrs.: *vide* **Mrs. Hungerford.**

"Aristocrats, the," Author of: *vide* **Gertrude Atherton.**

Arnold, Sir Edwin, † 1904.
The Light of Asia (with Portrait) 1 v.

Arnold, Matthew, † 1888.
Essays in Criticism 2 v. — Essays in Criticism (Second Series) 1 v.

Atherton, Gertrude Franklin (Am.).
American Wives and English Husbands 1 v. — The Californians 1 v. — Patience Sparhawk and her Times 2 v. — Senator North 2 v. — The Doomswoman 1 v. — The Aristocrats 1 v. — The Splendid Idle Forties 1 v. — The Conqueror 2 v. — A Daughter of the Vine 1 v. — His Fortunate Grace, etc. 1 v. — The Valiant Runaways 1 v. — The Bell in the Fog, and Other Stories 1 v. — The Travelling Thirds (in Spain) 1 v. — Rezánov 1 v. — Ancestors 2 v. — The Gorgeous Isle 1 v. — Tower of Ivory 2 v.

Austen, Jane, † 1817.
Sense and Sensibility 1 v. — Mansfield Park 1 v. — Pride and Prejudice 1 v. — Northanger Abbey, and Persuasion 1 v. — Emma 1 v.

"Autobiography of Lutfullah," Author of: *vide* **E. B. Eastwick.**

Avebury, Lord: *vide* **Sir John Lubbock.**

Bagot, Richard.
A Roman Mystery 2 v. — Casting of Nets 2 v. — The Just and the Unjust 2 v. — Donna Diana 2 v. — Love's Proxy 1 v. — The Passport 2 v. — Temptation 2 v. — The Lakes of Northern Italy 1 v. — Anthony Cuthbert 2 v.

Baring-Gould, S.
Jehalah 1 v. — John Herring 2 v. — Court Royal 2 v.

Barker, Lady: *v.* **Lady Broome.**

Barrett, Frank.
The Smuggler's Secret 1 v. — Out of the Jaws of Death 2 v.

Barrie, J. M.
Sentimental Tommy 2 v. — Margaret Ogilvy 1 v. — Tommy and Grizel 2 v. — The Little White Bird 1 v.

"Bayle's Romance, Miss," Author of: *vide* **W. Fraser Rae.**

Baynes, Rev. Robert H.
Lyra Anglicana, Hymns and Sacred Songs 1 v.

Beaconsfield, Lord: *vide* **Disraeli.**

Beaumont, Averil (Mrs. Hunt).
Thornicroft's Model 2 v.

Bell, Currer (Charlotte Brontë— Mrs. Nicholls), † 1855.
Jane Eyre 2 v. — Shirley 2 v. — Villette 2 v. — The Professor 1 v.

Bell, Ellis & Acton (Emily, † 1848, **and Anne,** † 1849, **Brontë).**
Wuthering Heights, and Agnes Grey 2 v.

Bellamy, Edward (Am.), † 1898.
Looking Backward 1 v.

Benedict, Frank Lee (Am.).
St. Simon's Niece 2 v.

Bennett, Arnold.
The Grand Babylon Hotel 1 v. — The Gates of Wrath 1 v. — A Great Man 1 v. — Sacred and Profane Love 1 v. — Whom God hath joined 1 v. — The Ghost 1 v. — The Grim Smile of the Five Towns 1 v. — Buried Alive 1 v. — The Old Wives' Tale 2 v. — The Glimpse 1 v. — Helen with the High Hand 1 v.

Bennett, A. & Phillpotts, Eden: *vide* **Eden Phillpotts.**

Benson, E. F.
Dodo 1 v. — The Rubicon 1 v. — Scarlet and Hyssop 1 v. — The Book of Months 1 v. — The Relentless City 1 v. — Mammon & Co. 2 v. — The Challoners 1 v. — An Act in a Backwater 1 v. — The Image in the Sand 2 v. — The Angel of Pain 2 v. — Paul 2 v. — The House of Defence 2 v. — Sheaves 2 v. — The Climber 2 v. — The Blotting Book 1 v. — A Reaping 1 v. — Daisy's Aunt 1 v.

Benson, Robert Hugh.
The Necromancers 1 v. — A Winnowing 1 v.

Besant, Sir Walter, † 1901.
The Revolt of Man 1 v. — Dorothy Forster 2 v. — Children of Gibeon 2 v. — The World went very well then 2 v. —

Katharine Regina 1 v. — Herr Paulus 2 v. — The Inner House 1 v. — The Bell of St. Paul's 2 v. — For Faith and Freedom 2 v. — Armorel of Lyonesse 2 v. — Verbena Camellia Stephanotis, etc. 1 v. — Beyond the Dreams of Avarice 2 v. — The Master Craftsman 2 v. — A Fountain Sealed 1 v. — The Orange Girl 2 v. — The Fourth Generation 1 v. — The Lady of Lynn 2 v.

Besant, Sir Walter, † 1901, & James Rice, † 1882.

The Golden Butterfly 2 v. — Ready-Money Mortiboy 2 v. — By Celia's Arbour 2 v.

Betham-Edwards, M.

The Sylvestres 1 v. — Felicia 2 v. — Brother Gabriel 2 v. — Forestalled 1 v. — Exchange no Robbery, and other Novelettes 1 v. — Disarmed 1 v. — Doctor Jacob 1 v. — Pearla 1 v. — Next of Kin Wanted 1 v. — The Parting of the Ways 1 v. — For One and the World 1 v. — The Romance of a French Parsonage 1 v. — France of To-day 1 v. — Two Aunts and a Nephew 1 v. — A Dream of Millions 1 v. — The Curb of Honour 1 v. — France of To-day (*Second Series*) 1 v. — A Romance of Dijon 1 v. — The Dream-Charlotte 1 v. — A Storm-Rent Sky 1 v. — Reminiscences 1 v. — The Lord of the Harvest 1 v. — Anglo-French Reminiscences, 1875—1899 1 v. — A Suffolk Courtship 1 v. — Mock Beggars' Hall 1 v. — East of Paris 1 v. — A Humble Lover 1 v. — Barham Brocklebank, M.D. 1 v. — Martha Rose, Teacher 1 v.

Bierce, Ambrose (Am.).

In the Midst of Life 1 v.

Birchenough, Mabel C.

Potsherds 1 v.

Bisland, E.: v. Rhoda Broughton.

Bismarck, Prince: *vide* Butler.

Vide also Wilhelm Görlach (Collection of German Authors, p. 29), and Whitman.

Black, William, † 1898.

A Daughter of Heth 2 v. — In Silk Attire 2 v. — The Strange Adventures of a Phaeton 2 v. — A Princess of Thule 2 v. — Kilmeny 1 v. — The Maid of Killeena, and other Stories 1 v. — Three Feathers 2 v. — Lady Silverdale's Sweetheart, and other Stories 1 v. — Madcap Violet 2 v. — Green Pastures and Piccadilly 2 v. — Macleod of Dare 2 v. — White Wings 2 v. — Sunrise 2 v. — The Beautiful Wretch 1 v. — Mr. Pisistratus Brown, M.P., in the Highlands; The Four Macnicols; The Pupil of Aurelius 1 v. — Shandon Bells (with Portrait) 2 v. — Judith Shakespeare 2 v. — The Wise Women of Inverness, etc. 1 v. — White Heather 2 v. — Sabina Zembra 2 v. — The Strange Adventures of a House-Boat 2 v. — In Far Lochaber 2 v. — The New Prince Fortunatus 2 v. — Stand Fast, Craig-Royston! 2 v. — Donald Ross of Heimra 2 v. — The Magic Ink, and other Tales 1 v. — Wolfenberg 2 v. — The Handsome Humes 2 v. — Highland Cousins 2 v. — Briseis 2 v. — Wild Eelin 1 v.

"Black-Box Murder, the," Author of.

The Black-Box Murder 1 v.

Blackmore, Richard Doddridge, † 1900.

Alice Lorraine 2 v. — Mary Anerley 3 v. — Christowell 2 v. — Tommy Upmore 2 v. — Perlycross 2 v.

"Blackwood."

Tales from "Blackwood" (*First Series*) 1 v. — Tales from "Blackwood" (*Second Series*) 1 v.

Blagden, Isa, † 1873.

The Woman I loved, and the Woman who loved me; A Tuscan Wedding 1 v.

Blessington, Countess of (Marguerite Gardiner), † 1849.

Meredith 1 v. — Strathern 2 v. — Memoirs of a Femme de Chambre 1 v. — Marmaduke Herbert 2 v. — Country Quarters (with Portrait) 2 v.

Bloomfield, Baroness.

Reminiscences of Court and Diplomatic Life (with the Portrait of Her Majesty the Queen) 2 v.

Boldrewood, Rolf.

Robbery under Arms 2 v. — Nevermore 2 v.

Braddon, Miss (Mrs. Maxwell).

Lady Audley's Secret 2 v. — Aurora Floyd 2 v. — Eleanor's Victory 2 v. — John Marchmont's Legacy 2 v. — Henry Dunbar 2 v. — The Doctor's Wife 2 v. — Only a Clod 2 v. — Sir Jasper's Tenant 2 v. — The Lady's Mile 2 v. — Rupert God-

2 v. — Dead-Sea Fruit 2 v. — Run to th 2 v. — Fenton's Quest 2 v. — The els of Arden 2 v. — Strangers and rims 2 v. — Lucius Davoren 3 v. — en at the Flood 3 v. — Lost for Love — A Strange World 2 v. — Hostages Fortune 2 v. — Dead Men's Shoes . — Joshua Haggard's Daughter 2 v. — avers and Weft 1 v. — In Great Waters, other Tales 1 v. — An Open Verdict — Vixen 3 v. — The Cloven Foot 3 v. he Story of Barbara 2 v. — Just as I 2 v. — Asphodel 3 v. — Mount Royal — The Golden Calf 2 v. — Flower and ed 1 v. — Phantom Fortune 3 v. — der the Red Flag 1 v. — Ishmael 3 v. Wyllard's Weird 3 v. — One Thing dful 2 v. — Cut by the County 1 v. — e and Unlike 2 v. — The Fatal Three . — The Day will come 2 v. — One , One Love 2 v. — Gerard 2 v. — Venetians 2 v. — All along the River — Thou art the Man 2 v. — The Christ- Hirelings, etc. 1 v. — Sons of Fire — London Pride 2 v. — Rough Justice — In High Places 2 v. — His Darling 1 v. — The Infidel 2 v. — The Conflict — The Rose of Life 2 v. — Dead Love Chains 1 v. — During Her Majesty's asure 1 v.

Brassey, Lady, † 1887.

Voyage in the "Sunbeam" 2 v. — shine and Storm in the East 2 v. — In Trades, the Tropics and the Roaring ties 2 v.

"Bread-Winners, the," Author of (Am.).

Bread-Winners 1 v.

Bret Harte: *vide* Harte.

Brock, Rev. William, † 1875.

Henry Havelock, K. C. B. 1 v.

Brontë, Charlotte: *vide* Currer Bell.

Brontë, Emily & Anne: *vide* Ellis & Acton Bell.

Brooks, Shirley, † 1874.

Silver Cord 3 v. — Sooner or Later

Broome, Lady (Lady Barker).

ion Life in New Zealand 1 v. — ion Amusements in New Zealand — A Year's Housekeeping in South Africa 1 v. — Letters to Guy, and A Distant Shore—Rodrigues 1 v. — Colonial Memories 1 v.

Broughton, Rhoda.

Cometh up as a Flower 1 v. — Not wisely, but too well 2 v. — Red as a Rose is She 2 v. — Tales for Christmas Eve 1 v. — Nancy 2 v. — Joan 2 v. — Second Thoughts 2 v. — Belinda 2 v. — Doctor Cupid 2 v. — Alas! 2 v. — Mrs. Bligh 1 v. — A Beginner 1 v. — Scylla or Charybdis? 1 v. — Dear Faustina 1 v. — The Game and the Candle 1 v. — Foes in Law 1 v. — Lavinia 1 v. — Mamma 1 v.

Broughton, Rhoda, & Elizabeth Bisland (Am.).

A Widower Indeed 1 v.

Brown, John, † 1882.

Rab and his Friends, and other Papers 1 v.

Browning, Elizabeth Barrett, † 1861.

A Selection from her Poetry (with Portrait) 1 v. — Aurora Leigh 1 v.

Browning, Robert, † 1889.

Poetical Works (with Portrait) 4 v.

Bullen, Frank T.

The Cruise of the "Cachalot" 2 v.

Bulwer, Edward, Lord Lytton, † 1873.

Pelham (with Portrait) 1 v. — Eugene Aram 1 v. — Paul Clifford 1 v. — Zanoni 1 v. — The Last Days of Pompeii 1 v. — The Disowned 1 v. — Ernest Maltravers 1 v. — Alice 1 v. — Eva, and The Pilgrims of the Rhine 1 v. — Devereux 1 v. — Godolphin and Falkland 1 v. — Rienzi 1 v. — Night and Morning 1 v. — The Last of the Barons 2 v. — Athens 2 v. — The Poems and Ballads of Schiller 1 v. — Lucretia 2 v. — Harold 2 v. — King Arthur 2 v. — The New Timon, and St. Stephen's 1 v. — The Caxtons 2 v. — My Novel 4 v. — What will he do with it? 4 v. — Dramatic Works 2 v. — A Strange Story 2 v. — Caxtoniana 2 v. — The Lost Tales of Miletus 1 v. — Miscellaneous Prose Works 4 v. — Odes and Epodes of Horace 2 v. — Kenelm Chillingly 4 v. — The Coming Race 1 v. — The Parisians 4 v. — Pausanias, the Spartan 1 v.

Bulwer, Henry Lytton (Lord Dalling), † 1872.
Historical Characters 2 v. — The Life of Viscount Palmerston 3 v.

Bunyan, John, † 1688.
The Pilgrim's Progress 1 v.

"Buried Alone," Author of (Charles Wood).
Buried Alone 1 v.

Burnett, Mrs. Frances Hodgson (Am.).
Through one Administration 2 v. — Little Lord Fauntleroy 1 v. — Sara Crewe, and Editha's Burglar 1 v. — The Pretty Sister of José 1 v. — A Lady of Quality 2 v. — His Grace of Osmonde 3 v. — The Shuttle 2 v.

Burney, Miss (Madame D'Arblay), † 1840.
Evelina 1 v.

Burns, Robert, † 1796.
Poetical Works (with Portrait) 1 v.

Burton, Richard F., † 1890.
A Pilgrimage to Mecca and Medina 3 v.

Bury, Baroness de: *vide* "All for Greed."

Butler, A. J.
Bismarck. His Reflections and Reminiscences. Translated from the great German edition, under the supervision of A. J. Butler. With two Portraits. 3 v.

Buxton, Mrs. B. H., † 1881.
Jennie of "The Prince's," 2 v. — Won 2 v. — Great Grenfell Gardens 2 v. — Nell—on and off the Stage 2 v. — From the Wings 2 v.

Byron, Lord, † 1824.
Poetical Works (with Portrait) 5 v.

Caffyn, Mrs. Mannington (Iota).
A Yellow Aster 1 v. — Children of Circumstance 2 v. — Anne Mauleverer 2 v.

Caine, Hall.
The Bondman 2 v. — The Manxman 2 v. — The Christian 2 v. — The Eternal City 3 v. — The Prodigal Son 2 v. — The White Prophet 2 v.

Cameron, Verney Lovett.
Across Africa 2 v.

Campbell Praed: *vide* Praed.

Carey, Rosa Nouchette, † 1909.
Not Like other Girls 2 v. — "But Men must Work" 1 v. — Sir Godfrey's Granddaughters 2 v. — The Old, Old Story 2 v. — Herb of Grace 2 v. — The Highway of Fate 2 v. — A Passage Perilous 2 v. — At the Moorings 2 v.

Carlyle, Thomas, † 1881.
The French Revolution 3 v. — Frederick the Great 13 v. — Oliver Cromwell's Letters and Speeches 4 v. — The Life of Schiller 1 v.

Carnegie, Andrew (Am.).
Problems of To-Day 1 v.

Carr, Alaric.
Treherne's Temptation 2 v.

Castle, Agnes & Egerton.
The Star Dreamer 2 v. — Incomparable Bellairs 1 v. — Rose of the World 1 v. — French Nan 1 v. — "If Youth but knew!" 1 v. — My Merry Rockhurst 1 v. — Flower o' the Orange 1 v. — Wroth 2 v.

Castle, Egerton.
Consequences 2 v. — "La Bella," and Others 1 v.

Charles, Mrs. Elizabeth Rundle, † 1896: *vide* Author of "Chronicles of the Schönberg-Cotta Family."

Charlesworth, Maria Louisa, † 1880.
Oliver of the Mill 1 v.

Chesterton, G. K.
The Man who was Thursday 1 v. — What's Wrong with the World 1 v.

Cholmondeley, Mary.
Diana Tempest 2 v. — Red Pottage 2 v. — Moth and Rust 1 v. — Prisoners 2 v. — The Lowest Rung 1 v.

Christian, Princess: *vide* Alice, Grand Duchess of Hesse.

"Chronicles of the Schönberg-Cotta Family," Author of (Mrs. E. Rundle Charles), † 1896.
Chronicles of the Schönberg-Cotta Family 2 v. — The Draytons and the Davenants 2 v. — On Both Sides of the Sea 2 v. — Winifred Bertram 1 v. — Diary of Mrs. Kitty Trevylyan 1 v. —

be Victory of the Vanquished 1 v. — he Cottage by the Cathedral and other 'arables 1 v. — Against the Stream 2 v. — The Bertram Family 2 v. — Conquering and to Conquer 1 v. — Lapsed, but not ost 1 v.

Churchill, Winston (Am.).
lr. Crewe's Career 2 v.

Clark, Alfred.
he Finding of Lot's Wife 1 v.

Clemens, Samuel L.: v. Twain.

Clifford, Mrs. W. K.
ove-Letters of a Worldly Woman 1 v. — Aunt Anne 2 v. — The Last Touches, and her Stories 1 v. — Mrs. Keith's Crime v. — A Wild Proxy 1 v. — A Flash of ummer 1 v. — A Woman Alone 1 v. — oodside Farm 1 v. — The Modern Way v. — The Getting Well of Dorothy 1 v. — Mere Stories 1 v.

Clive, Mrs. Caroline, † 1873:
vide Author of "Paul Ferroll."

Cobbe, Frances Power, † 1904.
e-Echoes 1 v.

Coleridge, C. R.
n English Squire 2 v.

Coleridge, M. E.
he King with two Faces 2 v.

Coleridge, Samuel Taylor, † 1834.
>ems 1 v.

Collins, Charles Allston, † 1873.
Cruise upon Wheels 2 v.

Collins, Mortimer, † 1876.
veet and Twenty 2 v. — A Fight with ortune 2 v.

Collins, Wilkie, † 1889.
ter Dark 1 v. — Hide and Seek 2 v. — Plot in Private Life, etc. 1 v. — The oman in White 2 v. — Basil 1 v. — No me 3 v. — The Dead Secret, and other les 2 v. — Antonina 2 v. — Armadale /. — The Moonstone 2 v. — Man and ife 3 v. — Poor Miss Finch 2 v. — Miss Mrs.? 1 v. — The New Magdalen 2 v. — e Frozen Deep 1 v. — The Law and the dy 2 v. — The Two Destinies 1 v. — My dy's Money, and Percy and the Prophet r. — The Haunted Hotel 1 v. — The llen Leaves 2 v. — Jezebel's Daughter r. — The Black Robe 2 v. — Heart and ience 2 v. — "I say No," 2 v. — The Evil nius 2 v. — The Guilty River, and The

Ghost's Touch 1 v. — The Legacy of Cain 2 v. — Blind Love 2 v.

"Cometh up as a Flower," Author of: vide Rhoda Broughton.

Conrad, Joseph.
An Outcast of the Islands 2 v. — Tales of Unrest 1 v. — The Secret Agent 1 v. — A Set of Six 1 v.

Conway, Hugh (F. J. Fargus), † 1885.
Called Back 1 v. — Bound Together 2 v. — Dark Days 1 v. — A Family Affair 2 v. — Living or Dead 2 v.

Cooper, James Fenimore (Am.), † 1851.
The Spy (with Portrait) 1 v. — The Two Admirals 1 v. — The Jack O'Lantern 1 v.

Cooper, Mrs.: vide Katharine Saunders.

Corelli, Marie.
Vendetta! 2 v. — Thelma 2 v. — A Romance of Two Worlds 2 v. — "Ardath" 3 v. — Wormwood. A Drama of Paris 2 v. — The Hired Baby, with other Stories and Social Sketches 1 v. — Barabbas; A Dream of the World's Tragedy 2 v. — The Sorrows of Satan 2 v. — The Mighty Atom 1 v. — The Murder of Delicia 1 v. — Ziska 1 v. — Boy. A Sketch. 2 v. — The Master-Christian 2 v. — "Temporal Power" 2 v. — God's Good Man 2 v. — Free Opinions 1 v. — Treasure of Heaven (with Portrait) 2 v. — Holy Orders 2 v.

Cotes, Mrs. Everard.
Those Delightful Americans 1 v. — Set in Authority 1 v. — Cousin Cinderella 1 v.

"County, the," Author of.
The County 1 v.

Craik, George Lillie, † 1866.
A Manual of English Literature and of the History of the English Language 2 v.

Craik, Mrs. (Miss Dinah M. Mulock), † 1887.
John Halifax, Gentleman 2 v. — The Head of the Family 2 v. — A Life for a Life 2 v. — A Woman's Thoughts about Women 1 v. — Agatha's Husband 1 v. — Romantic Tales 1 v. — Domestic Stories 1 v. — Mistress and Maid 1 v. — The Ogilvies 1 v. — Lord Erlistoun 1 v. — Christian's Mistake 1 v. — Bread upon the Waters 1 v. — A Noble Life 1 v. — Olive 2 v. — Two Marriages 1 v. — Studies

from Life 1 v. — Poems 1 v. — The Woman's Kingdom 2 v. — The Unkind Word, and other Stories 2 v. — A Brave Lady 2 v. — Hannah 2 v. — Fair France 1 v. — My Mother and I 1 v. — The Little Lame Prince 1 v. — Sermons out of Church 1 v. — The Laurel-Bush; Two little Tinkers 1 v. — A Legacy 2 v. — Young Mrs. Jardine 2 v. — His Little Mother, and other Tales and Sketches 1 v. — Plain Speaking 1 v. — Miss Tommy 1 v. — King Arthur 1 v.

Craik, Georgiana M. (Mrs. May).
Lost and Won 1 v. — Faith Unwin's Ordeal 1 v. — Leslie Tyrrell 1 v. — Winifred's Wooing, etc. 1 v. — Mildred 1 v. — Esther Hill's Secret 2 v. — Hero Trevelyan 1 v. — Without Kith or Kin 2 v. — Only a Butterfly 1 v. — Sylvia's Choice; Theresa 2 v. — Anne Warwick 1 v. — Dorcas 2 v. — Two Women 2 v.

Craik, Georgiana M., & M. C. Stirling.
Two Tales of Married Life (Hard to Bear, by Miss Craik; A True Man, by M. C. Stirling) 2 v.

Craven, Mrs. Augustus: *vide* **Lady Fullerton.**

Crawford, F. Marion (Am.), † 1909.
Mr. Isaacs 1 v. — Doctor Claudius 1 v. — To Leeward 1 v. — A Roman Singer 1 v. — An American Politician 1 v. — Zoroaster 1 v. — A Tale of a Lonely Parish 2 v. — Saracinesca 2 v. — Marzio's Crucifix 1 v. — Paul Patoff 2 v. — With the Immortals 1 v. — Greifenstein 2 v. — Sant' Ilario 2 v. — A Cigarette-Maker's Romance 1 v. — Khaled 1 v. — The Witch of Prague 2 v. — The Three Fates 2 v. — Don Orsino 2 v. — The Children of the King 1 v. — Pietro Ghisleri 2 v. — Marion Darche 1 v. — Katharine Lauderdale 2 v. — The Ralstons 2 v. — Casa Braccio 2 v. — Adam Johnstone's Son 1 v. — Taquisara 2 v. — A Rose of Yesterday 1 v. — Corleone 2 v. — Via Crucis 2 v. — In the Palace of the King 2 v. — Marietta, a Maid of Venice 2 v. — Cecilia 2 v. — The Heart of Rome 2 v. — Whosoever Shall Offend... 2 v. — Soprano 2 v. — A Lady of Rome 2 v. — Arethusa 2 v. — The Primadonna 2 v. — The Diva's Ruby 2 v. — The White Sister 1 v. — Stradella 1 v. — The Undesirable Governess 1 v.

Crockett, S. R.
The Raiders 2 v. — Cleg Kelly 2 v. —
The Grey Man 2 v. — Love Idylls 1 v. — The Dark o' the Moon 2 v.

Croker, B. M.
Peggy of the Bartons 2 v. — The Happy Valley 1 v. — The Old Cantonment, with Other Stories of India and Elsewhere 1 v. — A Nine Days' Wonder 1 v. — The Youngest Miss Mowbray 1 v. — The Company's Servant 2 v. — The Cat's-Paw 1 v. — Katherine the Arrogant 1 v. — Fame 1 v.

Cross, J. W.: *vide* **George Eliot's Life.**

Cudlip, Mrs. Pender: *vide* **A. Thomas.**

Cummins, Miss (Am.), † 1866.
The Lamplighter 1 v. — Mabel Vaughan 1 v. — El Fureidîs 1 v. — Haunted Hearts 1 v.

Cushing, Paul.
The Blacksmith of Voe 2 v.

"Daily News."
War Correspondence, 1877, by Archibald Forbes and others 3 v.

Danby, Frank.
The Heart of a Child 2 v. — An Incompleat Etonian 2 v.

"Dark," Author of.
Dark 1 v.

Davis, Richard Harding (Am.).
Gallegher, etc. 1 v. — Van Bibber and Others 1 v. — Ranson's Folly 1 v.

De Foe, Daniel, † 1731.
Robinson Crusoe 1 v.

Deland, Margaret (Am.).
John Ward, Preacher 1 v.

"Democracy," Author of (Am.).
Democracy 1 v.

"Demos," Author of: *vide* **George Gissing.**

De Quincey, Thomas.
Confessions of an English Opium-Eater 1 v.

"Diary and Notes": *vide* **Author of "Horace Templeton."**

Dickens, Charles, † 1870.
The Pickwick Club (with Portrait) 2 v. — American Notes 1 v. — Oliver Twist 1 v. — Nicholas Nickleby 2 v. — Sketches 1 v. — Martin Chuzzlewit 2 v. — A Christmas Carol; The Chimes; The Cricket on the Hearth 1 v. — Master Humphrey's Clock

(Old Curiosity Shop; Barnaby Rudge, etc.) 3 v. — Pictures from Italy 1 v. — Dombey and Son 3 v. — David Copperfield 3 v. — Bleak House 4 v. — A Child's History of England (2 v. 8º M. 2,70.) — Hard Times 1 v. — Little Dorrit (with Illustrations) 4 v. — The Battle of Life; The Haunted Man 1 v. — A Tale of two Cities 2 v. — Hunted Down; The Uncommercial Traveller 1 v. — Great Expectations 2 v. — Christmas Stories, etc. 1 v. — Our Mutual Friend (with Illustrations) 4 v. — Somebody's Luggage; Mrs. Lirriper's Lodgings; Mrs. Lirriper's Legacy 1 v. — Doctor Marigold's Prescriptions; Mugby Junction 1 v. — The Mystery of Edwin Drood (with Illustrations) 2 v. — The Mudfog Papers, 1 v. — The Letters of Charles Dickens, ed. by his Sister-in-law and his eldest Daughter 4 v. — *Vide* also Household Words, Novels and Tales, and John Forster.

Dickens, Charles, & Wilkie Collins.
No Thoroughfare; The Late Miss Hollingford 1 v.

Disraeli, Benjamin, Lord Beaconsfield, † 1881.
Coningsby 1 v. — Sybil 1 v. — Contarini Fleming (with Portrait) 1 v. — Alroy 1 v. — Tancred 2 v. — Venetia 2 v. — Vivian Grey 2 v. — Henrietta Temple 1 v. — Lothair 2 v. — Endymion 2 v.

Dixon, Ella Hepworth.
The Story of a Modern Woman 1 v. — One Doubtful Hour 1 v.

Dixon, W. Hepworth, † 1879.
Personal History of Lord Bacon 1 v. — The Holy Land 2 v. — New America 2 v. — Spiritual Wives 2 v. — Her Majesty's Tower 4 v. — Free Russia 2 v. — History of two Queens 6 v. — White Conquest 1 v. — Diana, Lady Lyle 2 v.

Dixon, Jr., Thomas, (Am.).
The Leopard's Spots 2 v.

Dougall, L. (Am.).
Beggars All 2 v.

Dowie, Ménie Muriel.
A Girl in the Karpathians 1 v.

Doyle, Sir A. Conan.
The Sign of Four 1 v. — Micah Clarke 1 v. — The Captain of the Pole-Star, and other Tales 1 v. — The White Company 1 v. — A Study in Scarlet 1 v. — The Great Shadow, and Beyond the City 1 v. — The Adventures of Sherlock Holmes 2 v. — The Refugees 2 v. — The Firm of Girdlestone 2 v. — The Memoirs of Sherlock Holmes 2 v. — Round the Red Lamp 1 v. — The Stark Munro Letters 1 v. — The Exploits of Brigadier Gerard 1 v. — Rodney Stone 2 v. — Uncle Bernac 1 v. — The Tragedy of the Korosko 1 v. — A Duet 1 v. — The Green Flag 1 v. — The Great Boer War 2 v. — The War in South Africa 1 v. — The Hound of the Baskervilles 1 v. — Adventures of Gerard 1 v. — The Return of Sherlock Holmes 2 v. — Sir Nigel 2 v. — Through the Magic Door 1 v. — Round the Fire Stories 1 v. — The Mystery of Cloomber 1 v.

Drummond, Professor Henry, † 1897.
The Greatest Thing in the World; Pax Vobiscum; The Changed Life 1 v.

Dufferin, the Earl of.
Letters from High Latitudes 1 v.

Duncan, Sara Jeannette: *vide* Mrs. Cotes.

Dunton: *vide* Th. Watts-Dunton.

Earl, the, and the Doctor.
South Sea Bubbles 1 v.

Eastwick, Edward B., † 1883.
Autobiography of Lutfullah 1 v.

Edgeworth, Maria, *vide* Series for the Young, p. 29.

Edwardes, Mrs. Annie.
Archie Lovell 2 v. — Steven Lawrence, Yeoman 2 v. — Ought we to visit her? 2 v. — A Vagabond Heroine 1 v. — Leah: A Woman of Fashion 2 v. — A Blue-Stocking 1 v. — Jet: Her Face or Her Fortune? 1 v. — Vivian the Beauty 1 v. — A Ballroom Repentance 2 v. — A Girton Girl 2 v. — A Playwright's Daughter, and Bertie Griffiths 1 v. — Pearl-Powder 1 v. The Adventuress 1 v.

Edwards, Amelia B., † 1892.
Barbara's History 2 v. — Miss Carew 2 v. — Hand and Glove 1 v. — Half a Million of Money 2 v. — Debenham's Vow 2 v. — In the Days of my Youth 2 v. — Untrodden Peaks and Unfrequented Valleys 1 v. — Monsieur Maurice 1 v. — A Night on the Borders of the Black Forest 1 v. — A Poetry-Book of Elder Poets

1 v. — A Thousand Miles up the Nile 2 v. — A Poetry-Book of Modern Poets 1 v. — Lord Brackenbury 2 v.

Edwards, M. Betham-: *vide* Betham.

Eggleston, Edward (Am.).
The Faith Doctor 2 v.

Elbon, Barbara (Am.).
Bethesda 2 v.

Eliot, George (Miss Evans — Mrs. Cross), † 1880.
Scenes of Clerical Life 2 v. — Adam Bede 2 v. — The Mill on the Floss 2 v. — Silas Marner 1 v. — Romola 2 v. — Felix Holt 2 v. — Daniel Deronda 4 v. — The Lifted Veil, and Brother Jacob 1 v. — Impressions of Theophrastus Such 1 v. — Essays and Leaves from a Note-Book 1 v. — George Eliot's Life, edited by her Husband, J. W. Cross 4 v.

"Elizabeth and her German Garden," Author of.
Elizabeth and her German Garden 1 v. — The Solitary Summer 1 v. — The Benefactress 2 v. — Princess Priscilla's Fortnight 1 v. — The Adventures of Elizabeth in Rügen 1 v. — Fräulein Schmidt and Mr. Anstruther 1 v.

Elliot, Mrs. Frances, † 1898.
Diary of an Idle Woman in Italy 2 v. — Old Court Life in France 2 v. — The Italians 2 v. — The Diary of an Idle Woman in Sicily 1 v. — Pictures of Old Rome 1 v. — The Diary of an Idle Woman in Spain 2 v. — The Red Cardinal 1 v. — The Story of Sophia 1 v. — Diary of an Idle Woman in Constantinople 1 v. — Old Court Life in Spain 2 v. — Roman Gossip 1 v.

Emerson, Ralph Waldo, † 1882.
Representative Men 1 v.

"Englishwoman's Love-Letters, an," Author of.
An Englishwoman's Love-Letters 1 v.

Erroll, Henry.
An Ugly Duckling 1 v.

Esler, E. Rentoul.
The Way they loved at Grimpat 1 v.

"Essays and Reviews," the Authors of.
Essays and Reviews. By various Authors 2 v.

"Estelle Russell," Author of.
Estelle Russell 2 v.

Esterre - Keeling, Elsa D'.
Three Sisters 1 v. — A Laughing Philosopher 1 v. — The Professor's Wooing 1 v. — In Thoughtland and in Dreamland 1 v. — Orchardscroft 1 v. — Appassionata 1 v. — Old Maids and Young 2 v. — The Queen's Serf 1 v.

"Euthanasia," Author of.
Euthanasia 1 v.

Ewing, Juliana Horatia, † 1885.
Jackanapes; The Story of a Short Life; Daddy Darwin's Dovecot 1 v. — A Flat Iron for a Farthing 1 v. — The Brownies, and other Tales 1 v.

"Expiated," Author of.
Expiated 2 v.

Fargus, F. J.: *vide* Hugh Conway.

Farrar, F. W. (Dean), † 1903.
Darkness and Dawn 3 v.

"Fate of Fenella, the," Authors of.
The Fate of Fenella, by 24 Authors 1 v.

Felkin, Alfred Laurence: *vide* E. T. Fowler.

Felkin, Mrs.: *vide* E. T. Fowler.

Fendall, Percy: *vide* F. C. Philips.

Fenn, George Manville.
The Parson o' Dumford 2 v. — The Clerk of Portwick 2 v.

Fielding, Henry, † 1754.
Tom Jones 2 v.

Findlater, Mary and Jane: *vide* Kate Douglas Wiggin.

Five Centuries
of the English Language and Literature:
John Wycliffe. — Geoffrey Chaucer. — Stephen Hawes. — Sir Thomas More. — Edmund Spenser. — Ben Jonson. — John Locke. — Thomas Gray (vol. 500, published 1860) 1 v.

Fleming, George (Am.).
Kismet 1 v. — Andromeda 2 v.

Forbes, Archibald, † 1900.
My Experiences of the War between France and Germany 2 v. — Soldiering and Scribbling 1 v. — Memories and Studies of War and Peace 2 v. — *Vide* also "Daily News," War Correspondence.

Forrest, R. E.
Eight Days 2 v.

Forrester, Mrs.
Viva 2 v. — Rhona 2 v. — Roy and Viola 2 v. — My Lord and My Lady 2 v. — I have Lived and Loved 2 v. — June 2 v. — Omnia Vanitas 1 v. — Although he was a Lord, and other Tales 1 v. — Corisande, and other Tales 1 v. — Once Again 2 v. — Of the World, Worldly 1 v. — Dearest 2 v. — The Light of other Days 1 v. — Too Late Repented 1 v.

Forster, John, † 1876.
The Life of Charles Dickens (with Illustrations and Portraits) 6 v. — Life and Times of Oliver Goldsmith 2 v.

Fothergill, Jessie.
The First Violin 2 v. — Probation 2 v. — Made or Marred, and "One of Three" 1 v. — Kith and Kin 2 v. — Peril 2 v. — Borderland 2 v.

"Found Dead," Author of: *vide* **James Payn.**

Fowler, Ellen Thorneycroft (Mrs. Alfred Laurence Felkin).
A Double Thread 2 v. — The Farringdons 2 v. — Fuel of Fire 1 v. — Place and Power 2 v. — In Subjection 2 v. — Miss Fallowfield's Fortune 1 v.

Fowler, Ellen Thorneycroft (Mrs. A. L. Felkin) & Alfred Laurence Felkin.
Kate of Kate Hall 2 v.

Fox, Caroline, † 1871.
Memories of Old Friends from her Journals and Letters, edited by Horace N. Pym 2 v.

"Frank Fairlegh," Author of (F. E. Smedley), † 1864.
Frank Fairlegh 2 v.

Francis, M. E.
The Duenna of a Genius 1 v.

Frederic, Harold (Am.), † 1898.
Illumination 2 v. — March Hares 1 v.

Freeman, Edward A., † 1892.
The Growth of the English Constitution 1 v. — Select Historical Essays 1 v. — Sketches from French Travel 1 v.

Froude, James Anthony, † 1894.
Oceana 1 v. — The Spanish Story of the Armada, and other Essays 1 v.

Fullerton, Lady Georgiana, † 1885.
Ellen Middleton 1 v. — Grantley Manor 2 v. — Lady Bird 2 v. — Too Strange not to be True 2 v. — Constance Sherwood 2 v. — A Stormy Life 2 v. — Mrs. Geralds' Niece 2 v. — The Notary's Daughter 1 v. — The Lilies of the Valley, and The House of Penarvan 1 v. — The Countess de Bonneval 1 v. — Rose Leblanc 1 v. — Seven Stories 1 v. — The Life of Luisa de Carvajal 1 v. — A Will and a Way, and The Handkerchief at the Window 2 v. — Eliane 2 v. (by Mrs. Augustus Craven, translated by Lady Fullerton). — Laurentia 1 v.

Galsworthy, John.
The Man of Property 2 v. — The Country House 1 v. — Fraternity 1 v. — Villa Rubein 1 v. — A Man of Devon, etc. 1 v. — A Motley 1 v.

Gardiner, Marguerite: *vide* **Lady Blessington.**

Gaskell, Mrs., † 1865.
Mary Barton 1 v. — Ruth 2 v. — North and South 1 v. — Lizzie Leigh, and other Tales 1 v. — The Life of Charlotte Brontö 2 v. — Lois the Witch, etc. 1 v. — Sylvia's Lovers 2 v. — A Dark Night's Work 1 v. — Wives and Daughters 3 v. — Cranford 1 v. — Cousin Phillis, and other Tales 1 v.

"Geraldine Hawthorne," Author of: *v.* Author of "Miss Molly."

Gerard, Dorothea (Madame Longard de Longgarde).
Lady Baby 2 v. — Recha 1 v. — Orthodox 1 v. — The Wrong Man 1 v. — A Spotless Reputation 1 v. — A Forgotten Sin 1 v. — One Year 1 v. — The Supreme Crime 1 v. — The Blood-Tax 1 v. — Holy Matrimony 1 v. — The Eternal Woman 1 v. — Made of Money 1 v. — The Bridge of Life 1 v. — The Three Essentials 1 v. — The Improbable Idyl 1 v. — The Compromise 2 v. — Itinerant Daughters 1 v. — Restitution 1 v. — Pomp and Circumstance 1 v. — The Grass Widow 1 v.

Gerard, E. (Emily de Laszowska).
A Secret Mission 1 v. — A Foreigner 2 v. — The Extermination of Love 2 v.

Giberne, Agnes.
The Curate's Home 1 v.

Gissing, George, † 1903.
Demos 2 v. — New Grub Street 2 v.

Gladstone, Rt. Hon. W. E., † 1898.
Rome and the Newest Fashions in Religion 1 v. — Bulgarian Horrors, and Russia in Turkistan, with other Tracts 1 v. — The Hellenic Factor in the Eastern Problem, with other Tracts 1 v.

Glyn, Elinor.
The Visits of Elizabeth 1 v. — The Reflections of Ambrosine 1 v. — The Vicissitudes of Evangeline 1 v. — Beyond the Rocks 1 v. — Three Weeks 1 v. — Elizabeth Visits America 1 v.

Godfrey, Hal: *vide* **Charlotte O'Conor Eccles.**

Goldsmith, Oliver, † 1774.
Select Works (with Portrait) 1 v.

Goodman, Edward J.
Too Curious 1 v.

Gordon, Julien (Am.).
A Diplomat's Diary 1 v.

Gordon, Major-Gen. C. G., † 1885.
His Journals at Kartoum (with eighteen Illustrations) 2 v.

Gore, Mrs., † 1861.
Castles in the Air 1 v. — The Dean's Daughter 2 v. — Progress and Prejudice 2 v. — Mammon 2 v. — A Life's Lessons 2 v. — The Two Aristocracies 2 v. — Heckington 2 v.

Grand, Sarah.
Our Manifold Nature 1 v. — Babs the Impossible 2 v. — Emotional Moments 1 v.

Grant, Miss.
Victor Lescar 2 v. — The Sun-Maid 2 v. — My Heart's in the Highlands 2 v. — Artiste 2 v. — Prince Hugo 2 v. — Cara Roma 2 v.

Gray, Maxwell.
The Silence of Dean Maitland 2 v. — The Reproach of Annesley 2 v.

Grenville: Murray, E. C. (Trois-Etoiles), † 1881.
The Member for Paris 2 v. — Young Brown 2 v. — The Boudoir Cabal 3 v. — French Pictures in English Chalk *(First Series)* 2 v. — The Russians of To-day 1 v. — French Pictures in English Chalk *(Second Series)* 2 v. — Strange Tales 1 v. — That Artful Vicar 2 v. — Six Months in the Ranks 1 v. — People I have met 1 v.

Grimwood, Ethel St. Clair.
My Three Years in Manipur (with Portrait) 1 v.

Grohman, W. A. Baillie.
Tyrol and the Tyrolese 1 v.

Gunter, A. C. (Am.), † 1907.
Mr. Barnes of New York 1 v.

Guthrie, F. Anstey: *vide* **Anstey.**

"Guy Livingstone," Author of (George Alfred Laurence), † 1876.
Guy Livingstone 1 v. — Sword and Gown 1 v. — Barren Honour 1 v. — Border and Bastille 1 v. — Maurice Dering 1 v. — Sans Merci 2 v. — Breaking a Butterfly 2 v. — Anteros 2 v. — Hagarene 2 v.

Habberton, John (Am.).
Helen's Babies & Other People's Children 1 v. — The Bowsham Puzzle 1 v. — One Tramp; Mrs. Mayburn's Twins 1 v.

Haggard, H. Rider.
King Solomon's Mines 1 v. — She 2 v. — Jess 2 v. — Allan Quatermain 2 v. — The Witch's Head 2 v. — Maiwa's Revenge 1 v. — Mr. Meeson's Will 1 v. — Colonel Quaritch, V. C. 2 v. — Cleopatra 2 v. — Allan's Wife 1 v. — Beatrice 2 v. — Dawn 2 v. — Montezuma's Daughter 2 v. — The People of the Mist 2 v. — Joan Haste 2 v. — Heart of the World 2 v. — The Wizard 1 v. — Doctor Therne 1 v. — Swallow 2 v. — Black Heart and White Heart, and Elissa 1 v. — Lysbeth 2 v. — A Winter Pilgrimage 2 v. — Pearl-Maiden 2 v. — Stella Fregelius 2 v. — The Brethren 2 v. — Ayesha. The Return of 'She' 2 v. — The Way of the Spirit 2 v. — Benita 1 v. — Fair Margaret 2 v. — The Lady of Blossholme 1 v. — Morning Star 1 v.

Haggard, H. Rider, & Andrew Lang.
The World's Desire 2 v.

Hake, A. E.: *vide* **Gen. Gordon.**

Hall, Mrs. S. C., † 1881.
Can Wrong be Right? 1 v. — Marian 2 v.

Hamerton, Philip Gilbert, † 1894.
Marmorne 1 v. — French and English 2 v.

Hardy, Miss Iza: *vide* Author of "Not Easily Jealous."

Hardy, Thomas.
The Hand of Ethelberta 2 v. — Far from the Madding Crowd 2 v. — The Return of the Native 2 v. — The Trumpet-Major 2 v. — A Laodicean 2 v. — Two on a Tower 2 v. — A Pair of Blue Eyes 2 v. — A Group of Noble Dames 1 v. — Tess of the D'Urbervilles 2 v. — Life's Little Ironies 1 v. — Jude the Obscure 2 v.

Harland, Henry, † 1905.
The Cardinal's Snuff-Box 1 v. — The Lady Paramount 1 v. — My Friend Prospero 1 v. — The Royal End 1 v.

Harraden, Beatrice.
Ships that pass in the Night 1 v. — In Varying Moods 1 v. — Hilda Strafford, and The Remittance Man 1 v. — The Fowler 2 v. — Katharine Frensham 2 v. — The Scholar's Daughter 1 v. — Interplay 2 v.

Harrison, Agnes.
Martin's Vineyard 1 v.

Harrison, Mrs.: *v.* Lucas Malet.

Harte, Bret (Am.), † 1902.
Prose and Poetry (Tales of the Argonauts: — The Luck of Roaring Camp; The Outcasts of Poker Flat, etc. — Spanish and American Legends; Condensed Novels; Civic and Character Sketches; Poems) 2 v. — Idyls of the Foothills 1 v. — Gabriel Conroy 2 v. — Two Men of Sandy Bar 1 v. — Thankful Blossom, and other Tales 1 v. — The Story of a Mine 1 v. — Drift from Two Shores 1 v. — An Heiress of Red Dog, and other Sketches 1 v. — The Twins of Table Mountain, and other Tales 1 v. — Jeff Briggs's Love Story, and other Tales 1 v. — Flip, and other Stories 1 v. — On the Frontier 1 v. — By Shore and Sedge 1 v. — Maruja 1 v. — Snow-bound at Eagle's, and Devil's Ford 1 v. — The Crusade of the "Excelsior" 1 v. — A Millionaire of Rough-and-Ready, and other Tales 1 v. — Captain Jim's Friend, and the Argonauts of North Liberty 1 v. — Cressy 1 v. — The Heritage of Dedlow Marsh, and other Tales 1 v. — A Waif of the Plains 1 v. — A Ward of the Golden Gate 1 v. — A Sappho of Green Springs, and other Tales 1 v. — A First Family of Tasajara 1 v. — Colonel Starbottle's Client, and some other People 1 v. — Susy 1 v. — Sally Dows, etc. 1 v. — A Protégée of Jack Hamlin's, etc. 1 v. — The Bell-Ringer of Angel's, etc. 1 v. — Clarence 1 v. — In a Hollow of the Hills, and The Devotion of Enriquez 1 v. — The Ancestors of Peter Atherly, etc. 1 v. — Three Partners 1 v. — Tales of Trail and Town 1 v. — Stories in Light and Shadow 1 v. — Mr. Jack Hamlin's Mediation, and other Stories 1 v. — From Sand-Hill to Pine 1 v. — Under the Redwoods 1 v. — On the Old Trail 1 v. — Trent's Trust 1 v.

Hawthorne, Nathaniel (Am.), † 1864.
The Scarlet Letter 1 v. — Transformation (The Marble Faun) 2 v. — Passages from his English Note-Books 2 v.

Hearn, Lafcadio, † 1906.
Kokoro 1 v. — Kwaidan 1 v. — Glimpses of Unfamiliar Japan *(First Series)* 1 v. — Glimpses of Unfamiliar Japan *(Second Series)* 1 v. — Gleanings in Buddha-Fields 1 v. — Out of the East 1 v. — The Romance of the Milky Way, and Other Studies and Stories 1 v.

Hector, Mrs.: *vide* Mrs. Alexander.

"Heir of Redclyffe, the," Author of: *vide* Charlotte M. Yonge.

Helps, Sir Arthur, † 1875.
Friends in Council 2 v. — Ivan de Biron 2 v.

Hemans, Mrs. Felicia, † 1835.
Select Poetical Works 1 v.

Hewlett, Maurice.
The Forest Lovers 1 v. — Little Novels of Italy 1 v. — The Life and Death of Richard Yea-and-Nay 2 v. — New Canterbury Tales 1 v. — The Queen's Quair; or, The Six Years' Tragedy 2 v. — Fond Adventures 1 v. — The Fool Errant 2 v. — The Stooping Lady 1 v. — The Spanish Jade 1 v. — Halfway House 2 v.

Hichens, Robert.
Flames 2 v. — The Slave 2 v. — Felix 2 v. — The Woman with the Fan 2 v. — The Garden of Allah 2 v. — The Black Spaniel, and Other Stories 1 v. — The Call of the Blood 2 v. — A Spirit in Prison 2 v. — Barbary Sheep 1 v. — Bella Donna 2 v.

Hobart Pasha, Admiral, † 1886.
Sketches from my Life 1 v.

Hobbes, John Oliver (Mrs. Craigie) (Am.), † 1906.
The Gods, Some Mortals and Lord

Wickenham 1 v. — The Serious Wooing 1 v. — The Dream and the Business 2 v.

Hoey, Mrs. Cashel.
A Golden Sorrow 2 v. — Out of Court 2 v.

Holdsworth, Annie E.
The Years that the Locust hath Eaten 1 v. — The Gods Arrive 1 v. — The Valley of the Great Shadow 1 v. — Great Lowlands 1 v. — A Garden of Spinsters 1 v.

Holme Lee: *vide* **Harriet Parr.**

Holmes, Oliver Wendell (Am.), † 1894.
The Autocrat of the Breakfast-Table 1 v. — The Professor at the Breakfast-Table 1 v. — The Poet at the Breakfast-Table 1 v. — Over the Teacups 1 v.

Hope, Anthony (Hawkins).
Mr. Witt's Widow 1 v. — A Change of Air 1 v. — Half a Hero 1 v. — The Indiscretion of the Duchess 1 v. — The God in the Car 1 v. — The Chronicles of Count Antonio 1 v. — Comedies of Courtship 1 v. — The Heart of Princess Osra 1 v. — Phroso 2 v. — Simon Dale 2 v. — Rupert of Hentzau 1 v. — The King's Mirror 2 v. — Quisanté 1 v. — Tristram of Blent 2 v. — The Intrusions of Peggy 2 v. — Double Harness 2 v. — A Servant of the Public 2 v. — Sophy of Kravonia 2 v. — Tales of Two People 2 v. — The Great Miss Driver 2 v.

Hopkins, Tighe.
An Idler in Old France 1 v. — The Man in the Iron Mask 1 v. — The Dungeons of Old Paris 1 v. — The Silent Gate 1 v. — The Women Napoleon Loved 1 v.

"Horace Templeton," Author of.
Diary and Notes 1 v.

Hornung, Ernest William.
A Bride from the Bush 1 v. — Under Two Skies 1 v. — Tiny Luttrell 1 v. — The Boss of Taroomba 1 v. — My Lord Duke 1 v. — Young Blood 1 v. — Some Persons Unknown 1 v. — The Amateur Cracksman 1 v. — The Rogue's March 1 v. — The Belle of Toorak 1 v. — Peccavi 1 v. — The Black Mask 1 v. — The Shadow of the Rope 1 v. — No Hero 1 v. — Denis Dent 1 v. — Irralie's Bushranger and The Unbidden Guest 1 v. — Stingaree 1 v. — A Thief in the Night 1 v. — Dead Men Tell No Tales 1 v. — Mr. Justice Raffles 1 v.

"Household Words."
Conducted by Charles Dickens. 1851-56. 36 v. — Novels and Tales reprinted from Household Words by Charles Dickens. 1856-59. 11 v.

Houstoun, Mrs.: *vide* **"Recommended to Mercy."**

"How to be Happy though Married," Author of.
How to be Happy though Married 1 v.

Howard, Blanche Willis (Am.), † 1898.
One Summer 1 v. — Aunt Serena 1 v. — Guenn 2 v. — Tony, the Maid, etc. 1 v. — The Open Door 2 v.

Howard, Blanche Willis, † 1898, & William Sharp, † 1905.
A Fellowe and His Wife 1 v.

Howells, William Dean (Am.).
A Foregone Conclusion 1 v. — The Lady of the Aroostook 1 v. — A Modern Instance 2 v. — The Undiscovered Country 1 v. — Venetian Life (with Portrait) 1 v. — Italian Journeys 1 v. — A Chance Acquaintance 1 v. — Their Wedding Journey 1 v. — A Fearful Responsibility, and Tonelli's Marriage 1 v. — A Woman's Reason 2 v. — Dr. Breen's Practice 1 v. — The Rise of Silas Lapham 2 v. — A Pair of Patient Lovers 1 v. — Miss Bellard's Inspiration 1 v.

Hughes, Thomas, † 1898.
Tom Brown's School-Days 1 v.

Hungerford, Mrs. (Mrs. Argles), † 1897.
Molly Bawn 2 v. — Mrs. Geoffrey 2 v. — Faith and Unfaith 2 v. — Portia 2 v. — Loÿs, Lord Berresford, and other Tales 1 v. — Her First Appearance, and other Tales 1 v. — Phyllis 2 v. — Rossmoyne 2 v. — Doris 2 v. — A Maiden all Forlorn, etc. 1 v. — A Passive Crime, and other Stories 1 v. — Green Pleasure and Grey Grief 2 v. — A Mental Struggle 2 v. — Her Week's Amusement, and Ugly Barrington 1 v. — Lady Branksmere 2 v. — Lady Valworth's Diamonds 1 v. — A Modern Circe 2 v. — Marvel 2 v. — The Hon. Mrs. Vereker 1 v. — Under-Currents 2 v. — In Durance Vile, etc. 1 v. — A Troublesome Girl, and other Stories 1 v. — A Life's Remorse 2 v. — A Born Coquette 2 v. — The Duchess 1 v. — Lady Verner's Flight 1 v. — A Conquering Heroine, and "When in Doubt" 1 v. — Nora Creina 2 v. — A Mad Prank, and other Stories 1 v. — The Hoyden 2 v. — The Red House Mystery 1 v. — An Unsatis-

factory Lover 1 v. — Peter's Wife 2 v. — The Three Graces 1 v. — A Tug of War 1 v. — The Professor's Experiment 2 v. — A Point of Conscience 2 v. — A Lonely Girl 1 v. — Lovice 1 v. — The Coming of Chloe 1 v.

Hunt, Mrs.: *vide* **Beaumont.**

Hunt, Violet.
The Human Interest 1 v. — White Rose of Weary Leaf 2 v. — The Wife of Altamont 1 v.

Hutten, Baroness von (Am.).
The Halo 1 v. — Kingsmead 1 v. — The Lordship of Love 2 v.

Ingelow, Jean, † 1897.
Off the Skelligs 3 v. — Poems 2 v. — Fated to be Free 2 v. — Sarah de Berenger 2 v. — Don John 2 v.

Inglis, the Hon. Lady.
The Siege of Lucknow 1 v.

Ingram, John H.: *vide* **Poe.**

Iota: *vide* **Mrs. Caffyn.**

Irving, Washington (Am.), † 1859.
The Sketch Book (with Portrait) 1 v. — The Life of Mahomet 1 v. — Lives of the Successors of Mahomet 1 v. — Oliver Goldsmith 1 v. — Chronicles of Wolfert's Roost 1 v. — Life of George Washington 5 v.

Jackson, Mrs. Helen (H. H.) (Am.), † 1885.
Ramona 2 v.

Jacobs, W. W.
Many Cargoes 1 v. — The Skipper's Wooing, and The Brown Man's Servant 1 v. — Sea Urchins 1 v. — A Master of Craft 1 v. — Light Freights 1 v. — At Sunwich Port 1 v. — The Lady of the Barge 1 v. — Odd Craft 1 v. — Dialstone Lane 1 v. — Captains All 1 v. — Short Cruises 1 v. — Salthaven 1 v. — Sailors' Knots 1 v.

James, Charles T. C.
Holy Wedlock 1 v.

James, G. P. R., † 1860.
Morley Ernstein (with Portrait) 1 v. — Forest Days 1 v. — The False Heir 1 v. — Arabella Stuart 1 v. — Rose d'Albret 1 v. — Arrah Neil 1 v. — Agincourt 1 v. — The Smuggler 1 v. — The Step-Mother 2 v. — Beauchamp 1 v. — Heidelberg 1 v. — The Gipsy 1 v. — The Castle of Ehrenstein 1 v. — Darnley 1 v. — Russell 2 v. — The Convict 2 v. — Sir Theodore Broughton 2 v.

James, Henry (Am.).
The American 2 v. — The Europeans 1 v. — Daisy Miller; An International Episode; Four Meetings 1 v. — Roderick Hudson 2 v. — The Madonna of the Future, etc. 1 v. — Eugene Pickering, etc. 1 v. — Confidence 1 v. — Washington Square, etc. 2 v. — The Portrait of a Lady 3 v. — Foreign Parts 1 v. — French Poets and Novelists 1 v. — The Siege of London; The Point of View; A Passionate Pilgrim 1 v. — Portraits of Places 1 v. — A Little Tour in France 1 v.

James, Winifred.
Bachelor Betty 1 v.

Jeaffreson, J. Cordy.
A Book about Doctors 2 v. — A Woman in spite of Herself 2 v. — The Real Lord Byron 3 v.

Jenkin, Mrs. Charles, † 1885.
"Who Breaks—Pays" 1 v. — Skirmishing 1 v. — Once and Again 2 v. — Two French Marriages 2 v. — Within an Ace 1 v. — Jupiter's Daughters 1 v.

Jenkins, Edward.
Ginx's Baby, his Birth and other Misfortunes; Lord Bantam 2 v.

"Jennie of 'The Prince's,'"
Author of: *vide* **B. H. Buxton.**

Jerome, K. Jerome.
The Idle Thoughts of an Idle Fellow 1 v. — Diary of a Pilgrimage, and Six Essays 1 v. — Novel Notes 1 v. — Sketches in Lavender, Blue and Green 1 v. — The Second Thoughts of an Idle Fellow 1 v. — Three Men on the Bummel 1 v. — Paul Kelver 2 v. — Tea-Table Talk 1 v. — Tommy and Co. 1 v. — Idle Ideas in 1905 1 v. — The Passing of the Third Floor Back 1 v. — The Angel and the Author—and Others 1 v. — They and I, 1 v.

Jerrold, Douglas, † 1857.
History of St. Giles and St. James 2 v. — Men of Character 2 v.

"John Halifax, Gentleman,"
Author of: *vide* **Mrs. Craik.**

Johnny Ludlow: *vide* **Mrs. Henry Wood.**

Johnson, Samuel, † 1784.
Lives of the English Poets 2 v.

Jolly, Emily.
Colonel Dacre 2 v.

"Joshua Davidson," Author of: vide Mrs. E. Lynn Linton.

Kavanagh, Miss Julia, † 1877.
Nathalie 2 v. — Daisy Burns 2 v. — Grace Lee 2 v. — Rachel Gray 1 v. — Adèle 3 v. — A Summer and Winter in the Two Sicilies 2 v. — Seven Years, and other Tales 2 v. — French Women of Letters 1 v. — English Women of Letters 1 v. — Queen Mab 2 v. — Beatrice 2 v. — Sybil's Second Love 2 v. — Dora 2 v. — Silvia 2 v. — Bessie 2 v. — John Dorrien 3 v. — Two Lilies 2 v. — Forget-me-nots 2 v. — *Vide* Series for the Young, p. 29.

Keary, Annie, † 1879.
Oldbury 2 v. — Castle Daly 2 v.

Keeling, D'Esterre-: *vide* Esterre.

Kempis, Thomas a.
The Imitation of Christ. Translated from the Latin by W. Benham, B.D. 1 v.

Kimball, Richard B. (Am.), †
Saint Leger 1 v. — Romance of Student Life Abroad 1 v. — Undercurrents 1 v. — Was he Successful? 1 v. — To-Day in New York 1 v.

Kinglake, A. W., † 1891.
Eothen 1 v. — The Invasion of the Crimea 14 v.

Kingsley, Charles, † 1875.
Yeast 1 v. — Westward ho! 2 v. — Two Years ago 2 v. — Hypatia 2 v. — Alton Locke 2 v. — Hereward the Wake 2 v. — At Last 2 v. — His Letters and Memories of his Life, edited by his Wife 2 v.

Kingsley, Henry, † 1876.
Ravenshoe 2 v. — Austin Elliot 1 v. — Geoffry Hamlyn 2 v. — The Hillyars and the Burtons 2 v. — Leighton Court 1 v. — Valentin 1 v. — Oakshott Castle 1 v. — Reginald Hetherege 2 v. — The Grange Garden 2 v.

Kinross, Albert.
An Opera and Lady Grasmere 1 v.

Kipling, Rudyard.
Plain Tales from the Hills 1 v. — The Second Jungle Book 1 v. — The Seven Seas 1 v. — "Captains Courageous" 1 v. — The Day's Work 1 v. — A Fleet in Being 1 v. — Stalky & Co. 1 v. — From Sea to Sea 2 v. — The City of Dreadful Night 1 v. — Kim 1 v. — Just So Stories 1 v. — The Five Nations 1 v. — Traffics and Discoveries 1 v. — Puck of Pook's Hill 1 v. — Actions and Reactions 1 v. — Rewards and Fairies 1 v.

Laffan, May.
Flitters, Tatters, and the Counsellor 1 v.

Lamb, Charles, † 1834.
The Essays of Elia and Eliana 1 v.

Lang, Andrew: *vide* H. Rider Haggard.

Langdon, Mary (Am.).
Ida May 1 v.

"**Last of the Cavaliers, the,**" Author of (Miss Piddington).
The Last of the Cavaliers 2 v. — The Gain of a Loss 2 v.

Łaszowska, Mme de: *vide* E. Gerard.

Laurence, George Alfred: *vide* "Guy Livingstone."

Lawless, the Hon. Emily.
Hurrish 1 v.

"**Leaves from the Journal of our Life in the Highlands:**" *vide* Victoria R. I.

Lee, Holme, †1900: *vide* Harriet Parr.

Lee, Vernon.
Pope Jacynth, etc. 1 v. — Genius Loci, and The Enchanted Woods 1 v. — Hortus Vitae, and Limbo 1 v. — The Spirit of Rome, and Laurus Nobilis 1 v.

Le Fanu, J. S., † 1873.
Uncle Silas 2 v. — Guy Deverell 2 v.

Lemon, Mark, † 1870.
Wait for the End 2 v. — Loved at Last 2 v. — Falkner Lyle 2 v. — Leyton Hall, and other Tales 2 v. — Golden Fetters 2 v.

"**Letters of Her Mother to Elizabeth, the,**" Author of: *vide* W. R. H. Trowbridge.

Lever, Charles, † 1872.
The O'Donoghue 1 v. — The Knight of Gwynne 3 v. — Arthur O'Leary 2 v. — Harry Lorrequer 2 v. — Charles O'Malley 3 v. — Tom Burke of "Ours" 3 v. — Jack Hinton 2 v. — The Daltons 4 v. — The Dodd Family Abroad 3 v. — The Martins of Cro' Martin 3 v. — The Fortunes of Glencore 2 v. — Roland Cashel

3 v. — Davenport Dunn 3 v. — Confessions of Con Cregan 2 v. — One of Them 2 v. — Maurice Tiernay 2 v. — Sir Jasper Carew 2 v. — Barrington 2 v. — A Day's Ride 2 v. — Luttrell of Arran 2 v. — Tony Butler 2 v. — Sir Brook Fossbrooke 2 v. — The Bramleighs of Bishop's Folly 2 v. — A Rent in a Cloud 1 v. — That Boy of Norcott's 1 v. — St. Patrick's Eve; Paul Gosslett's Confessions 1 v. — Lord Kilgobbin 2 v.

Levett-Yeats, S.
The Honour of Savelli 1 v. — The Chevalier d'Auriac 1 v. — The Traitor's Way 1 v. — The Lord Protector 1 v. — Orrain 1 v.

Lewes, G. H., † 1878.
Ranthorpe 1 v. — The Physiology of Common Life 2 v. — On Actors and the Art of Acting 1 v.

Linton, Mrs. E. Lynn, † 1898.
The true History of Joshua Davidson 1 v. — Patricia Kemball 2 v. — The Atonement of Leam Dundas 2 v. — The World well Lost 2 v. — Under which Lord? 2 v. — With a Silken Thread, and other Stories 1 v. — Todhunters' at Loanin' Head, and other Stories 1 v. — "My Love!" 2 v. — The Girl of the Period, and other Social Essays 1 v. — Ione 2 v.

Lockhart, Laurence W. M., † 1882.
Mine is Thine 2 v.

Loftus, Lord Augustus.
Diplomatic Reminiscences 1837-1862 (with Portrait) 2 v.

Longard, Mme de: *vide* D. Gerard.

Longfellow, Henry Wadsworth (Am.), † 1882.
Poetical Works (with Portrait) 3 v. — The Divine Comedy of Dante Alighieri 3 v. — The New-England Tragedies 1 v. — The Divine Tragedy 1 v. — Flower-de-Luce, and Three Books of Song 1 v. — The Masque of Pandora, and other Poems 1 v.

Lonsdale, Margaret.
Sister Dora (with Portrait) 1 v.

Lorimer, George Horace (Am.).
Letters from a Self-Made Merchant to his Son 1 v. — Old Gorgon Graham 1 v. — Jack Spurlock, Prodigal 1 v.

"Lost Battle, a," Author of.
A Lost Battle 2 v.

Lowndes, Mrs. Belloc.
The Uttermost Farthing 1 v. — Studies in Wives 1 v.

Lubbock, Sir John (Lord Avebury).
The Pleasures of Life 1 v. — The Beauties of Nature (with Illustrations) 1 v. — The Use of Life 1 v. — Scenery of Switzerland (with Illustrations) 2 v. — Essays and Addresses 1900-1903 1 v. — On Peace and Happiness 1 v.

"Lutfullah": *vide* Eastwick.

Lyall, Edna, † 1903.
We Two 2 v. — Donovan 2 v. — In the Golden Days 2 v. — Knight-Errant 2 v. — Won by Waiting 2 v. — Wayfaring Men 2 v. — Hope the Hermit 2 v. — Doreen 2 v. — In Spite of All 2 v. — The Hinderers 1 v.

Lytton, Lord: *vide* E. Bulwer.

Lytton, Robert Lord (Owen Meredith), † 1891.
Poems 2 v. — Fables in Song 2 v.

Maartens, Maarten.
The Sin of Joost Avelingh 1 v. — An Old Maid's Love 2 v. — God's Fool 2 v. — The Greater Glory 2 v. — My Lady Nobody 2 v. — Her Memory 1 v. — Some Women I have known 1 v. — My Poor Relations 2 v. — Dorothea 2 v. — The Healers 2 v. — The Woman's Victory, and Other Stories 2 v. — The New Religion 2 v. — Brothers All 1 v.—The Price of Lis Doris 2 v. — Harmen Pols: Peasant 1 v.

McAulay, Allan: *vide* Kate Douglas Wiggin.

Macaulay, Lord, † 1859.
History of England (with Portrait) 10 v. — Critical and Historical Essays 5 v. — Lays of Ancient Rome 1 v. — Speeches 2 v. — Biographical Essays 1 v. — William Pitt, Atterbury 1 v. — (See also Trevelyan).

McCarthy, Justin.
The Waterdale Neighbours 2 v. — Dear Lady Disdain 2 v. — Miss Misanthrope 2 v. — A History of our Own Times 5 v. — Donna Quixote 2 v. — A Short History of our Own Times 2 v. — A History of the Four Georges. Vols. 1 & 2. — A History of our Own Times. Vols. 6 & 7 (supplemental). — A History of the Four Georges and of William IV. Vols. 3, 4 & 5 (supplemental). — A Short History of our Own Times. Vol. 3 (supplemental).

Mac Donald, George, † 1905.
Alec Forbes of Howglen 2 v. — Annals of a Quiet Neighbourhood 2 v. — David Elginbrod 2 v. — The Vicar's Daughter 2 v. — Malcolm 2 v. — St. George and St. Michael 2 v. — The Marquis of Lossie 2 v. — Sir Gibbie 2 v. — Mary Marston 2 v. — The Gifts of the Child Christ, and other Tales 1 v. — The Princess and Curdie 1 v.

Mackarness, Mrs., † 1881.
Sunbeam Stories 1 v. — A Peerless Wife 2 v. — A Mingled Yarn 2 v.

Mackay, Eric, † 1898.
Love Letters of a Violinist, and other Poems 1 v.

Mc Knight, Charles (Am.).
Old Fort Duquesne 2 v.

Maclaren, Ian, † 1907.
Beside the Bonnie Brier Bush 1 v. — The Days of Auld Langsyne 1 v. — His Majesty Baby 1 v.

Macleod, Fiona, † 1905.
Wind and Wave 1 v. — The Sunset of Old Tales 1 v.

Macleod, Norman, † 1872.
The Old Lieutenant and his Son 1 v.

Macpherson, James, † 1796: *vide* **Ossian.**

Macquoid, Mrs.
Patty 2 v. — Miriam's Marriage 2 v. — Pictures across the Channel 2 v. — Too Soon 1 v. — My Story 2 v. — Diane 2 v. — Beside the River 2 v. — A Faithful Lover 2 v.

"Mademoiselle Mori," Author of (Miss Roberts).
Mademoiselle Mori 2 v. — Denise 1 v. — Madame Fontenoy 1 v. — On the Edge of the Storm 1 v. — The Atelier du Lys 2 v. — In the Olden Time 2 v.

Mahon, Lord: *vide* **Stanhope.**

Maine, E. S.
Scarscliff Rocks 2 v.

Malet, Sir Edward, G.C.B., G.C.M.G.
Shifting Scenes 1 v.

Malet, Lucas (Mrs. Mary St. Leger Harrison).
Colonel Enderby's Wife 2 v. — The History of Sir Richard Calmady 3 v. — The Far Horizon 2 v. — The Score 1 v.

Malmesbury, the Earl of, G.C.B.
Memoirs of an Ex-Minister 3 v.

Mann, Mary E.
A Winter's Tale 1 v. — The Cedar Star 1 v.

Mansfield, Robert Blachford.
The Log of the Water Lily 1 v.

Mark Twain: *vide* **Twain.**

"Marmorne," Author of: *vide* **P. G. Hamerton.**

Marryat, Capt., † 1848.
Jacob Faithful (with Portrait) 1 v. — Percival Keene 1 v. — Peter Simple 1 v. — Japhet in Search of a Father 1 v. — Monsieur Violet 1 v. — The Settlers in Canada 1 v. — The Mission 1 v. — The Privateer's-Man 1 v. — The Children of the New-Forest 1 v. — Valerie 1 v. — Mr. Midshipman Easy 1 v. — The King's Own 1 v.

Marryat, Florence, † 1899.
Love's Conflict 2 v. — For Ever and Ever 2 v. — The Confessions of Gerald Estcourt 2 v. — Nelly Brooke 2 v. — Véronique 2 v. — Petronel 2 v. — Her Lord and Master 2 v. — The Prey of the Gods 1 v. — Life and Letters of Captain Marryat 1 v. — Mad Dumaresq 2 v. — No Intentions 2 v. — Fighting the Air 2 v. — A Star and a Heart; An Utter Impossibility 1 v. — The Poison of Asps, and other Stories 1 v. — A Lucky Disappointment, and other Stories 1 v. — "My own Child" 2 v. — Her Father's Name 2 v. — A Harvest of Wild Oats 2 v. — A Little Stepson 1 v. — Written in Fire 2 v. — Her World against a Lie 2 v. — A Broken Blossom 2 v. — The Root of all Evil 2 v. — The Fair-haired Aida 2 v. — With Cupid's Eyes 2 v. — My Sister the Actress 2 v. — Phyllida 2 v. — How they loved Him 2 v. — Facing the Footlights (with Portrait) 2 v. — A Moment of Madness, and other Stories 1 v. — The Ghost of Charlotte Cray, and other Stories 1 v. — Peeress and Player 2 v. — Under the Lilies and Roses 2 v. — The Heart of Jane Warner 2 v. — The Heir Presumptive 2 v. — The Master Passion 2 v. — Spiders of Society 2 v. — Driven to Bay 2 v. — A Daughter of the Tropics 2 v. — Gentleman and Courtier 2 v. — On Circumstantial Evidence 2 v. — Mount Eden. A Romance 2 v. — Blindfold 2 v. — A Scarlet Sin 1 v. — A Bankrupt Heart 2 v. — The Spirit World 1 v. — The Beautiful Soul 1 v. — At Heart a Rake 2 v. — The Strange Transfiguration of Hannah Stubbs 1 v. — The Dream that Stayed

2 v. — A Passing Madness 1 v. — The Blood of the Vampire 1 v. — A Soul on Fire 1 v. — Iris the Avenger 1 v.

Marsh, Mrs. Anne (Caldwell), † 1874.
Ravenscliffe 2 v. — Emilia Wyndham 2 v. — Castle Avon 2 v. — Aubrey 2 v. — The Heiress of Haughton 2 v. — Evelyn Marston 2 v. — The Rose of Ashurst 2 v.

Marshall, Mrs. Emma, † 1899.
Mrs. Mainwaring's Journal 1 v. — Benvenuta 1 v. — Lady Alice 1 v. — Dayspring 1 v. — Life's Aftermath 1 v. — In the East Country 1 v. — No. XIII; or, The Story of the Lost Vestal 1 v. — In Four Reigns 1 v. — On the Banks of the Ouse 1 v. — In the City of Flowers 1 v. — Alma 1 v. — Under Salisbury Spire 1 v. — The End Crowns All 1 v. —Winchester Meads 1 v. — Eventide Light 1 v. — Winifrede's Journal 1 v. — Bristol Bells 1 v. — In the Service of Rachel Lady Russell 1 v. — A Lily among Thorns 1 v. — Penshurst Castle 1 v. — Kensington Palace 1 v. — The White King's Daughter 1 v. — The Master of the Musicians 1 v. — An Escape from the Tower 1 v. — A Haunt of Ancient Peace 1 v. — Castle Meadow 1 v. — In the Choir of Westminster Abbey 1 v. — The Young Queen of Hearts 1 v. — Under the Dome of St. Paul's 1 v. — The Parson's Daughter 1 v.

Mason, A. E. W.
The Four Feathers 2 v. — Miranda of the Balcony 1 v. — The Courtship of Morrice Buckler 2 v. — The Truants 2 v. — The Watchers 1 v. — Running Water 1 v. — The Broken Road 1 v. — At the Villa Rose 1 v.

Mathers, Helen (Mrs. Henry Reeves).
"Cherry Ripe!" 2 v. — "Land o' the Leal" 1 v. — My Lady Green Sleeves 2 v. — As he comes up the Stair, etc. 1 v. — Sam's Sweetheart 2 v. — Eyre's Acquittal 2 v. — Found Out 1 v. — Murder or Manslaughter? 1 v. — The Fashion of this World (80 Pf.) — Blind Justice, and "Who, being dead, yet Speaketh" 1 v. — What the Glass Told, and A Study of a Woman 1 v. — Bam Wildfire 2 v. — Becky 2 v. — Cinders 1 v. — "Honey" 1 v. — Griff of Griffithscourt 1 v.— The New Lady Teazle, and Other Stories and Essays 1 v. — The Ferryman 1 v. — Tally Ho! 2 v. — Pigskin and Petticoat 2 v. — Gay Lawless 1 v. — Love the Thief 1 v.

Maurice, Colonel.
The Balance of Military Power in Europe 1 v.

Maurier, George du, † 1896.
Trilby 2 v. — The Martian 2 v.

Maxwell, Mrs.: v. **Miss Braddon.**

Maxwell, W. B.
The Ragged Messenger 2 v.—The Guarded Flame 2 v.

"Mehalah": v. **Baring-Gould.**

Melville, George J. Whyte, † 1878.
Kate Coventry 1 v. — Holmby House 2 v. — Digby Grand 1 v. — Good for Nothing 2 v. — The Queen's Maries 2 v. — The Gladiators 2 v. — The Brookes of Bridlemere 2 v. — Cerise 2 v. — The Interpreter 2 v. — The White Rose 2 v. — M. or N. 1 v. — Contraband 1 v. — Sarchedon 2 v. — Uncle John 2 v. — Katerfelto 1 v. — Sister Louise 1 v. — Rosine 1 v. — Roys' Wife 2 v. — Black but Comely 2 v.—Riding Recollections 1 v.

Memorial Volumes: vide Five Centuries (vol. 500); The New Testament (vol. 1000); Henry Morley (vol. 2000).

Meredith, George, † 1909.
The Ordeal of Richard Feverel 2 v. — Beauchamp's Career 2 v. — The Tragic Comedians 1 v. — Lord Ormont and his Aminta 2 v.—The Amazing Marriage 2 v. — The Egoist 2 v.

Meredith, Owen: vide **Robert Lord Lytton.**

Merrick, Leonard.
The Man who was good 1 v. — This Stage of Fools 1 v. — Cynthia 1 v. — One Man's View 1 v. — The Actor-Manager 1 v. — The Worldlings 1 v. — When Love flies out o' the Window 1 v. — Conrad in Quest of His Youth 1 v. — The Quaint Companions 1 v.—Whispers about Women 1 v. — The House of Lynch 1 v. — The Man who Understood Women, and Other Stories 1 v.

Merriman, Henry Seton, † 1903.
Young Mistley 1 v. — Prisoners and Captives 2 v. — From One Generation to Another 1 v. — With Edged Tools 2 v. — The Sowers 2 v. — Flotsam 1 v. — In Kedar's Tents 1 v. — Roden's Corner 1 v. — The Isle of Unrest 1 v. — The Velvet Glove 1 v. — The Vultures 1 v. — Barlasch

of the Guard 1 v. — Tomaso's Fortune, and Other Stories 1 v. — The Last Hope 2 v.

Merriman, H. S., & S. G. Tallentyre.
The Money-Spinner, etc. 1 v.

Milne, James.
The Epistles of Atkins 1 v.

Milton, John, † 1674.
Poetical Works 1 v.

"Miss Molly," Author of.
Geraldine Hawthorne 1 v.

"Molly Bawn," Author of: *vide* **Mrs. Hungerford.**

Montgomery, Florence.
Misunderstood 1 v. — Thrown Together 2 v. — Thwarted 1 v. — Wild Mike 1 v. — Seaforth 2 v. — The Blue Veil 1 v. — Transformed 1 v. — The Fisherman's Daughter, etc. 1 v. — Colonel Norton 2 v. — Prejudged 1 v. — An Unshared Secret, and Other Tales 1 v.

Moore, Frank Frankfort.
"I Forbid the Banns" 2 v. — A Gray Eye or So 2 v. — One Fair Daughter 2 v. — They Call it Love 2 v. — The Jessamy Bride 1 v. — The Millionaires 1 v. — Nell Gwyn—Comedian 1 v.—A Damsel or Two 1 v. — Castle Omeragh 2 v. — Shipmates in Sunshine 2 v. — The Original Woman 1 v. — The White Causeway 1 v.— The Artful Miss Dill 1 v. — The Marriage Lease 1 v. — An Amateur Adventuress 1 v. — Priscilla and Charybdis 1 v. — The Food of Love 1 v. — The Laird of Craig Athol 1 v.

Moore, George.
Celibates 1 v. — Evelyn Innes 2 v. — Sister Teresa 2 v.—The Untilled Field 1 v. — Confessions of a Young Man 1 v. — The Lake 1 v. — Memoirs of my Dead Life 1 v.

Moore, Thomas, † 1852.
Poetical Works (with Portrait) 5 v.

Morgan, Lady, † 1859.
Memoirs 3 v.

Morley, Henry, † 1894.
Of English Literature in the Reign of Victoria. With Facsimiles of the Signatures of Authors in the Tauchnitz Edition (v. 2000, published 1881) 1 v.

Morris, William.
A Selection from his Poems. Edited with a Memoir by F. Hueffer 1 v.

Morrison, Arthur.
Tales of Mean Streets 1 v. — A Child of the Jago 1 v. — To London Town 1 v. — Cunning Murrell 1 v. — The Hole in the Wall 1 v. — The Green Eye of Goona 1 v. — Divers Vanities 1 v. — Green Ginger 1 v.

Muirhead, James Fullarton.
The Land of Contrasts 1 v.

Mulock, Miss: *vide* **Mrs. Craik.**

Murray, David Christie.
Rainbow Gold 2 v.

Murray, Grenville: *v.* **Grenville.**

"My Little Lady," Author of: *vide* **E. Frances Poynter.**

New Testament, the.
The Authorised English Version, with Introduction and Various Readings from the three most celebrated Manuscripts of the Original Text, by Constantine Tischendorf (vol. 1000, published 1869) 1 v.

Newby, Mrs. C. J.
Common Sense 2 v.

Newman, Dr. J. H. (Cardinal Newman), † 1890.
Callista 1 v.

Nicholls, Mrs.: *vide* **Currer Bell.**

"Nina Balatka," Author of: *vide* **Anthony Trollope.**

"No Church," Author of (F. Robinson).
No Church 2 v. — Owen:—a Waif 2 v.

Noel, Lady Augusta.
From Generation to Generation 1 v. - Hithersea Mere 2 v.

Norris, Frank (Am.), † 1902.
The Octopus 2 v. — The Pit 2 v.

Norris, W. E.
My Friend Jim 1 v. — A Bachelor's Blunder 2 v. — Major and Minor 2 v. - The Rogue 2 v. — Miss Shafto 2 v. — Mrs. Fenton 1 v. — Misadventure 2 v. — Saint Ann's 1 v. — A Victim of Good Luck 1 v. — The Dancer in Yellow 1 v. — Clarissa Furiosa 2 v. — Marietta's Marriage 2 v. — The Fight for the Crown 1 v. — The Widower 1 v.—Giles Ingilby 1 v. — The Flower of the Flock 1 v. — His Own Father 1 v. — The Credit of the County 1 v. — Lord Leonard the Luckless 1 v. — Nature's Comedian 1 v. — Nigel's Vocation 1 v. — Barham of Beltana 1 v. — Harry and Ursula 1 v. — The Square Peg 1 v. - Pauline 1 v. — The Perjurer 1 v. — Not Guilty 1 v.

Norton, Hon. Mrs., † 1877.
Stuart of Dunleath 2 v. — Lost and Saved 2 v. — Old Sir Douglas 2 v.

"Not Easily Jealous," Author of (Miss Iza Hardy).
Not Easily Jealous 2 v.
   "Novels and Tales": *vide* "Household Words."

O'Conor Eccles, Charlotte (Hal Godfrey).
The Rejuvenation of Miss Semaphore 1 v. — The Matrimonial Lottery 1 v.

Oldmeadow, Ernest.
Susan 1 v.

Oliphant, Laurence, † 1888.
Altiora Peto 2 v. — Masollam 2 v.

Oliphant, Mrs., † 1897.
The Last of the Mortimers 2 v. — Mrs. Margaret Maitland 1 v. — Agnes 2 v. — Madonna Mary 2 v. — The Minister's Wife 2 v. — The Rector and the Doctor's Family 1 v. — Salem Chapel 2 v. — The Perpetual Curate 2 v. — Miss Marjoribanks 2 v. — Ombra 2 v. — Memoir of Count de Montalembert 2 v. — May 2 v. — Innocent 2 v. — For Love and Life 2 v. — A Rose in June 1 v. — The Story of Valentine and his Brother 2 v. — Whiteladies 2 v. — The Curate in Charge 1 v. — Phœbe, Junior 2 v. — Mrs. Arthur 2 v. — Carità 2 v. — Young Musgrave 2 v. — The Primrose Path 2 v. — Within the Precincts 3 v. — The Greatest Heiress in England 2 v. — He that will not when he may 2 v. — Harry Joscelyn 2 v. — In Trust 2 v. — It was a Lover and his Lass 3 v. — The Ladies Lindores 3 v. — Hester 3 v. — The Wizard's Son 3 v. — A Country Gentleman and his Family 2 v. — Neighbours on the Green 1 v. — The Duke's Daughter 1 v. — The Fugitives 1 v. — Kirsteen 2 v. — Life of Laurence Oliphant and of Alice Oliphant, his Wife 2 v. — The Little Pilgrim in the Unseen 1 v. — The Heir Presumptive and the Heir Apparent 2 v. — The Sorceress 2 v. — Sir Robert's Fortune 2 v. — The Ways of Life 1 v. — Old Mr. Tredgold 2 v.

"One who has kept a Diary": *vide* George W. E. Russell.

Osbourne, Lloyd (Am.).
Baby Bullet 1 v. — Wild Justice 1 v. — The Motormaniacs 1 v. — Harm's Way 1 v.

Ossian.
The Poems of Ossian. Translated by James Macpherson 1 v.

Ouida, † 1908.
Idalia 2 v. — Tricotrin 2 v. — Puck 2 v. — Chandos 2 v. — Strathmore 2 v. — Under two Flags 2 v. — Folle-Farine 2 v. — A Leaf in the Storm; A Dog of Flanders; A Branch of Lilac; A Provence Rose 1 v. — Cecil Castlemaine's Gage, and other Novelettes 1 v. — Madame la Marquise, and other Novelettes 1 v. — Pascarèl 2 v. — Held in Bondage 2 v. — Two little Wooden Shoes 1 v. — Signa (with Portrait) 3 v. — In a Winter City 1 v. — Ariadnê 2 v. — Friendship 2 v. — Moths 3 v. — Pipistrello, and other Stories 1 v. — A Village Commune 2 v. — In Maremma 3 v. — Bimbi 1 v. — Wanda 3 v. — Frescoes and other Stories 1 v. — Princess Napraxine 3 v. — Othmar 3 v. — A Rainy June (60 Pf.). Don Gesualdo (60 Pf.). — A House Party 1 v. — Guilderoy 2 v. — Syrlin 3 v. — Ruffino, and other Stories 1 v. — Santa Barbara, etc. 1 v. — Two Offenders 1 v. — The Silver Christ, etc. 1 v. — Toxin, and other Papers 1 v. — Le Selve, and Tonia 1 v. — The Massarenes 2 v. — An Altruist, and Four Essays 1 v. — La Strega, and other Stories 1 v. — The Waters of Edera 1 v. — Street Dust, and Other Stories 1 v. — Critical Studies 1 v. — Helianthus 2 v.

"Outcasts, the," Author of: *vide* "Roy Tellet."

Pain, Barry.
The Exiles of Faloo 1 v.

Parker, Sir Gilbert.
The Battle of the Strong 2 v. — Donovan Pasha, & Some People of Egypt 1 v. — The Seats of the Mighty 2 v. — The Weavers 2 v.

Parr, Harriet (Holme Lee), † 1900.
Basil Godfrey's Caprice 2 v. — For Richer, for Poorer 2 v. — The Beautiful Miss Barrington 2 v. — Her Title of Honour 1 v. — Echoes of a Famous Year 1 v. — Katherine's Trial 1 v. — The Vicissitudes of Bessie Fairfax 2 v. — Ben Milner's Wooing 1 v. — Straightforward 2 v. — Mrs. Denys of Cote 2 v. — A Poor Squire 1 v.

Parr, Mrs.
Dorothy Fox 1 v. — The Prescotts of Pamphillon 2 v. — The Gosau Smithy, etc. 1 v. — Robin 2 v. — Loyalty George 2 v.

Paston, George.
A Study in Prejudices 1 v. — A Fair Deceiver 1 v.

Pasture, Mrs. Henry de la.
The Lonely Lady of Grosvenor Square 1 v.

— The Grey Knight 1 v. — Catherine's Child 1 v.

Paul, Mrs.: *vide* Author of "Still Waters."

"Paul Ferroll," Author of (Mrs. Caroline Clive), † 1873.
Paul Ferroll 1 v. — Year after Year 1 v. — Why Paul Ferroll killed his Wife 1 v.

Payn, James, † 1898.
Found Dead 1 v. — Gwendoline's Harvest 1 v. — Like Father, like Son 2 v. — Not Wooed, but Won 2 v. — Cecil's Tryst 1 v. — A Woman's Vengeance 2 v. — Murphy's Master 1 v. — In the Heart of a Hill, and other Stories 1 v. — At Her Mercy 2 v. — The Best of Husbands 2 v. — Walter's Word 2 v. — Halves 2 v. — Fallen Fortunes 2 v. — What He cost Her 2 v. — By Proxy 2 v. — Less Black than we're Painted 2 v. — Under one Roof 2 v. — High Spirits 1 v. — High Spirits *(Second Series)* 1 v. — A Confidential Agent 2 v. — From Exile 2 v. — A Grape from a Thorn 2 v. — Some Private Views 1 v. — For Cash Only 2 v. — Kit: A Memory 2 v. — The Canon's Ward (with Portrait) 2 v. — Some Literary Recollections 1 v. — The Talk of the Town 1 v. — The Luck of the Darrells 2 v. — The Heir of the Ages 2 v. — Holiday Tasks 1 v. — Glow-Worm Tales *(First Series)* 1 v. — Glow-Worm Tales *(Second Series)* 1 v. — A Prince of the Blood 2 v. — The Mystery of Mirbridge 2 v. — The Burnt Million 2 v. — The Word and the Will 2 v. — Sunny Stories, and some Shady Ones 1 v. — A Modern Dick Whittington 2 v. — A Stumble on the Threshold 2 v. — A Trying Patient 1 v. — Gleams of Memory, and The Eavesdropper 1 v. — In Market Overt 1 v. — The Disappearance of George Driffell, and other Tales 1 v. — Another's Burden etc. 1 v. — The Backwater of Life, or Essays of a Literary Veteran 1 v.

Peard, Frances Mary.
One Year 2 v. — The Rose-Garden 1 v. — Unawares 1 v. — Thorpe Regis 1 v. — A Winter Story 1 v. — A Madrigal, and other Stories 1 v. — Cartouche 1 v. — Mother Molly 1 v. — Schloss and Town 2 v. — Contradictions 2 v. — Near Neighbours 1 v. — Alicia Tennant 1 v. — Madame's Granddaughter 1 v. — Donna Teresa 1 v. — Number One and Number Two 1 v. — The Ring from Jaipur 1 v. — The Flying Months 1 v.

Pemberton, Max.
The Impregnable City 1 v. — A Woman of Kronstadt 1 v. — The Phantom Army 1 v. — The Garden of Swords 1 v. — The Footsteps of a Throne 1 v. — Pro Patriâ 1 v. — The Giant's Gate 2 v. — I crown thee King 1 v. — The House under the Sea 1 v. — The Gold Wolf 1 v. — Doctor Xavier 1 v. — Red Morn 1 v. — Beatrice of Venice 2 v. — Mid the Thick Arrows 2 v. — My Sword for Lafayette 1 v. — The Lady Evelyn 1 v. — The Diamond Ship 1 v. — The Lodestar 1 v. — Wheels of Anarchy 1 v. — Love the Harvester 1 v. — The Adventures of Captain Jack 1 v. — White Walls 1 v. — The Show Girl 1 v.

Percy, Bishop Thomas, † 1811.
Reliques of Ancient English Poetry 3 v.

Perrin, Alice.
Idolatry 1 v. — The Charm 1 v.

Philips, F. C.
As in a Looking Glass 1 v. — The Dean and his Daughter 1 v. — Lucy Smith 1 v. — A Lucky Young Woman 1 v. — Jack and Three Jills 1 v. — Little Mrs. Murray 1 v. — Young Mr. Ainslie's Courtship 1 v. — Social Vicissitudes 1 v. — Extenuating Circumstances, and A French Marriage 1 v. — More Social Vicissitudes 1 v. — Constance 2 v. — That Wicked Mad'moiselle, etc. 1 v. — A Doctor in Difficulties, etc. 1 v. — Black and White 1 v. — "One Never Knows" 2 v. — Of Course 1 v. — Miss Ormerod's Protégé 1 v. — My little Husband 1 v. — Mrs. Bouverie 1 v. — A Question of Colour, and other Stories 1 v. — A Devil in Nun's Veiling 1 v. — A Full Confession, and other Stories 1 v. — The Luckiest of Three 1 v. — Poor Little Bella 1 v. — Eliza Clarke, Governess, and Other Stories 1 v. — Marriage, etc. 1 v. — Schoolgirls of To-day, etc. 1 v. — If Only, etc. 1 v. — An Unfortunate Blend 1 v. — A Barrister's Courtship 1 v.

Philips, F. C. & Percy Fendall.
A Daughter's Sacrifice 1 v. — Margaret Byng 1 v. — Disciples of Plato 1 v. — A Honeymoon—and After 1 v.

Philips, F. C. & C. J. Wills.
The Fatal Phryne 1 v. — The Scudamores 1 v. — A Maiden Fair to See 1 v. — Sybil Ross's Marriage 1 v.

Phillpotts, Eden.
Lying Prophets 2 v. — The Human Boy 1 v. — Sons of the Morning 2 v. — The Good Red Earth 1 v. — The Striking Hours 1 v. — The Farm of the Dagger 1 v. —

The Golden Fetich 1 v. — The Whirlwind 2 v. — The Human Boy Again 1 v.

Phillpotts, E. & Arnold Bennett.
The Sinews of War 1 v. — The Statue 1 v.

Piddington, Miss: *vide* Author of "The Last of the Cavaliers."

Poe, Edgar Allan (Am.), † 1849.
Poems and Essays, edited with a new Memoir by John H. Ingram 1 v. — Tales, edited by John H. Ingram 1 v.

Pope, Alexander, † 1744.
Select Poetical Works (with Portrait) 1 v.

Poynter, Miss E. Frances.
My Little Lady 2 v. — Ersilia 2 v. — Among the Hills 1 v. — Madame de Presnel 1 v.

Praed, Mrs. Campbell.
Zéro 1 v. — Affinities 1 v. — The Head Station 2 v.

Prentiss, Mrs. E. (Am.), † 1878.
Stepping Heavenward 1 v.

Prince Consort, the, † 1861.
His Principal Speeches and Addresses (with Portrait) 1 v.

Pryce, Richard.
Miss Maxwell's Affections 1 v. — The Quiet Mrs. Fleming 1 v. — Time and the Woman 1 v.

Pym, H. N.: *vide* Caroline Fox.

Quiller-Couch, A. T. ("Q").
Noughts and Crosses 1 v. — I Saw Three Ships 1 v. — Dead Man's Rock 1 v. — Ia and other Tales 1 v. — The Ship of Stars 1 v. — The Adventures of Harry Revel 1 v. — Fort Amity 1 v. — Shakespeare's Christmas, and Other Stories 1 v. — The Mayor of Troy 1 v. — Merry-Garden, and Other Stories 1 v.

Quincey: *vide* De Quincey.

Rae, W. Fraser, † 1905.
Westward by Rail 1 v. — Miss Bayle's Romance 2 v. — The Business of Travel 1 v.

Raimond, C. E. (Miss Robins) (Am.).
The Open Question 2 v. — The Magnetic North 2 v. — A Dark Lantern 2 v. — The Convert 2 v. — The Florentine Frame 1 v.

"Rajah's Heir, the," Author of.
The Rajah's Heir 2 v.

Reade, Charles, † 1884.
"It is never too late to mend" 2 v. — "Love me little, love me long" 1 v. — The Cloister and the Hearth 2 v. — Hard Cash 3 v. — Put Yourself in his Place 2 v. — A Terrible Temptation 2 v. — Peg Woffington 1 v. — Christie Johnstone 1 v. — A Simpleton 2 v. — The Wandering Heir 1 v. — A Woman-Hater 2 v. — Readiana 1 v. — Singleheart and Doubleface 1 v.

"Recommended to Mercy," Author of (Mrs. Houstoun).
"Recommended to Mercy" 2 v. — Zoe's "Brand" 2 v.

Reeves, Mrs.: *v.* Helen Mathers.

Rhys, Grace.
Mary Dominic 1 v. — The Wooing of Sheila 1 v.

Rice, James: *v.* Walter Besant.

Richards, Alfred Bate, † 1876.
So very Human 3 v.

Richardson, S., † 1761.
Clarissa Harlowe 4 v.

Riddell, Mrs. (F. G. Trafford).
George Geith of Fen Court 2 v. — Maxwell Drewitt 2 v. — The Race for Wealth 2 v. — Far above Rubies 2 v. — The Earl's Promise 2 v. — Mortomley's Estate 2 v.

Ridge, W. Pett.
Name of Garland 1 v.

"Rita."
Souls 1 v. — The Jesters 1 v. — The Masqueraders 2 v. — Queer Lady Judas 2 v. — Prince Charming 1 v. — The Pointing Finger 1 v. — A Man of no Importance 1 v. — The Millionaire Girl, and Other Stories 1 v. — The House called Hurrish 1 v. — Calvary 2 v. — That is to say— 1 v.

Ritchie, Mrs. Anne Thackeray: *vide* Miss Thackeray.

Roberts, Miss: *vide* Author of "Mademoiselle Mori."

Robertson, Rev. F. W., † 1853.
Sermons 4 v.

Robins, Miss: *vide* Raimond.

Robinson, F.: *v.* "No Church."

Roosevelt, Theodore (Am.).
Outdoor Pastimes of an American Hunter (with Portrait) 1 v.

Ross, Charles H.
The Pretty Widow 1 v. — A London Romance 2 v.

Ross, Martin: *vide* Somerville.

Rossetti, Dante Gabriel, † 1882.
Poems 1 v. — Ballads and Sonnets 1 v.

"Roy Tellet."
The Outcasts 1 v. — A Draught of Lethe 1 v. — Pastor and Prelate 2 v.

Ruffini, J., † 1881.
Lavinia 2 v. — Doctor Antonio 1 v. — Lorenzo Benoni 1 v. — Vincenzo 2 v. — A Quiet Nook in the Jura 1 v. — The Paragreens on a Visit to Paris 1 v. — Carlino, and other Stories 1 v.

Ruskin, John, * 1819, † 1900.
Sesame and Lilies 1 v. — The Stones of Venice (with Illustrations) 2 v. — Unto this Last and Munera Pulveris 1 v. — The Seven Lamps of Architecture (with 14 Illustrations) 1 v. — Mornings in Florence 1 v. — St. Mark's Rest 1 v.

Russell, W. Clark.
A Sailor's Sweetheart 2 v. — The "Lady Maud" 2 v. — A Sea Queen 2 v.

Russell, George W. E.
Collections and Recollections. By One who has kept a Diary 2 v. — A Londoner's Log-Book 1 v.

Sala, George Augustus, † 1895.
The Seven Sons of Mammon 2 v.

Saunders, John.
Israel Mort, Overman 2 v. — The Shipowner's Daughter 2 v. — A Noble Wife 2 v.

Saunders, Katherine (Mrs. Cooper).
Joan Merryweather, and other Tales 1 v. — Gideon's Rock, and other Tales 1 v. — The High Mills 2 v. — Sebastian 1 v.

Savage, Richard Henry (Am.), † 1903.
My Official Wife 1 v. — The Little Lady of Lagunitas (with Portrait) 2 v. — Prince Schamyl's Wooing 1 v. — The Masked Venus 2 v. — Delilah of Harlem 2 v. — The Anarchist 2 v. — A Daughter of Judas 1 v. — In the Old Chateau 1 v. — Miss Devereux of the Mariquita 2 v. — Checked Through 2 v. — A Modern Corsair 2 v. — In the Swim 2 v. — The White Lady of Khaminavatka 2 v. — In the House of His Friends 2 v. — The Mystery of a Shipyard 2 v. — A Monte Cristo in Khaki 1 v.

Schreiner, Olive.
Trooper Peter Halket of Mashonaland 1 v.

Scott, Sir Walter, † 1832.
Waverley (with Portrait) 1 v. — The Antiquary 1 v. — Ivanhoe 1 v. — Kenilworth 1 v. — Quentin Durward 1 v. — Old Mortality 1 v. — Guy Mannering 1 v. — Rob Roy 1 v. — The Pirate 1 v. — The Fortunes of Nigel 1 v. — The Black Dwarf; A Legend of Montrose 1 v. — The Bride of Lammermoor 1 v. — The Heart of Midlothian 2 v. — The Monastery 1 v. — The Abbot 1 v. — Peveril of the Peak 2 v. — Poetical Works 2 v. — Woodstock 1 v. — The Fair Maid of Perth 1 v. — Anne of Geierstein 1 v.

Seeley, Prof. J. R., † 1895.
Life and Times of Stein (with a Portrait of Stein) 4 v. — The Expansion of England 1 v. — Goethe 1 v.

Sewell, Elizabeth, † 1906.
Amy Herbert 2 v. — Ursula 2 v. — A Glimpse of the World 2 v. — The Journal of a Home Life 2 v. — After Life 2 v. — The Experience of Life 2 v.

Shakespeare, William, † 1616.
Plays and Poems (with Portrait) (Second Edition) 7 v. — Doubtful Plays 1 v.
Shakespeare's Plays may also be had in 37 numbers, at ℳ 0,30. each number.

Sharp, William, † 1905: v. Miss Howard, Fiona Macleod and Swinburne.

Shelley, Percy Bysshe, † 1822.
A Selection from his Poems 1 v.

Sheppard, Nathan (Am.), † 1888.
Shut up in Paris 1 v.

Sheridan, Richard Brinsley, † 1816.
The Dramatic Works 1 v.

Shorthouse, J. Henry.
John Inglesant 2 v. — Blanche, Lady Falaise 1 v.

Slatin Pasha, Rudolf C., C.B.
Fire and Sword in the Sudan (with two Maps in Colours) 3 v.

Smedley, F. E.: vide Author of "Frank Fairlegh."

Smollett, Tobias, † 1771.
Roderick Random 1 v. — Humphry Clinker 1 v. — Peregrine Pickle 2 v.

"Society in London," Author of.
Society in London. By a Foreign Resident 1 v.

Somerville, E. Œ., & Martin Ross.
Naboth's Vineyard 1 v. — All on the Irish Shore 1 v.

"Spanish Brothers, the," Author of.
The Spanish Brothers 2 v.
Stanhope, Earl (Lord Mahon), † 1875.
The History of England 7 v. — Reign of Queen Anne 2 v.
Stanton, Theodore (Am.).
A Manual of American Literature 1 v.
Steel, Flora Annie.
The Hosts of the Lord 2 v. — In the Guardianship of God 1 v.
Steevens, G. W., † 1900.
From Capetown to Ladysmith 1 v.
Sterne, Laurence, † 1768.
Tristram Shandy 1 v. — A Sentimental Journey (with Portrait) 1 v.
Stevenson, Robert Louis, † 1894.
Treasure Island 1 v. — Dr. Jekyll and Mr. Hyde, and An Inland Voyage 1 v. — Kidnapped 1 v. — The Black Arrow 1 v. — The Master of Ballantrae 1 v. — The Merry Men, etc. 1 v. — Across the Plains, etc. 1 v. — Island Nights' Entertainments 1 v. — Catriona 1 v. — Weir of Hermiston 1 v. — St. Ives 2 v. — In the South Seas 2 v. — Tales and Fantasies 1 v.
"Still Waters," Author of (Mrs. Paul).
Still Waters 1 v. — Dorothy 1 v. — De Cressy 1 v. — Uncle Ralph 1 v. — Maiden Sisters 1 v. — Martha Brown 1 v. — Vanessa 1 v.
Stirling, M. C.: vide G. M. Craik.
Stockton, Frank R. (Am.).
The House of Martha 1 v.
"Story of a Penitent Soul, the," Author of.
The Story of a Penitent Soul 1 v.
"Story of Elizabeth, the," Author of: vide Miss Thackeray.
Stowe, Mrs. Harriet Beecher (Am.), † 1896.
Uncle Tom's Cabin (with Portrait) 2 v. — A Key to Uncle Tom's Cabin 2 v. — Dred 2 v. — The Minister's Wooing 1 v. — Oldtown Folks 2 v.
"Sunbeam Stories," Author of: vide Mrs. Mackarness.
Swift, Jonathan (Dean Swift), † 1745.
Gulliver's Travels 1 v.

Swinburne, Algernon Charles, † 1909.
Atalanta in Calydon: and Lyrical Poems (edited, with an Introduction, by William Sharp) 1 v. — Love's Cross-Currents 1 v. — Chastelard and Mary Stuart 1 v.
Symonds, John Addington, † 1893.
Sketches in Italy 1 v. — New Italian Sketches 1 v.
Tallentyre, S. G.: v. H. S. Merriman.
Tasma.
Uncle Piper of Piper's Hill 2 v.
Tautphoeus, Baroness, † 1893.
Cyrilla 2 v. — The Initials 2 v. — Quits 2 v. — At Odds 2 v.
Taylor, Col. Meadows, † 1876.
Tara; a Mahratta Tale 3 v.
Templeton: vide Author of "Horace Templeton."
Tennyson, Alfred (Lord), † 1892.
Poetical Works 8 v. — Queen Mary 1 v. — Harold 1 v. — Becket; The Cup; The Falcon 1 v. — Locksley Hall, sixty Years after; The Promise of May; Tiresias and other Poems 1 v. — A Memoir. By His Son (with Portrait) 4 v.
Testament, the New: vide New.
Thackeray, William Makepeace, † 1863.
Vanity Fair 3 v. — Pendennis 3 v. — Miscellanies 8 v. — Henry Esmond 2 v. — The English Humourists of the Eighteenth Century 1 v. — The Newcomes 4 v. — The Virginians 4 v. — The Four Georges; Lovel the Widower 1 v. — The Adventures of Philip 2 v. — Denis Duval 1 v. — Roundabout Papers 2 v. — Catherine 1 v. — The Irish Sketch Book 2 v. — The Paris Sketch Book (with Portrait) 2 v.
Thackeray, Miss (Lady Ritchie).
The Story of Elizabeth 1 v. — The Village on the Cliff 1 v. — Old Kensington 2 v. — Bluebeard's Keys, and other Stories 1 v. — Five Old Friends 1 v. — Miss Angel 1 v. — Out of the World, and other Tales 1 v. — Fulham Lawn, and other Tales 1 v. — From an Island. A Story and some Essays 1 v. — Da Capo, and other Tales 1 v. — Madame de Sévigné; From a Stage Box; Miss Williamson's Divagations 1 v. — A Book of Sibyls 1 v. — Mrs. Dymond 2 v. — Chapters from some Memoirs 1 v.

Thomas a Kempis: *v*. Kempis.

Thomas, A. (Mrs. Pender Cudlip).
Denis Donne 2 v. — On Guard 2 v. — Walter Goring 2 v. — Played Out 2 v. — Called to Account 2 v. — Only Herself 2 v. — A Narrow Escape 2 v.

Thomson, James, † 1748.
Poetical Works (with Portrait) 1 v.

"Thoth," Author of.
Thoth 1 v.

Thurston, E. Temple.
The Greatest Wish in the World 1 v. — Mirage 1 v.

"Tim," Author of.
Tim 1 v.

Trafford, F. G.: *v*. Mrs. Riddell.

Trevelyan, George Otto.
The Life and Letters of Lord Macaulay (with Portrait) 4 v. — Selections from the Writings of Lord Macaulay 2 v. — The American Revolution (with a Map) 2 v.

Trois-Etoiles: *vide* Grenville.

Trollope, Anthony, † 1882.
Doctor Thorne 2 v. — The Bertrams 2 v. — The Warden 1 v. — Barchester Towers 2 v. — Castle Richmond 2 v. — The West Indies 1 v. — Framley Parsonage 2 v. — North America 3 v. — Orley Farm 3 v. — Rachel Ray 2 v. — The Small House at Allington 3 v. — Can you forgive her? 3 v. — The Belton Estate 1 v. — Nina Balatka 1 v. — The Last Chronicle of Barset 3 v. — The Claverings 2 v. — Phineas Finn 3 v. — He knew he was right 3 v. — The Vicar of Bullhampton 2 v. — Sir Harry Hotspur of Humblethwaite 1 v. — Ralph the Heir 2 v. — The Golden Lion of Granpere 1 v. — Australia and New Zealand 3 v. — Lady Anna 2 v. — Harry Heathcote of Gangoil 1 v. — The Way we live now 4 v. — The Prime Minister 4 v. — The American Senator 3 v. — South Africa 2 v. — Is He Popenjoy? 3 v. — An Eye for an Eye 1 v. — John Caldigate 3 v. — Cousin Henry 1 v. — The Duke's Children 3 v. — Dr. Wortle's School 1 v. — Ayala's Angel 3 v. — The Fixed Period 1 v. — Marion Fay 2 v. — Kept in the Dark 1 v. — Frau Frohmann, and other Stories 1 v. — Alice Dugdale, and other Stories 1 v. — La Mère Bauche, and other Stories 1 v. — The Mistletoe Bough, and other Stories 1 v. — An Autobiography 1 v. — An Old Man's Love 1 v.

Trollope, T. Adolphus, † 1892.
The Garstangs of Garstang Grange 2 v. — A Siren 2 v.

Trowbridge, W. R. H.
The Letters of Her Mother to Elizabeth 1 v. — A Girl of the Multitude 1 v. — That Little Marquis of Brandenburg 1 v. — A Dazzling Reprobate 1 v.

Twain, Mark (Samuel L. Clemens) (Am.), † 1910.
The Adventures of Tom Sawyer 1 v. — The Innocents Abroad; or, The New Pilgrims' Progress 2 v. — A Tramp Abroad 2 v. — "Roughing it" 1 v. — The Innocents at Home 1 v. — The Prince and the Pauper 2 v. — The Stolen White Elephant, etc. 1 v. — Life on the Mississippi 2 v. — Sketches (with Portrait) 1 v. — Huckleberry Finn 2 v. — Selections from American Humour 1 v. — A Yankee at the Court of King Arthur 2 v. — The American Claimant 1 v. — The £ 1 000 000 Bank-Note and other new Stories 1 v. — Tom Sawyer Abroad 1 v. — Pudd'nhead Wilson 1 v. — Personal Recollections of Joan of Arc 2 v. — Tom Sawyer, Detective, and other Tales 1 v. — More Tramps Abroad 2 v. — The Man that corrupted Hadleyburg, etc. 2 v. — A Double-Barrelled Detective Story, etc. 1 v. — The $30,000 Bequest, and Other Stories 1 v. — Christian Science 1 v. — Captain Stormfield's Visit to Heaven & Is Shakespeare Dead? 1 v.

"Two Cosmos, the," Author of.
The Two Cosmos 1 v.

Vachell, Horace Annesley.
Brothers 2 v. — The Face of Clay 1 v. — Her Son 1 v. — The Hill 1 v. — The Waters of Jordan 1 v. — An Impending Sword 1 v. — The Paladin 1 v.

"Venus and Cupid," Author of.
Venus and Cupid 1 v.

"Vera," Author of.
Vera 1 v. — The Hôtel du Petit St. Jean 1 v. — Blue Roses 2 v. — Within Sound of the Sea 2 v. — The Maritime Alps and their Seaboard 2 v. — Ninette 1 v.

Victoria R. I.
Leaves from the Journal of our Life in the Highlands from 1848 to 1861 1 v. — More Leaves, etc. from 1862 to 1882 1 v.

"Virginia," Author of.
Virginia 1 v.

Vizetelly, Ernest Alfred.
With Zola in England 1 v.

Walford, L. B.
Mr. Smith 2 v. — Pauline 2 v. — Cousins 2 v. — Troublesome Daughters 2 v. — Leddy Marget 1 v.

Wallace, D. Mackenzie.
Russia 3 v.

Wallace, Lew. (Am.), † 1905.
Ben-Hur 2 v.

Warburton, Eliot, † 1852.
The Crescent and the Cross 2 v. — Darien 2 v.

Ward, Mrs. Humphry.
Robert Elsmere 3 v. — David Grieve 3 v. — Miss Bretherton 1 v. — Marcella 3 v. — Bessie Costrell 1 v. — Sir George Tressady 2 v. — Helbeck of Bannisdale 2 v. — Eleanor 2 v. — Lady Rose's Daughter 2 v. — The Marriage of William Ashe 2 v. — Fenwick's Career 2 v. — Diana Mallory 2 v. — Daphne; or, "Marriage à la Mode" 1 v. — Canadian Born 1 v.

Warner, Susan *vide*: **Wetherell.**

Warren, Samuel, † 1877.
Diary of a late Physician 2 v. — Ten Thousand a-Year 3 v. — Now and Then 1 v. — The Lily and the Bee 1 v.

"Waterdale Neighbours, the,"
Author of: *v.* Justin McCarthy.

Watts-Dunton, Theodore.
Aylwin 2 v.

Wells, H. G.
The Stolen Bacillus, etc. 1 v. — The War of the Worlds 1 v. — The Invisible Man 1 v. — The Time Machine, and The Island of Doctor Moreau 1 v. — When the Sleeper wakes 1 v. — Tales of Space and Time 1 v. — The Plattner Story, and Others 1 v. — Love and Mr. Lewisham 1 v. — The Wheels of Chance 1 v. — Anticipations 1 v. — The First Men in the Moon 1 v. — The Sea Lady 1. — Mankind in the Making 2 v. — Twelve Stories and a Dream 1 v. — The Food of the Gods 1 v. — A Modern Utopia 1 v. — Kipps 2 v. — In the Days of the Comet 1 v. — The Future in America 1 v. — New Worlds for Old 1 v. — The War in the Air 1 v. — Tono-Bungay 2 v. — First and Last Things 1.

Westbury, Hugh.
Acte 2 v.

Wetherell, Elizabeth (Susan Warner) (Am.), † 1885.
The wide, wide World 2 v. — Queechy 2 v. — The Hills of the Shatemuc 2 v. — Say and Seal 2 v. — The Old Helmet 2 v.

Weyman, Stanley J.
The House of the Wolf 1 v. — The Story of Francis Cludde 2 v. — A Gentleman of France 2 v. — The Man in Black 1 v. — Under the Red Robe 1 v. — My Lady Rotha 2 v. — From the Memoirs of a Minister of France 1 v. — The Red Cockade 2 v. — Shrewsbury 2 v. — The Castle Inn 2 v. — Sophia 2 v. — Count Hannibal 2 v. — In Kings' Byways 1 v. — The Long Night 2 v. — The Abbess of Vlaye 2 v. — Starvecrow Farm 2 v. — Chippinge 2 v. — Laid up in Lavender 1 v.

Wharton, Edith (Am.).
The House of Mirth 2 v. — The Fruit of the Tree 2 v.

"Whim, a," Author of.
A Whim, and its Consequences 1 v.

Whitby, Beatrice.
The Awakening of Mary Fenwick 2 v. — In the Suntime of her Youth 2 v.

White, Percy.
Mr. Bailey-Martin 1 v. — The West End 2 v. — The New Christians 1 v. — Park Lane 2 v. — The Countess and The King's Diary 1 v. — The Triumph of Mrs. St. George 2 v. — A Millionaire's Daughter 1 v. — A Passionate Pilgrim 1 v. — The System 2 v. — The Patient Man 1 v. — Mr. John Strood 1 v. — The Eight Guests 2 v. — Mr. Strudge 1 v. — Love and the Poor Suitor 1 v. — The House of Intrigue 1 v. — Love and the Wise Men 1 v. — An Averted Marriage 1 v. — The Lost Halo 1 v.

White, Walter.
Holidays in Tyrol 1 v.

Whiteing, Richard.
The Island; or, An Adventure of a Person of Quality 1 v. — No. 5 John Street 1 v. — The Life of Paris 1 v. — The Yellow Van 1 v. — Ring in the New 1 v. — All Moonshine 1 v. — Little People 1 v.

Whitman, Sidney.
Imperial Germany 1 v. — The Realm of the Habsburgs 1 v. — Teuton Studies 1 v. — Reminiscences of the King of Roumania 1 v. — Conversations with Prince Bismarck 1 v. — Life of the Emperor Frederick 2 v.

"Who Breaks—Pays," Author of: *vide* **Mrs. Jenkin.**

Whyte Melville, George J.: *vide* **Melville.**

Wiggin, Kate Douglas (Am.).
Timothy's Quest 1 v. — A Cathedral

Courtship, and Penelope's English Experiences 1 v. — Penelope's Irish Experiences 1 v. — Rebecca of Sunnybrook Farm 1 v. — The Affair at the Inn 1 v. (By K. D. Wiggin, M. & J. Findlater, and Allan McAulay.) — Rose o' the River 1 v. — New Chronicles of Rebecca 1 v. — The Old Peabody Pew, and Susanna and Sue 1 v.

Wilde, Oscar, † 1900.
The Picture of Dorian Gray 1 v. — De Profundis and The Ballad of Reading Gaol 1 v. — A House of Pomegranates 1 v. — Lord Arthur Savile's Crime, and Other Prose Pieces 1 v.—Lady Windermere's Fan 1 v.—An Ideal Husband 1 v.—Salome 1 v. — The Happy Prince, and Other Tales 1 v. — A Woman of No Importance 1 v. — The Importance of Being Earnest 1 v.

Wilkins, Mary E. (Am.).
Pembroke 1 v. — Madelon 1 v. — Jerome 2 v. — Silence, and other Stories 1 v. — The Love of Parson Lord, etc. 1 v.

Williamson, C. N. & A. M. (Am.).
The Lightning Conductor 1 v.—Lady Betty across the Water 1 v.—The Motor Maid 1 v.

Wills, C. J., *vide* F. C. Philips.

Winter, Mrs. J. S.
Regimental Legends 1 v.

Wood, Charles: *vide* Author of "Buried Alone."

Wood, H. F.
The Passenger from Scotland Yard 1 v.

Wood, Mrs. Henry (Johnny Ludlow), † 1887.
East Lynne 3 v. — The Channings 2 v. — Mrs. Halliburton's Troubles 2 v. — Verner's Pride 3 v. — The Shadow of Ashlydyat 3 v. — Trevlyn Hold 2 v. — Lord Oakburn's Daughters 2 v. — Oswald Cray 2 v. — Mildred Arkell 2 v. — St. Martin's Eve 2 v. — Elster's Folly 2 v. — Lady Adelaide's Oath 2 v. — Orville College 1 v. — A Life's Secret 1 v. — The Red Court Farm 2 v. — Anne Hereford 1 v. — Roland Yorke 2 v. — George Canterbury's Will 2 v. — Bessy Rane 2 v. — Dene Hollow 2 v. — The Foggy Night at Offord; Martyn Ware's Temptation; The Night-Walk over the Mill Stream 1 v. — Within the Maze 2 v. — The Master of Greylands 2 v. — Johnny Ludlow 2 v. — Told in the Twilight 2 v. — Adam Grainger 1 v. — Edina 2 v. — Pomeroy Abbey 2 v. — Court Netherleigh 2 v. — (The following by Johnny Ludlow): Lost in the Post, and Other Tales 1 v.—A Tale of Sin, and Other Tales 1 v. — Anne, and Other Tales 1 v. — The Mystery of Jessy Page, and Other Tales 1 v. — Helen Whitney's Wedding, and Other Tales 1 v. — The Story of Dorothy Grape, and Other Tales 1 v.

Woodroffe, Daniel.
Tangled Trinities 1 v.—The Beauty-Shop 1 v.

Woods, Margaret L.
A Village Tragedy 1 v. — The Vagabonds 1 v. — Sons of the Sword 2 v. — The Invader 1 v.

Wordsworth, William, † 1850.
Select Poetical Works 2 v.

Wraxall, Lascelles, † 1865.
Wild Oats 1 v.

Yates, Edmund, † 1894.
Land at Last 2 v. — Broken to Harness 2 v. — The Forlorn Hope 2 v. — Black Sheep 2 v. — The Rock Ahead 2 v. — Wrecked in Port 2 v. — Dr. Wainwright's Patient 2 v. — Nobody's Fortune 2 v. — Castaway 2 v. — A Waiting Race 2 v. — The yellow Flag 2 v. — The Impending Sword 2 v. — Two, by Tricks 1 v. — A Silent Witness 2 v. — Recollections and Experiences 2 v.

Yeats: *vide* Levett-Yeats.

Yonge, Charlotte M., † 1901.
The Heir of Redclyffe 2 v. — Heartsease 2 v. — The Daisy Chain 2 v. — Dynevor Terrace 2 v. — Hopes and Fears 2 v. — The Young Step-Mother 2 v. — The Trial 2 v. — The Clever Woman of the Family 2 v. — The Dove in the Eagle's Nest 2 v. — The Danvers Papers; The Prince and the Page 1 v. — The Chaplet of Pearls 2 v. — The two Guardians 1 v. — The Caged Lion 2 v. — The Pillars of the House 5 v. — Lady Hester 1 v. — My Young Alcides 2 v. — The Three Brides 2 v. — Womankind 2 v. — Magnum Bonum 2 v. — Love and Life 2 v. — Unknown to History 2 v. — Stray Pearls (with Portrait) 2 v. — The Armourer's Prentices 2 v. — The Two Sides of the Shield 2 v. — Nuttie's Father 2 v. — Beechcroft at Rockstone 2 v. — A Reputed Changeling 2 v. — Two Penniless Princesses 2 v. — That Stick 1 v. — Grisly Grisell 1 v. — The Long Vacation 2 v. — Modern Broods 1 v.

"Young Mistley," Author of: *vide* Henry Seton Merriman.

Zangwill, I.
Dreamers of the Ghetto 2 v. — Ghetto Comedies 2 v. — Ghetto Tragedies 2 v. "Z. Z."
The World and a Man 2 v.

Series for the Young.

30 Volumes. Published with Continental Copyright on the same conditions as the Collection of English and American Authors. Vide p. 1.

— Price 1 M. 60 Pf. or 2 Fr. per Volume. —

Barker, Lady (Lady Broome).
Stories About:— 1 v.

Charlesworth, Maria Louisa, † 1880.
Ministering Children 1 v.

Craik, Mrs. (Miss Mulock), † 1887.
Our Year 1 v. — Three Tales for Boys 1 v. — Three Tales for Girls 1 v.

Craik, Georgiana M. (Mrs. May).
Cousin Trix, and her Welcome Tales 1 v.

Edgeworth, Maria, † 1849.
Moral Tales 1 v. — Popular Tales 2 v.

Kavanagh, Bridget & Julia, † 1877.
The Pearl Fountain, and other Fairy-Tales 1 v.

Lamb, Charles & Mary, † 1834 and 1847.
Tales from Shakspeare 1 v.

Marryat, Captain, † 1848.
Masterman Ready 1 v.

Marshall, Mrs. Emma, † 1899.
Rex and Regina 1 v.

Montgomery, Florence.
The Town-Crier; to which is added: The Children with the Indian-Rubber Ball 1 v.

"Ruth and her Friends," Author of.
Ruth and her Friends. A Story for Girls 1 v.

Wood, Mrs. Henry, † 1887.
William Allair 1 v.

Yonge, Charlotte M., † 1901.
Kenneth; or, the Rear-Guard of the Grand Army 1 v. — The Little Duke. Ben Sylvester's Word 1 v. — The Stokesley Secret 1 v. — Countess Kate 1 v. — A Book of Golden Deeds 2 v. — Friarswood Post-Office 1 v. — Henrietta's Wish 1 v. — Kings of England 1 v. — The Lances of Lynwood; the Pigeon Pie 1 v. — P's and Q's 1 v. — Aunt Charlotte's Stories of English History 1 v. — Bye-Words 1 v. — Lads and Lasses of Langley, etc. 1 v.

Collection of German Authors.

51 Volumes. Translations from the German, published with universal copyright. These volumes may be imported into any country.

— Price 1 M. 60 Pf. or 2 Fr. per Volume. —

Auerbach, Berthold, † 1882.
On the Heights, *(Second Edition)* 3 v. — Brigitta 1 v. — Spinoza 2 v.

Ebers, Georg, † 1898.
An Egyptian Princess 2 v. — Uarda 1 v. — Homo Sum 2 v. — The Sisters [Die Schwestern] 2 v. — Joshua 2 v. — Per Aspera 2 v.

Fouqué, De la Motte, † 1843.
Undine, Sintram, etc. 1 v.

Freiligrath, Ferdinand, † 1876.
Poems *(Second Edition)* 1 v.

Görlach, Wilhelm.
Prince Bismarck (with Portrait) 1 v.

Goethe, W. v., † 1832.
Faust 1 v. — Wilhelm Meister's Apprenticeship 2 v.

Gutzkow, Karl, † 1878.
Through Night to Light 1 v.

Hackländer, F. W., † 1877.
Behind the Counter [Handel und Wandel] 1 v.

Hauff, Wilhelm, † 1827.
Three Tales 1 v.

Heyse, Paul.
L'Arrabiata, etc. 1 v. — The Dead Lake, etc. 1 v. — Barbarossa, etc. 1 v.

Hillern, Wilhelmine von.
The Vulture Maiden [die Geier-Wally] 1 v. — The Hour will come 2 v.

Kohn, Salomon.
Gabriel 1 v.

Lessing, G. E., † 1781.
Nathan the Wise and Emilia Galotti 1 v.

Lewald, Fanny, † 1889.
Stella 2 v.

Marlitt, E., † 1887.
The Princess of the Moor [Das Haideprinzesschen] 2 v.

Nathusius, Maria, † 1857.
Joachim v. Kamern, and Diary of a Poor Young Lady 1 v.

Reuter, Fritz, † 1874.
In the Year '13 1 v. — An old Story of my Farming Days [Ut mine Stromtid] 3 v.

Richter, J. P. Friedrich (Jean Paul), † 1825.
Flower, Fruit and Thorn Pieces 2 v.

Scheffel, Victor von, † 1886.
Ekkehard 2 v.

Taylor, George.
Klytia 2 v.

Zschokke, Heinrich, † 1848.
The Princess of Brunswick-Wolfenbüttel, etc. 1 v.

Students' Series for School, College, and Home.
Ausgaben
mit deutschen Anmerkungen und Special-Wörterbüchern.

Br. = Broschiert. Kart. = Kartoniert.

Bulwer, Edward, Lord Lytton, † 1873.
The Lady of Lyons. Von Dr. *Fritz Bischoff*. Br. ℳ 0,50. Kart. ℳ 0,60.

Burnett, Frances Hodgson (Am.).
Little Lord Fauntleroy. Von Dr. *Ernst Groth*. Br. ℳ 1,50. Kart. ℳ 1,60. — Anmerkungen und Wörterbuch. Br. ℳ 0,40.
Sara Crewe. Von *Bertha Connell*. Br. ℳ 0,50. Kart. ℳ 0,60. — Anmerkungen und Wörterbuch. Br. ℳ 0,40.

Carlyle, Thomas, † 1881.
The Reign of Terror (French Revolution). Von Dr. *Ludwig Herrig*. Br. ℳ 1,00. Kart. ℳ 1,10.

Craik, Mrs. (Miss Mulock), † 1887.
A Hero. A Tale for Boys. Von Dr. *Otto Dost*. Br. ℳ 0,80. Kart. ℳ 0,90.— Wörterbuch. Br. ℳ 0,40.

Dickens, Charles, † 1870.
Sketches. First Series. Von Dr. *A. Hoppe*. Br. ℳ 1,20. Kart. ℳ 1,30.
Sketches. Second Series. Von Dr. *A. Hoppe*. Br. ℳ 1,40. Kart. ℳ 1,50.—Wörterbuch (First and Second Series). Br. ℳ 1,00.
A Christmas Carol in Prose. Being a Ghost Story of Christmas. Von Dr. *G. Tanger*. Br. ℳ 1,00. Kart. ℳ 1,10.

Eliot, George (Miss Evans—Mrs. Cross), † 1880.
The Mill on the Floss. Von Dr. *H. Conrad*. Br. ℳ 1,70. Kart. ℳ 1,80.

Ewing, Juliana Horatia, † 1885.
Jackanapes. Von *E. Roos*. Br. ℳ 0,50. Kart. ℳ 0,60. — Wörterbuch. Br. ℳ 0,20.
The Brownies; and The Land of Lost Toys. Von Dr. *A. Müller*. Br. ℳ 0,60. Kart. ℳ 0,70. — Wörterbuch. Br. ℳ 0,30.
Timothy's Shoes; An Idyll of the Wood; Benjy in Beastland. Von *E. Roos*. Br. ℳ 0,70. Kart. ℳ 0,80. — Wörterbuch. Br. ℳ 0,30.

Franklin, Benjamin (Am.), † 1790.
His Autobiography. Von Dr. *Karl Feyerabend*. I. Teil. Die Jugendjahre (1706—1730). Br. ℳ 1,00. Kart. ℳ 1,10.
II. Teil. Die Mannesjahre (1731 bis 1757). Mit einer Beigabe: The Way to Wealth. Von Dr. *Karl Feyerabend*. Br. ℳ 1,20. Kart. ℳ 1,30.

Freeman, Edward A. † 1892.
Three Historical Essays. Von Dr. *C. Balser*. Br. ℳ 0,70. Kart. ℳ 0,80.

Harte, Bret (Am.), † 1902.
Tales of the Argonauts. Von Dr. *G. Tanger*. Br. ℳ 1,40. Kart. ℳ 1,50.

Hawthorne, Nathaniel (Am.),
† 1864.
Wonder Book for Boys and Girls. Von
E. Roos. Br. ℳ 0,70. Kart. ℳ 0,80. —
Anmerkungen und Wörterbuch. Br. ℳ 0,40.

Hughes, Thomas, † 1898.
Tom Brown's School Days. Von Dr. *I.
Schmidt.* 2 Parts. Br. ℳ 3,00. Kart.
ℳ 3,20. Part I. apart. Br. ℳ 1,70.
Kart. ℳ 1,80. Part. II. apart. Br. ℳ 1,30.
Kart. ℳ 1,40.

Longfellow, Henry Wadsworth (Am.), † 1882.
Tales of a Wayside Inn. Von Dr. *H.
Varnhagen.* 2 Bände. Br. ℳ 2,00.
Kart. ℳ 2,20. 1. Band apart. Br. ℳ 1,00.
Kart. ℳ 1,10. 2. Band apart. Br. ℳ 1,00.
Kart. ℳ 1,10.

Macaulay, Lord, Thomas Babington, † 1859.
England before the Restoration. (History of England. Chapter I.) Von Dr. *W.
Ihne.* Br. ℳ 0,70. Kart. ℳ 0,80.
England under Charles the Second.
(History of England. Chapter II.) Von
Dr. *W. Ihne.* Br. ℳ 1,00. Kart. ℳ 1,10.
The Rebellions of Argyle and Monmouth. (History of England. Chapter V.)
Von Dr. *Immanuel Schmidt.* Br. ℳ 1,00.
Kart. ℳ 1,10.
Lord Clive. (Histor. Essay.) Von Prof.
Dr. *R. Thum.* Br. ℳ 1,40. Kart. ℳ 1,50.
Ranke's History of the Popes. (Historical Essay.) Von Prof. Dr. *R. Thum.*
Br. ℳ 0,60. Kart. ℳ 0,70.
Warren Hastings. (Historical Essay.)
Von Prof. Dr. *R. Thum.* Br. ℳ 1,50.
Kart. ℳ 1,60.

MᶜCarthy, Justin.
The Indian Mutiny. (Chap. 32—35 of "A
History of our own Times.") Von Dr. *A.
Hamann.* Br. ℳ 0,60. Kart. ℳ 0,70.
— Wörterbuch. Br. ℳ 0,20.

Montgomery, Florence.
Misunderstood. Von Dr. *R. Palm.* Br.
ℳ 1,60. Kart. ℳ 1,70. — Wörterbuch.
Br. ℳ 0,40.

Scott, Sir Walter, † 1832.
The Talisman. Von Dr. *R. Dressel.*
Br. ℳ 1,60. Kart. ℳ 1,70.
Tales of a Grandfather. First Series.
Von Dr. *H. Löschhorn.* Br. ℳ 1,50.
Kart. ℳ 1,60. —Wörterbuch. Br. ℳ 0,50.
Tales of a Grandfather. Second Series.
Von Dr. *H. Löschhorn.* Br. ℳ 1,70.
Kart. ℳ 1,80.

Shakespeare, William, † 1616.
Twelfth Night; or, What you will. Von
Dr. *H. Conrad.* Br. ℳ 1,40. Kart. ℳ 1,50.
Julius Cæsar. Von Dr. *Immanuel
Schmidt.* Br. ℳ 1,00. Kart. ℳ 1,10.
Macbeth. Von Dr. *Immanuel Schmidt.*
Br. ℳ 1,00. Kart. ℳ 1,10.

Stanhope, Earl (Lord Mahon),
† 1875.
Prince Charles Stuart. (History of England from the Peace of Utrecht to the
Peace of Versailles. 1713—1783.) Von
Dr. *Martin Krummacher.* Br. ℳ 1,20.
Kart. ℳ 1,30.
The Seven Years' War. Von Dr. *M.
Krummacher.* Br. ℳ 1,20. Kart. ℳ 1,30.

Tennyson, Alfred Lord, † 1892.
Enoch Arden and other Poems. Von
Dr. *A. Hamann.* Br. ℳ 0,70. Kart.
ℳ 0,80. — Wörterbuch. Br. ℳ 0,20.

Thackeray, W. M. † 1863.
Samuel Titmarsh and The great Hoggarty Diamond. Von *George Boyle.*
Br. ℳ 1,20. Kart. ℳ 1,30.

Yonge, Charlotte M., † 1901.
The Little Duke, or, Richard the Fearless. Von *E. Roos.* Br. ℳ 0,90. Kart.
ℳ 1,00. — Wörterbuch. Br. ℳ 0,20.

Manuals of Conversation (same size as Tauchnitz Edition).
Each Volume, bound ℳ 2,25.

Für Deutsche.
Englische Conversationssprache von
A. Schlessing. 4. Stereotypaufl.
Französische Conversationssprache
von *L. Rollin.* 2. Stereotypaufl.
Russische Conversationssprache
von Dr. *Z. Koiransky.*

For English students.
German Language of Conversation
by *A. Schlessing.*

À l'usage des étudiants français.
Conversation Allemande par MM.
L. Rollin et *Wolfgang Weber.*

Tauchnitz Dictionaries.

For sale and for use in all countries.

Crown 8vo.

English-German and German-English. (JAMES.) *Forty-second Edition entirely rewritten and greatly enlarged.* Sewed ℳ 4,50. Bound in cloth ℳ 5,00. Bound in half-morocco ℳ 5,50.

English-French and French-English. (JAMES & MOLÉ.) *Seventeenth entirely new and modern Edition.* Sewed ℳ 5,00. Bound ℳ 6,00

English-Italian and Italian-English. (JAMES & GRASSI.) *Thirteenth Edition.* Sewed ℳ 5,00. Bound in half-morocco ℳ 6,25.

Tolhausen, Technological Dictionary in three Languages. Complete in three parts. Each part with a new large Supplement including all modern terms and expressions in Electricity, Telegraphy and Telephony. Sewed ℳ 29,00 Bound in cloth ℳ 32,00. Bound in half-morocco ℳ 33,50.
    Vol. I. Français-Allemand-Anglais. *5ième Édition.* Avec un grand Supplément de 1901. Broché ℳ 10,00. Relié en toile ℳ 11,00. Relié en demi-maroquin ℳ 11,50. Supplément séparément ℳ 2,00.
    Vol. II. English-German-French. *5th Edition.* With a large Supplement published in 1902. Sewed ℳ 10,00. Bound in cloth ℳ 11,00. Bound in half-morocco ℳ 11,50. Supplement separately ℳ 2,00.
    Vol. III. Deutsch-Englisch-Französisch. *5. Auflage.* Mit einem Nachtrage von 1902. Brosch. ℳ 9,00. Geb. in Leinen ℳ 10,00. Geb. in Halbfrz. ℳ 10,50. Nachtrag einzeln ℳ 1,00.

Pocket Dictionaries (same size as Tauchnitz Edition).
Bound ℳ 2,25. Sewed ℳ 1,50.

These Dictionaries are constantly revised and kept carefully up to date.

English-German and German-English. *Thirty-first Edition.*
English-French and French-English. *Thirty-second Edition.*
English-Italian and Italian-English. *Twenty-third Edition.*
English-Spanish and Spanish-English. *Thirtieth Edition.*
Latin-English and English-Latin *Sixteenth Edition.*
Französisch-Deutsch und Deutsch-Französisch. *Zwölfte Auflage*
Italienisch-Deutsch und Deutsch-Italienisch. *Achte Auflage.*
Espagnol-Français et Français-Espagnol. *Cinquième Édition.*

Russisch-Deutsch und Deutsch-Russisch. (KOIRANSKY.)
5. Auflage. Br. ℳ 3,00. Geb. ℳ 4,00. Geb. in Halbmarokko ℳ 5,50

Imperial 4°.

Italienisch-Deutsch und Deutsch-Italienisch. (RIGUTINI & BULLE.) 2 Bände. 1. Band. *4. Auflage.* 2. Band. *3. Auflage.* Brosch. ℳ 18,00 Geb. ℳ 20,00. Halbmarokko ℳ 23,00.

Spanisch-Deutsch und Deutsch-Spanisch. (TOLHAUSEN.) 2 Bände *5. Auflage.* Brosch. ℳ 15,00. Geb. ℳ 17,50. Halbmarokko ℳ 20,50

Imperial 8°.

Hebrew and Chaldee Lexicon. (FÜRST.) Translated from the German *Fifth Edition.* ℳ 19,00.

Handwörterbuch der Deutschen Sprache. (WEBER.) *25., völlig neu bearbeitete und den Regeln der neuesten Rechtschreibung angepasste Auflage.* Br. ℳ 6,00. Halbleinw. ℳ 7,00. Halbfranz ℳ 7,50.

Handbuch der Fremdwörter. (WEBER.) *17. Auflage.* Br. ℳ 3,00.

BERNHARD TAUCHNITZ, LEIPZIG.

January 1910.

Tauchnitz Edition.

Latest Volumes:

4134/35. Priscilla and Charybdis. By Frank Frankfort Moore.
4136. The Score. By Lucas Malet.
4137. The House of Intrigue. By Percy White.
4138. The Mystery of Cloomber. By A. Conan Doyle.
4139. The Flying Months. By Frances Mary Peard.
4140. The House called Hurrish. By "Rita."
4141. The Happy Prince, and Other Tales. By Oscar Wilde.
4142. Love the Thief. By Helen Mathers.
4143. On Peace and Happiness. By Lord Avebury (Sir John Lubbock).
4144. Actions and Reactions. By Rudyard Kipling.
4145. Mr. Justice Raffles. By E. W. Hornung.
4146. Mere Stories. By Mrs. W. K. Clifford.
4147. They and I. By Jerome K. Jerome.
4148. Stradella. By F. Marion Crawford.
4149. The Paladin. By Horace Annesley Vachell.
4150. The Glimpse. By Arnold Bennett.
4151. Sailors' Knots. By W. W. Jacobs.
4152. A Reaping. By E. F. Benson.
4153. The Food of Love. By Frank Frankfort Moore.
4154. The Adventures of Captain Jack. By Max Pemberton.
4155/56. The White Prophet. By Hall Caine.
4157. A Woman of No Importance. By Oscar Wilde.
4158. The Lady of Blossholme. By H. Rider Haggard.
4159. Love and the Wise Men. By Percy White.
4160. The Florentine Frame. By Elizabeth Robins.

The Tauchnitz Edition is sold by all Booksellers and Railway Libraries on the Continent, price of each volume ℳ 1,60 or francs 2,00 sewed, ℳ 2,20 or francs 2.75 cloth (Original-Leinenband), ℳ 3,00 or francs 3,75 in elegant soft binding (Original-Geschenkband). A complete Catalogue of the Tauchnitz Edition is attached to this work.

www.ingramcontent.com/pod-product-compliance
Lightning Source LLC
Chambersburg PA
CBHW021204230426
43667CB00006B/554